The LITTLE BLACK SONGBOOK

The Beatles

Published by
Wise Publications
14-15 Berners Street, London W1T 3LJ, UK.
Exclusive distributors:
Music Sales Limited
Distribution Centre,
Newmarket Road, Bury St Edmunds, Suffolk IP33 3YB, UK.
Music Sales Pty Limited
20 Resolution Drive, Caringbah, NSW 2229, Australia.

Order No. NO91102
ISBN 978-1-84609-216-9

Cover designed by Michael Bell Design.
Cover photographs courtesy of Harry Goodwin.
Music arranged by Rikky Rooksby.
Printed in the E.U.

www.musicsales.com

Wise Publications
part of The Music Sales Group
London / New York / Paris / Sydney / Copenhagen / Berlin / Madrid / Hong Kong / Tokyo

Across The Universe

Words & Music by
John Lennon & Paul McCartney

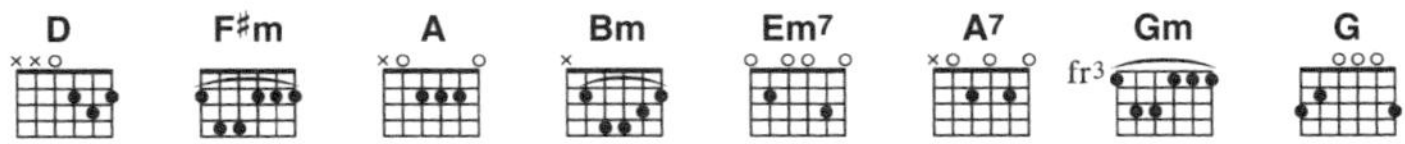

Tune guitar down one semitone

Intro | D | F♯m | A ||

Verse 1

```
D                         Bm                      F♯m
Words are flying out like endless rain into a paper cup,
         Em7                                A7
They slither wildly as they slip away across the universe.
D                        Bm                      F♯m
Pools of sorrow, waves of joy are drifting through my opened mind,
       Em7               Gm
Possessing and caressing me.
```

Chorus 1

```
D                      A7
Jai Guru Deva, Om.
A
Nothing's gonna change my world,
G                                          D
Nothing's gonna change my world.
A
Nothing's gonna change my world,
G                                          D
Nothing's gonna change my world.
```

Verse 2

```
                  Bm                      F♯m                                    Em7
Images of broken light which dance before me like a million eyes,
                                         A7
They call me on and on across the universe.
D                          Bm              F♯m
Thoughts meander like a restless wind inside a letter box,
           Em7                                       A7
They tumble blindly as they make their way across the universe.
```

Chorus 2

D A7
Jai Guru Deva, Om.
A
Nothing's gonna change my world,
G D
Nothing's gonna change my world.
A
Nothing's gonna change my world,
G D
Nothing's gonna change my world.

Verse 3

Bm F♯m
Sounds of laughter, shades of life are ringing through my opened ears,
Em7 Gm
Inciting and inviting me.
D Bm F♯m Em7
Limitless, undying love which shines around me like a million suns,
A7
It calls me on and on across the universe.

Chorus 3

D A7
Jai Guru Deva, Om.
A
Nothing's gonna change my world,
G D
Nothing's gonna change my world.
A
Nothing's gonna change my world,
G D
Nothing's gonna change my world.

Outro

(D)
𝄆 Jai Guru Deva. 𝄇 *Repeat to fade*

All I've Got To Do

Words & Music by
John Lennon & Paul McCartney

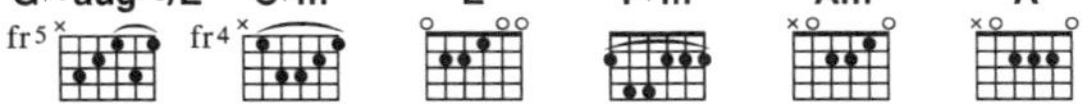

Intro | G♯7aug♭9/E ||

Verse 1

C♯m E
Whenever I ____ want you around, yeah,
C♯m F♯m
All I gotta do ____ is call you on the phone

And you'll come running home,
Am E
Yeah, that's all I ____ gotta do.

Verse 2

C♯m E
And when I, ____ I wanna kiss you, yeah,
C♯m F♯m
All I gotta do ____ is whisper in your ear

The words you long to hear,
Am E
And I'll ____ be kissing you.

Chorus 1

A
And the same goes for me,

Whenever you want me at all,
C♯m
I'll be here, yes I will, whenever you call,
A E C♯m
You just gotta call on me, yeah,
A E
You just gotta call on me.

Verse 3

N.C. C♯m E
And when I, ____ I wanna kiss you, yeah,

C♯m F♯m
All I gotta do ____ is call you on the phone

And you'll come running home,

Am E
Yeah, that's all I ____ gotta do.

Chorus 2

A
And the same goes for me,

Whenever you want me at all,

C♯m
I'll be here, yes I will, whenever you call,

A E C♯m
You just gotta call on me, yeah,

A E
You just gotta call on me,

A E
You just gotta call on me.

Outro

C♯m E C♯m
Mmm. ________ *Fade out*

All My Loving

Words & Music by
John Lennon & Paul McCartney

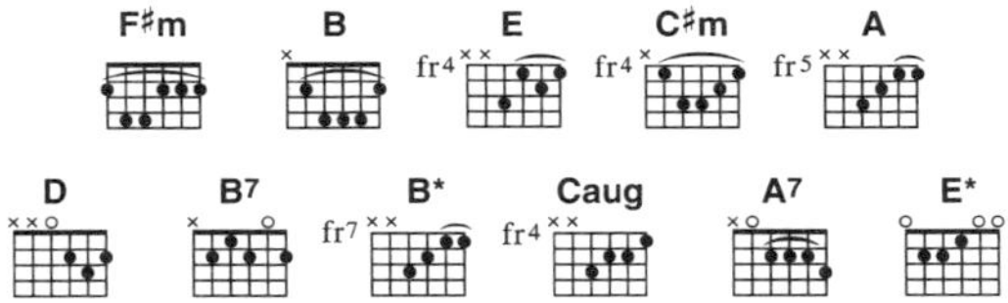

Verse 1

N.C. F♯m B
Close your eyes and I'll kiss you,
E C♯m
Tomorrow I'll miss you,
A F♯m D B7
Remember, I'll always be true.
F♯m B
And then while I'm away
E C♯m
I'll write home every day,
A B* E
And I'll send all my loving to you.

Verse 2

N.C. F♯m B
I'll pretend that I'm kissing
E C♯m
The lips I am missing
A F♯m D B7
And hope that my dreams will come true.
F♯m B
And then while I'm away
E C♯m
I'll write home every day,
A B E
And I'll send all my loving to you.

Chorus 1

C♯m Caug E
All my loving I will send to you,
C♯m Caug E
All my loving, darling I'll be true.

Solo

```
| A7    | A7    | E*    | E*    |
| B7    | B7    | E*    | E*    ||
```

Verse 3

```
N.C.         F#m          B
Close your eyes and I'll kiss you,
  E              C#m
Tomorrow I'll miss you,
  A              F#m         D     B7
Remember, I'll always be true.
           F#m          B
And then while I'm away
             E              C#m
I'll write home every day,
            A            B          E
And I'll send all my loving to you.
```

Chorus 2

```
           C#m    Caug            E
All my loving I will send to you,
           C#m     Caug             E
All my loving, darling I'll be true.
           C#m
All my loving,
           E
All my loving oo-ooh,
           C#m
All my loving
                 E*
I will send to you.
```

All Together Now

Words & Music by
John Lennon & Paul McCartney

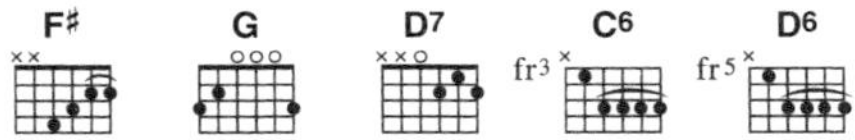

Intro F♯ ‖: G | G | G | G :‖

Verse 1
G D7
One, two, three, four, can I have a little more?
G D7 G
Five, six, seven, eight, nine, ten, I love you.

Verse 2
G D7
A, B, C, D, can I bring my friend to tea?
G D7 G
E, F, G, H, I, J, I love you.

Bridge 1
(Boom boom boom
C6
Boom boom boom.) Sail the ship,
G
(Boom boom boom.) Chop the tree,
C6
(Boom boom boom.) Skip the rope,
D6 D7
(Boom boom boom.) Look at me! ____

(All together now.)

Chorus 1
G
All together now, (all together now.)

All together now, (all together now.)
D7
All together now, (all together now.)
G
All together now, (all together now.)

```
               G                                D7
Verse 3        Black, white, green, red, can I take my friend to bed?
               G                                        D7          G
               Pink, brown, yellow, orange and blue, I love you.

               (All together now.)

                  G
Chorus 2       𝄆 All together now, (all together now.)

               All together now, (all together now.)
               D7
               All together now, (all together now.)
               G
               All together now, (all together now.)   𝄇


Bridge 2       (Boom boom boom
               C6
               Boom boom boom.) Sail the ship,
               G
               (Boom boom boom.) Chop the tree,
               C6
               (Boom boom boom.) Skip the rope,
               D6                D7
               (Boom boom boom.) Look at me! ____

               (All together now.)

                  G
Chorus 3       𝄆 All together now, (all together now.)

               All together now, (all together now.)
               D7
               All together now, (all together now.)
               G
               All together now, (all together now.)   𝄇

               G
Chorus 4       All together now, (all together now.)

               All together now, (all together now.)
               D7
               All together now, (all together now.)
                             G
               All together now. ____
```

All You Need Is Love

Words & Music by
John Lennon & Paul McCartney

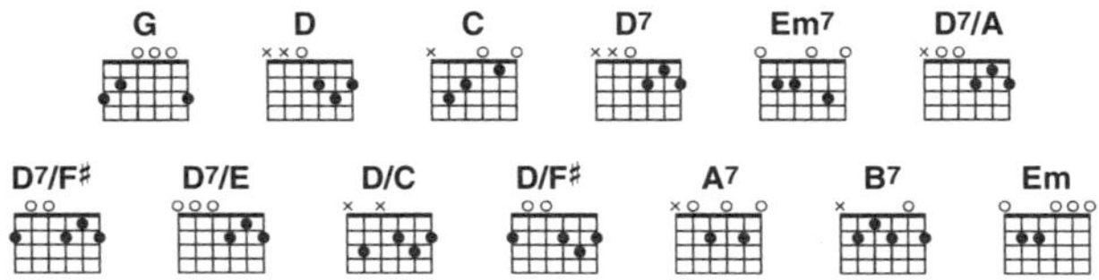

Intro

```
| G    D    | G           | C    D7   ||

G       D      Em7
Love, love, love,

G       D      Em7
Love, love, love,

D7/A  G        D7/F♯  D7/E
Love, love, love.

| D    D/C  | D           ||
```

Verse 1

```
G                                D/F♯               Em7
   There's nothing you can do that can't be done,
G                     D/F♯                Em7
   Nothing you can sing that can't be sung,
D7/A                  G
   Nothing you can say,
                   D/F♯                  D7/E
But you can learn how to play the game,
     D     D/C     D
It's easy.
```

Verse 2

```
G                     D/F♯                   Em7
   Nothing you can make that can't be made,
G              D/F♯                 Em7
   No-one you can save that can't be saved,
D7/A                  G
   Nothing you can do,
                 D/F♯                    D7/E
But you can learn how to be you in time,
     D     D/C     D
It's easy.
```

Chorus 1

```
G            A7       D      D7
  All you need is love,
G            A7       D      D7
  All you need is love,
G            B7       Em     Em7
  All you need is love, love,
C            D7              G
  Love is all you need.
```

Link

```
G        D        Em7
(Love, love, love,)
G        D        Em7
(Love, love, love,)
D7/A     G        D7/F#    D7/E
(Love, love, love.)

| D   D/C  | D          ||
```

Chorus 2

As Chorus 1

Verse 3

```
G                           D/F#                        Em7
  There's nothing you can know that isn't known,
G                                D/F#                Em7
  There's nothing you can see that isn't shown,
D7/A                             G
  There's nowhere you can be
              D/F#                           D7/E
That isn't where you're meant to be,
     D       D/C      D
It's easy.
```

Chorus 3

As Chorus 1

Chorus 4

As Chorus 1

Coda

```
G
Love is all you need.

(Love is all you need.)
    (G)
||: Love is all you need.

(Love is all you need.) :||  Repeat to fade
```

And I Love Her

Words & Music by
John Lennon & Paul McCartney

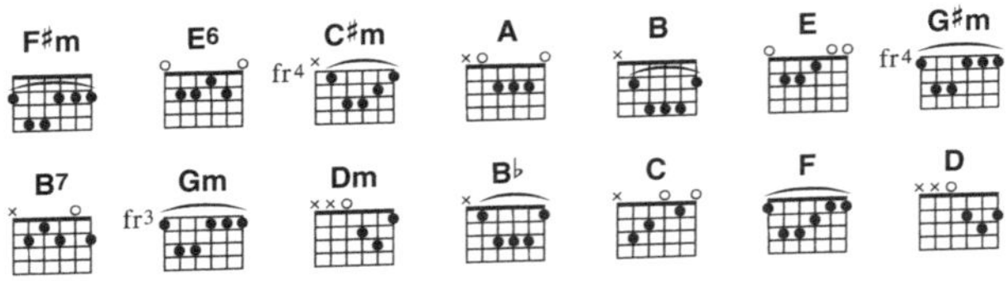

Intro | F♯m | F♯m | E6 | E6 ||

Verse 1

```
F♯m           C♯m
   I give her all my love,
F♯m             C♯m
   That's all I do,
F♯m             C♯m
   And if you saw my love,
A                 B
   You'd love her too,
  E
I love her.
```

Verse 2

```
F♯m               C♯m
   She gives me everything,
F♯m             C♯m
   And tenderly,
F♯m               C♯m
   The kiss my lover brings,
A               B
She brings to me,
        E
And I love her.
```

Bridge

```
C♯m          B
   A love like ours
C♯m              G♯m
   Could never die
C♯m            G♯m
   As long as I
           B         B7
Have you near me.
```

Verse 3

```
F♯m                 C♯m
   Bright are the stars that shine,
F♯m              C♯m
   Dark is the sky,
F♯m              C♯m
   I know this love of mine
A                B
   Will never die,
        E
And I love her.
```

Solo

| Gm | Dm | Gm | Dm | Gm |

| Dm | B♭ | C | F | F ||

Verse 4

```
Gm                 Dm
   Bright are the stars that shine,
Gm              Dm
   Dark is the sky,
Gm              Dm
   I know this love of mine
B♭               C
   Will never die,
        F
And I love her.
```

Coda

| Gm | Gm | F | F |

| Gm | Gm | D ||

And Your Bird Can Sing

Words & Music by
John Lennon & Paul McCartney

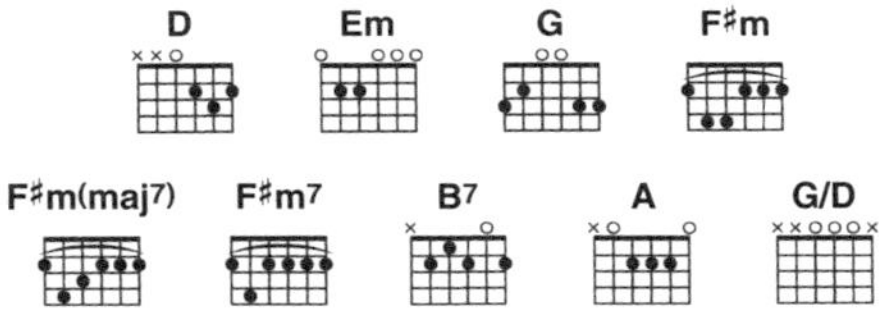

Capo second fret

Intro | D | D | D | D ||

Verse 1

```
    D
You tell me that you've got everything you want,

And your bird can sing,
                  Em
But you don't get me,
G             D
  You don't get me.
```

Verse 2

```
D
You say you've seen seven wonders,

And your bird is green,
                  Em
But you can't see me,
G             D
  You can't see me.
```

Bridge 1

```
F♯m                     F♯m(maj7)
When your prized possessions
F♯m7                B7
Start to weigh you down,
D               Em
Look in my direction,
                         A
I'll be 'round, I'll be 'round.
```

Solo 1 | D | D | D | D |
| Em | G | D | D ||

Bridge 2

F♯m F♯m(maj7)
When your bird is broken,
F♯m7 B7
Will it bring you down?
D Em
You may be awoken,
A
I'll be 'round, I'll be 'round,

Verse 3

D
You tell me that you've heard every sound there is,

And your bird can swing,
Em
But you can't hear me,
G D
You can't hear me.

Solo 2 | D | D | D | D |
| Em | G | D | D ||

Coda | D | D | D | G/D ||

Another Girl

Words & Music by
John Lennon & Paul McCartney

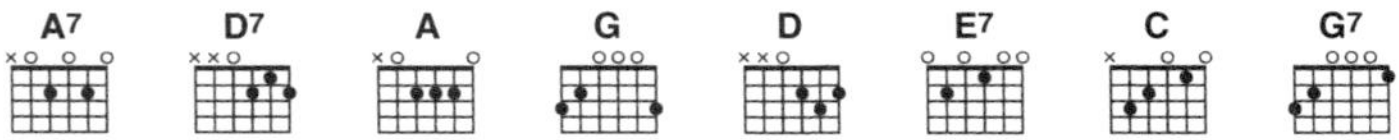


```
          N.C.          A7   D7          A7   D7          A
Intro     For I have got   another girl,   another girl.

          (A)                       G                  A
Verse 1   You're making me say that I've got
                             D
          Nobody but you,
          A                 G                  A
             But as from today, well I've got
                                  D
          Somebody that's new.
          D7                                              E7
          I ain't no fool and I don't take what I don't want,
          N.C.          A7   D7          A7   D7          A
          For I have got   another girl,   another girl.

          (A)                        G                  A
Verse 2   She's sweeter than all the girls and
                               D
          I've met quite a few,
          A                  G                   A
             Nobody in all the world can
                                    D
          Do what she can do.
          D7                                                     E7
          And so I'm telling you this time you'd better stop,
          N.C.          A7   D7          A7   D7
          For I have got   another girl.
```

Bridge 1

```
             C                G7              C
Another girl who will love me till the end,
G7                        C
   Through thick and thin,
           E7             A      E7
She will always be my friend.
```

Verse 3

```
A                    G                    A
   I don't wanna say that I've been
                     D
Unhappy with you,
A                   G                     A
   But as from today, well I've seen
                         D
Somebody that's new.
D7                                                    E7
I ain't no fool and I don't take what I don't want,
N.C.          A7   D7          A7    D7
For I have got   another girl.
```

Bridge 2

```
             C                G7              C
Another girl who will love me till the end,
G7                        C
   Through thick and thin,
           E7             A      E7
She will always be my friend.
```

Verse 4

```
A                    G                    A
   I don't wanna say that I've been
                     D
Unhappy with you,
A                   G                     A
   But as from today, well I've seen
                         D
Somebody that's new.
D7                                                    E7
I ain't no fool and I don't take what I don't want,
N.C.          A7   D7          A7
For I have got   another girl.
D7              A7   D7          A
   Another girl,   another girl.
```

Any Time At All

Words & Music by
John Lennon & Paul McCartney

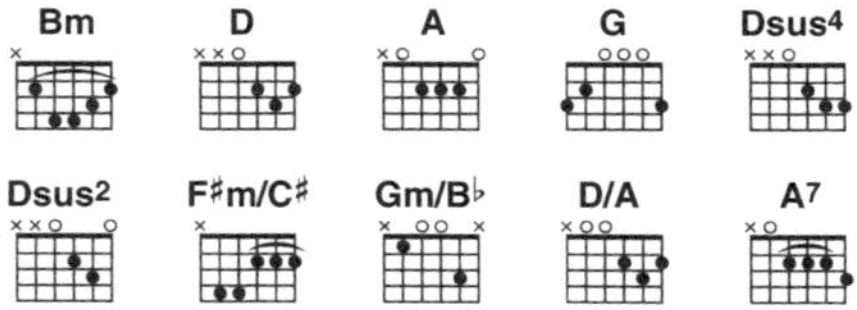

Chorus 1

N.C. Bm D
Any time at all,
A
Any time at all,
Bm
Any time at all,
G
All you've got to do is call
A Dsus4 D Dsus2 D
And I'll be there.

Verse 1

D F♯m/C♯
If you need somebody to love,
Bm Gm/B♭
Just look into my eyes,
D/A A D
I'll be there to make you feel right.

Verse 2

F♯m/C♯
If you're feeling sorry and sad,
Bm Gm/B♭
I'd really sympathise.
D/A A Dsus4 D Dsus2 D
Don't you be sad, just call me tonight.

Chorus 2

As Chorus 1

Verse 3

D F♯m/C♯
If the sun has faded away,
Bm Gm/B♭
I'll try to make it shine.
D/A A D
There is nothing I won't do.

Verse 4

F♯m/C♯
When you need a shoulder to cry on,
Bm Gm/B♭
I hope it will be mine.
D/A A Dsus4 D Dsus2 D
Call me tonight, and I'll come to you.

Chorus 3

As Chorus 1

Solo

| A | A7 | A | A7 | G | A |

| G | A | Dsus4 D Dsus2 | D ||

Chorus 4

N.C. Bm D
Any time at all,
A
Any time at all,
Bm
Any time at all,
G
All you've got to do is call
A Dsus4 D Dsus2 D
And I'll be there.
G
Any time at all,
A
All you've got to do is call
Dsus4 D Dsus2 D
And I'll be there.

Ask Me Why

Words & Music by
John Lennon & Paul McCartney

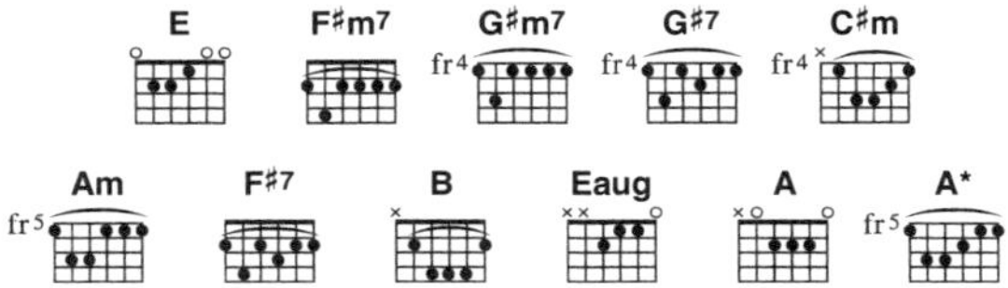


```
Intro         | E          ||

              E    F♯m7  G♯m7  F♯m7
Verse 1       I    love   you, ______
                                         E
              'Cause you tell me things I want to know.
              E    F♯m7   G♯m7   F♯m7
              And it's    true ______
                                        E
              That it really only goes to show
              G♯7
              That I know
                   C♯m            Am                      F♯7    B
              That I, I, I, I should never, never, never be blue. ____

              E      F♯m7    G♯m7    F♯m7
Verse 2       Now you're  mine ______
                                          E
              My happiness still makes me cry.
              E      F♯m7  G♯m7   F♯m7
              And in       time ______
                                                E
              You'll understand the reason why
              G♯7
              If I cry
                  C♯m
              It's not because I'm sad,
                                Am                      E      Eaug
              But you're the only love that I've ever had.
```

Bridge 1

A B E Eaug
I can't believe it's happened to me,
A B E N.C. (B)
I can't conceive of any more misery.

Chorus 1

E F♯m7 G♯m7
Ask me why,
A*
I'll say I love you
G♯m7 A* E
And I'm always thinking of you. ___

Verse 3

E F♯m7 G♯m7 F♯m7
I love you, ___
E
'Cause you tell me things I want to know.
E F♯m7 G♯m7 F♯m7
And it's true ___
E
That it really only goes to show
G♯7
That I know
C♯m Am F♯7 B
That I, I, I, I should never, never, never be blue. ___

Chorus 2

E F♯m7 G♯m7
Ask me why,
A*
I'll say I love you
G♯m7 A* E Eaug
And I'm always thinking of you. ___

Bridge 2

As Bridge 1

Chorus 3

E F♯m7 G♯m7
Ask me why,
A*
I'll say I love you
G♯m7 A* E
And I'm always thinking of you. ___
A* E
You, ___
A* G♯m7
You. ___

Baby You're A Rich Man

Words & Music by
John Lennon & Paul McCartney

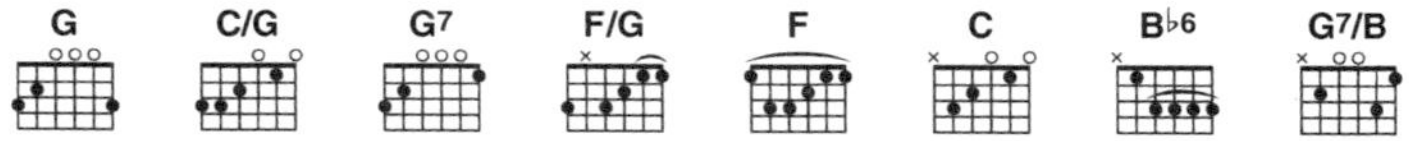

Intro | G | C/G | G | C/G | G7 | C/G | G7 | C/G ||

Verse 1

```
G                         C/G                   G7
How does it feel to be one of the beautiful people?
G                                 F/G
Now that you know who you are,
F              G        C
What do you want to be?
G                                  F/G
And have you travelled very far?
F          G       C
Far as the eye can see.
```

Verse 2

```
G                         C/G                   G7
How does it feel to be one of the beautiful people?
G                                F/G
How often have you been there?
F      G          C
Often enough to know.
G                                     F/G
What did you see when you were there?
F              G       C
Nothing that doesn't show.
```

Chorus 1

```
G
Baby you're a rich man,
C
Baby you're a rich man,
G                          C
Baby you're a rich man too.
     B♭6            G7/B        C
You keep all your money in a big brown bag
         G7
Inside a zoo.
                C
What a thing to do.
```

cont.

G
Baby you're a rich man,
C
Baby you're a rich man,
G   C
Baby you're a rich man too.

Verse 3

G   C/G   G7
How does it feel to be one of the beautiful people?
G   F/G
Tuned to a natural E,
F   G   C
Happy to be that way.
G   F/G
Now that you've found another key,
F   G   C
What are you going to play?

Chorus 2

G
Baby you're a rich man,
C
Baby you're a rich man,
G   C
Baby you're a rich man too.
      B♭6   G7/B   C
You keep all your money in a big brown bag
         G7
Inside a zoo.
                          C
What a thing to do.
G
Baby you're a rich man,
C
Baby you're a rich man,
G   C
Baby you're a rich man too.

Outro

   G
𝄆 Baby you're a rich man,
C
Baby you're a rich man,
G   C
Baby you're a rich man too. 𝄇 *Repeat and fade*

Baby's In Black

Words & Music by
John Lennon & Paul McCartney

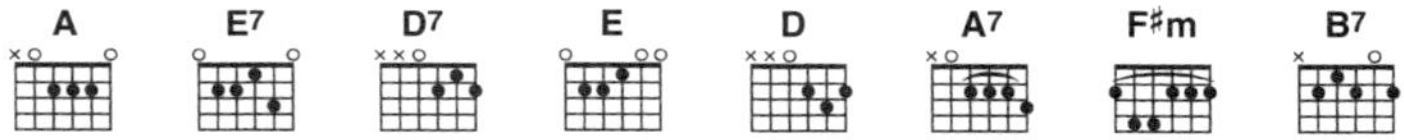

Intro | (A) (A/E) | A ||

Chorus 1

```
A          E7
Oh dear, what can I do?
D7                     E
Baby's in black and I'm feeling blue,
        A  D          A
Tell me, oh, what can I do?
```

Verse 1

```
A
She thinks of him,
      A7               D
And so she dresses in black,
                               A
And though he'll never come back,
E                A
She's dressed in black.
```

Chorus 2 As Chorus 1

Verse 2

```
A
I think of her,
     A7                 D
But she thinks only of him,
                           A
And though it's only a whim,
E            A
She thinks of him.
```

Bridge 1

```
F♯m       B7
Oh, how long will it take,
D       E7                       A
Till she sees the mistake she has made.
```

Chorus 3

```
        E7
Oh dear, what can I do?
D7                E
Baby's in black and I'm feeling blue,
         A  D        A
Tell me, oh, what can I do?
```

Solo

| A | E | D | E | A D | A ||

Bridge 2

```
F#m      B7
Oh, how long will it take,
D       E7                      A
Till she sees the mistake she has made.
```

Chorus 4

```
     E7
Dear, what can I do?
D7                E
Baby's in black and I'm feeling blue,
         A  D        A
Tell me, oh, what can I do?
```

Verse 3

```
A
She thinks of him,
    A7              D
And so she dresses in black,
                            A
And though he'll never come back,
E               A
She's dressed in black.
```

Chorus 5

```
A       E7
Oh dear, what can I do?
D7                E
Baby's in black and I'm feeling blue,
         A  D        A
Tell me, oh, what can I do?
```

Back In The USSR

Words & Music by
John Lennon & Paul McCartney

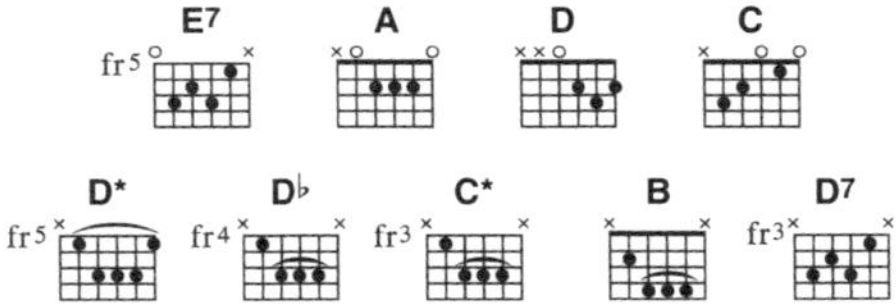

Intro | E7 | E7 | E7 | E7 ||

Verse 1
A D
Flew in from Miami Beach B. O. A. C.,
C D
Didn't get to bed last night.
A D
On the way the paper bag was on my knee,
C D
Man, I had a dreadful flight.

Chorus 1
A
I'm back in the U. S. S. R., __
C D
You don't know how lucky you are boy.
(D) N.C. A E7
Back in the U. S. S. R.

Verse 2
A D
Been away for so long I hardly knew the place,
C D
Gee it's good to be back home.
A D
Leave it till tomorrow to unpack my case,
C D
Honey, disconnect the phone.

```
                                     A
Chorus 2     I'm back in the U. S. S. R., ___
             C                               D
               You don't know how lucky you are boy.
             (D) N.C.                                               A
                Back in the U.S., back in the U.S., back in the U. S. S. R. ___

                         D
Bridge 1     Well the Ukraine girls really knock me out,
                  A
             They leave the West behind,
                 D*       D♭          C*       B
             And Moscow girls make me sing and shout
                 E7                          D7          A        E7
             That Georgia's always on my mi-mi-mi-mi-mi-mi-mi-mind.

Solo         |: A      | D      | C      | D      :|

                                     A
Chorus 3     I'm back in the U. S. S. R., ___
             C                               D
               You don't know how lucky you are boys.
             (D) N.C.              A
                Back in the U. S. S. R. ___

Bridge 2     As Bridge 1

             A                                    D
Verse 3      Show me round your snow-peaked mountains way down south,
             C                   D
             Take me to your daddy's farm.
             A                  D
             Let me hear your balalaikas ringing out,
             C                     D
             Come and keep your comrade warm.

                                     A
Chorus 4     I'm back in the U. S. S. R., ___
             C                               D
               You don't know how lucky you are boy.
             (D) N.C.              A
                Back in the U. S. S. R. ___
                     E7           A
             Oh, let me tell you honey.

                      Play 3 times
             |: A      | A      :| A      ||
```

The Ballad Of John And Yoko

Words & Music by
John Lennon & Paul McCartney

E E7 A B7 E6

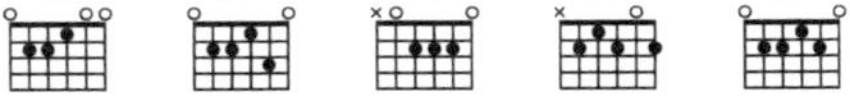

Intro | E | E ||

Verse 1

E
Standing in the dock at Southampton,

Trying to get to Holland or France.

E7
The man in the mac said, "You've got to go back."

You know they didn't give us a chance.

Chorus 1

A
Christ! You know it ain't easy,

E
You know how hard it can be.

B7
The way things are going,

E
They're gonna crucify me.

Verse 2

E
Finally made the plane into Paris,

Honeymooning down by the Seine.

E7
Peter Brown called to say,

"You can make it OK, you can get married in Gibraltar, near Spain."

Chorus 2 As Chorus 1

Verse 3

E
Drove from Paris to the Amsterdam Hilton,

Talking in our beds for a week.

E7
The newspeople said, "Say, what you doing in bed?"

I said, "We're only trying to get us some peace."

Chorus 3 As Chorus 1

Bridge

```
A
Saving up your money for a rainy day,

Giving all your clothes to charity.

Last night the wife said, "Oh boy when you're dead,

You don't take nothing with you but your soul."
    B7
Think!
```

Verse 4

```
E
Made a lightning trip to Vienna,

Eating chocolate cake in a bag.
    E7
The newspapers said, "She's gone to his head,

They look just like two gurus in drag."
```

Chorus 4 As Chorus 1

Verse 5

```
E
Caught the early plane back to London,

Fifty acorns tied in a sack.
    E7
The men from the press said,

"We wish you success, it's good to have the both of you back."
```

Chorus 5 As Chorus 1

Coda

```
                               B7                            E
The way things are going,  they're gonna crucify me.

| B7    | B7    | E     | E6        ||
```

Because

Words & Music by
John Lennon & Paul McCartney

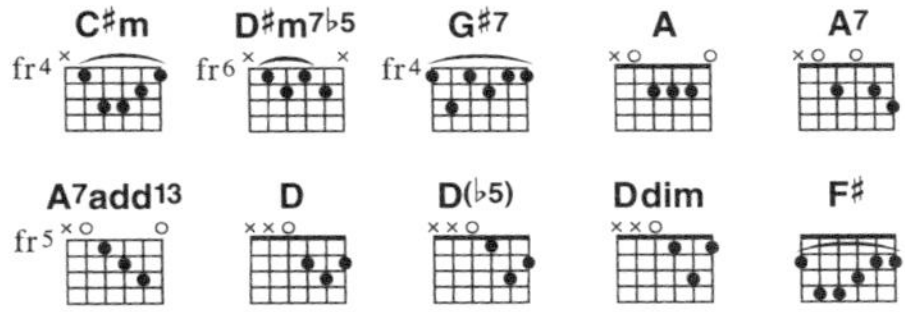

Intro

```
| C♯m      | C♯m      | D♯m7♭5   | G♯7       |
| A        | C♯m      | A7       | A7add13   ||
```

```
D       D(♭5)  Ddim
Ah. ________
```

Verse 1

```
     C♯m
Because the world is round
                 D♯m7♭5   G♯7
It turns me on, ________
   A              C♯m       A7          A7add13
Because the world is round, ________
D       D(♭5)  Ddim
Ah. ________
```

Verse 2

```
     C♯m
Because the wind is high
                   D♯m7♭5      G♯7
It blows my mind, ________
   A              C♯m       A7       A7add13
Because the wind is high, ________
D       D(♭5)  Ddim
Ah. ________
```

Bridge

(Ddim) F♯
Love is old, love is new,
G♯7
Love is all, love is you.

Verse 3

C♯m
Because the sky is blue
D♯m7♭5 G♯7
It makes me cry, ______
A C♯m A7 A7add13
Because the sky is blue, ______
D D(♭5) Ddim
Ah. ____________

Instrumental

| C♯m | C♯m | D♯m7♭5 | G♯7 |
(Ah.) __ (Ah.) ____________

| A | C♯m | A7 | A7add13 |
(Ah.) __ Ah. ____________

| D | D(♭5) Ddim ||
Ah. ____________

Being For The Benefit Of Mr Kite

Words & Music by
John Lennon & Paul McCartney

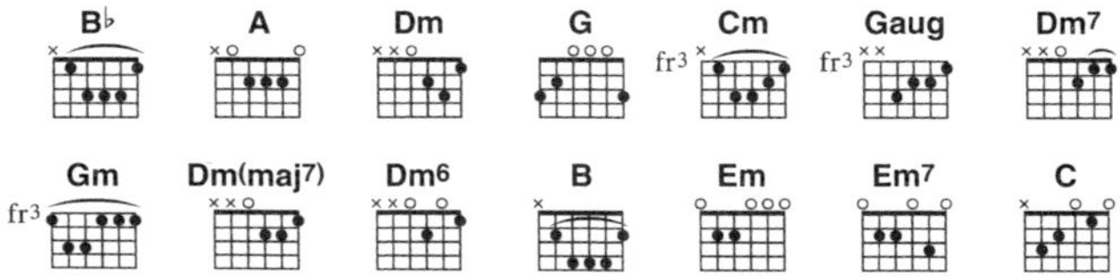

Intro | B♭ | A | Dm G ||

Verse 1

```
            Cm          Gaug
For the benefit of Mr. Kite,
B♭                Dm              G              Gaug
There will be a show tonight on trampoline.
       Cm              Gaug
The Hendersons will all be there,
B♭               Dm               A
Late of Pablo Fanques fair, what a scene,
        Dm                 Dm7
Over men and horses, hoops and garters,
B♭                   A                  Dm
Lastly through a hog's head of real fire.
          Gm        A                     Dm
In this way Mr. K. will challenge the world.
```

Link | Gm A | Dm G ||

Verse 2

```
       Cm          Gaug
The celebrated Mr. K.
B♭                         Dm          G              Gaug
Performs his feat on Saturday at Bishopsgate.
       Cm              Gaug
The Hendersons will dance and sing
    B♭              Dm                  A
As Mr. Kite flies through the ring, don't be late!
```

cont.

```
             Dm          Dm7
Messrs K. and H. assure the public
B♭                 A              Dm
Their production will be second to none.
       Gm              A
And of course, Henry the Horse dances the (waltz!)
```

Instrumental

```
| Dm  Dm(maj7) | Dm7  Dm6 | A      | A      |
 waltz!
| Dm  Dm(maj7) | Dm7  Dm6 | B      | Em  Em7 |
| C   B  | Em  Em7 | C   B  | Em     | G      ||
```

Verse 3

```
      Cm              Gaug
The band begins at ten to six,
        B♭        Dm                   G              Gaug
When Mr. K. performs his tricks without a sound.
      Cm         Gaug
And Mr. H. will demonstrate
     B♭              Dm          A
Ten summersets he'll undertake on solid ground.
          Dm                  Dm7
Having been some days in preparation,
  B♭                 A              Dm
A splendid time is guaranteed for all.
         Gm        A                   Dm      Gm  A
And tonight Mr. Kite is topping the bill. ________
```

Outro

```
| Dm  Dm(maj7) | Dm7  Dm6 | A      | A      |
| Dm  Dm(maj7) | Dm7  Dm6 | B      |
|: Em  Em7 | C   B  | Em  Em7 | C   B  :| Em      ||
```

Birthday

Words & Music by
John Lennon & Paul McCartney

A7 D7 E7 E C G A

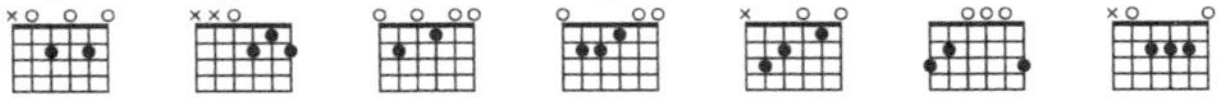

Intro | (A7) | (A7) | (A7) | (A7) | (D7) | (D7) |
| (A7) | (A7) | (E7) | (E7) | (A7) | (A7) ||

Verse 1
A7 N.C.
You say it's your birthday,
A7 N.C.
It's my birthday too, yeah.
D7 N.C.
You say it's your birthday,
A7 N.C.
We're gonna have a good time.
E7 N.C.
I'm glad it's your birthday,
A7 N.C.
Happy birthday to you.

Link | *Drums for 8 bars* | E | E ||

Bridge
E
Yes, we're going to a party, party,

Yes, we're going to a party, party,

Yes, we're going to a party, party.

Middle 1
C G
I would like you to dance,
C G
(Birthday) Take a cha-cha-cha-chance,
C G
(Birthday) I would like you to dance,
C G E
(Birthday) Dance! ____

Instrumental | (A7) | (A7) | (A7) | (A7) | (D7) | (D7) |

| (A7) | (A7) | (E7) | (E7) | (A7) | (A7) |

| (A) | (A) (G) | (A) | (A) (G) ||

Middle 2

```
C           G
  I would like you to dance,
C                   G
(Birthday) Take a cha-cha-cha-chance,
C                   G
(Birthday) I would like you to dance,
C           G       E
(Birthday) Dance! ____
```

Verse 2

```
A7
  You say it's your birthday,

It's my birthday too, yeah.
D7
  You say it's your birthday,
A7
  We're gonna have a good time.
E7
  I'm glad it's your birthday,
A7
  Happy birthday to you.
```

Coda | A | A ||

Blackbird

Words & Music by
John Lennon & Paul McCartney

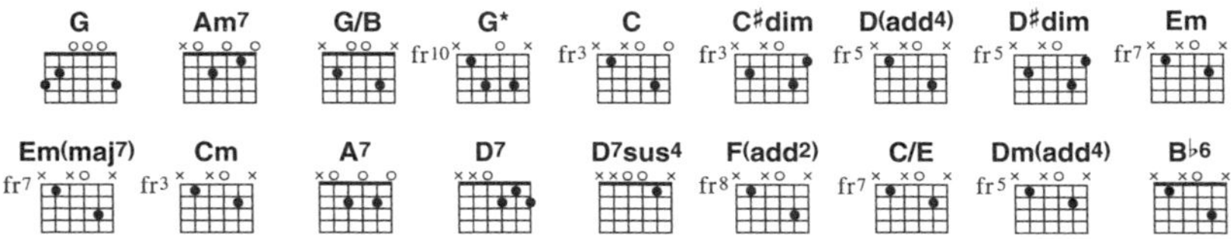

Intro | G Am7 G/B | G* ||

Verse 1

G Am7 G/B G*
Blackbird singing in the dead of night,
C C♯dim D D♯dim Em Em(maj7)
Take these broken wings and learn to fly.
D C♯dim C Cm
All your life,
G/B A7 D7 G
You were only waiting for this moment to arise.

Link 1 | C G/B A7 | D7sus4 G ||

Verse 2

G Am7 G/B G*
Blackbird singing in the dead of night,
C C♯dim D D♯dim Em Em(maj7)
Take these sunken eyes and learn to see.
D C♯dim C Cm
All your life,
G/B A7 D7 G
You were only waiting for this moment to be free.

Bridge 1

F C/E Dm C B♭6 C
Black - bird, fly. ___
F C/E Dm C B♭6 A7
Black - bird, fly.
D7sus4 G
Into the light of a dark black night.

Link 2 | G Am7 G/B | G* | C C♯dim D D♯dim | Em Em(maj7) |
(night.)
| D C♯dim | C Cm | G/B A7 | D7sus4 G ||

Bridge 2
F C/E Dm C B♭6 C
Black - bird, fly. ___
F C/E Dm C B♭6 A7
Black - bird, fly.
D7sus4 G
Into the light of a dark black night.

Link 3 | G Am7 G/B | G* | G | G |
(night.)

| G Am7 G/B | C G/B A7 | D7sus4 ||

Verse 3
G Am7 G/B G*
Blackbird singing in the dead of night,
C C♯dim D D♯dim Em Em(maj7)
Take these broken wings and learn to fly.
D C♯dim C Cm
All your life,
G/B A7 D7sus4 G
You were only waiting for this moment to arise.

Coda
C G/B A7 D7sus4 G
You were only waiting for this moment to arise.
C G/B A7 D7sus4 G
You were only waiting for this moment to arise.

Blue Jay Way

Words & Music by
George Harrison

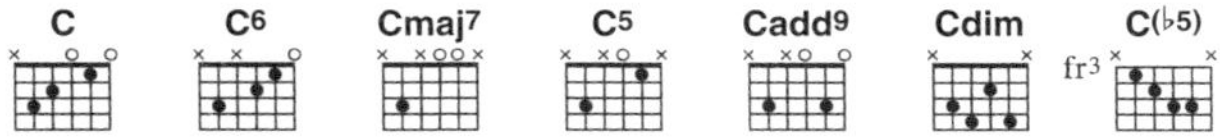

Intro

| (C) | (C) | C6 Cmaj7 | C5 Cmaj7 |
| Cmaj7 C6 Cmaj7 Cadd9 | C Cmaj7 | C ||

Verse 1

N.C. C
There's a fog upon L.A.
Cdim C
And my friends have lost their way.
Cdim C(♭5)
We'll be over soon, they said,
Cdim C
Now they've lost themselves instead.

Chorus 1

C6 Cmaj7 C5 Cmaj7
Please don't be long,
C6 Cmaj7 C5 Cmaj7
Please don't you be very long,
C6 Cmaj7 C5 Cmaj7
Please don't be long,
C6 C5 Cmaj7 C6 C5 C
Or I may be a - sleep. __

Verse 2

N.C. C
Well it only goes to show,
Cdim C
And I told them where to go:
Cdim C(♭5)
Ask a policeman on the street,
Cdim C
There's so many there to meet.

Chorus 2 As Chorus 1

Verse 3

```
N.C.                      C
   Now it's past my bed, I know,
Cdim                   C
   And I'd really like to go.
Cdim                         C(♭5)
   Soon will be the break of day,
Cdim                       C
   Sitting here in Blue Jay Way.
```

Chorus 3 As Chorus 1

Chorus 4

```
C6     Cmaj7  C5  Cmaj7
Please don't  be  long,
C6     Cmaj7      C5        Cmaj7
Please don't you be very long,
C6     Cmaj7  C5  Cmaj7
Please don't  be  long,
```

Link

```
| C5   | C5   ||
```

Chorus 5 As Chorus 4

Link

```
| C5   | C5   ||
```

Chorus 6 As Chorus 4

Chorus 7

```
C
Don't be long, don't be long,

Don't be long,

Don't be long, ___

Don't be long, don't be long,

Don't be long.
```

Can't Buy Me Love

Words & Music by
John Lennon & Paul McCartney

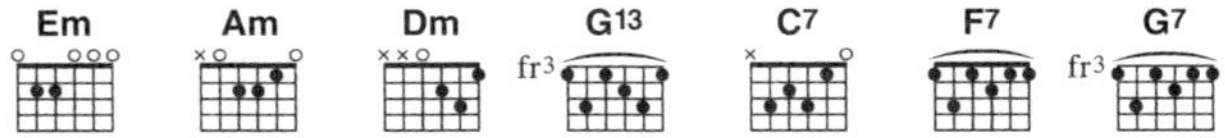

Intro

Em Am Em Am
Can't buy me love, ___ love, ___
Dm G13
Can't buy me love. ___

Verse 1

C7
I'll buy you a diamond ring my friend,

If it makes you feel all right.
F7
I'll get you anything my friend,
C7
If it makes you feel all right.
G7 F7
'Cause I don't care too much for money,
C7
(For) money can't buy me love.

Verse 2

C7
I'll give you all I've got to give,

If you say you love me too.
F7
I may not have a lot to give,
C7
But what I've got I'll give to you.
G7 F7
I don't care too much for money.
C7
(For) money can't buy me love.

```
                        Em    Am
Chorus 1      Can't buy me love, ___
              C7
              Everybody tells me so.
                        Em    Am
              Can't buy me love, ___
              Dm          G13
              No, no, no, no.

              C7
Verse 3       Say you don't need no diamond rings

              And I'll be satisfied.
              F7
              Tell me that you want the kind of things
                  C7
              That money just can't buy.
              G7             F7
              I don't care too   much for money.
                                         C7
              (For) money can't buy me love.

Solo          | C7    | C7    | C7    | C7    |

              | F7    | F7    | C7    | C7    |

              | G7    | F7    | C7    | C7    ||

Chorus 2      As Chorus 1

Verse 4       As Verse 3

                        Em    Am    Em    Am
Outro         Can't buy me love, ___ love, ___
                        Dm    G13
              Can't buy me love ___
              C7
              Oh.
```

Carry That Weight

Words & Music by
John Lennon & Paul McCartney

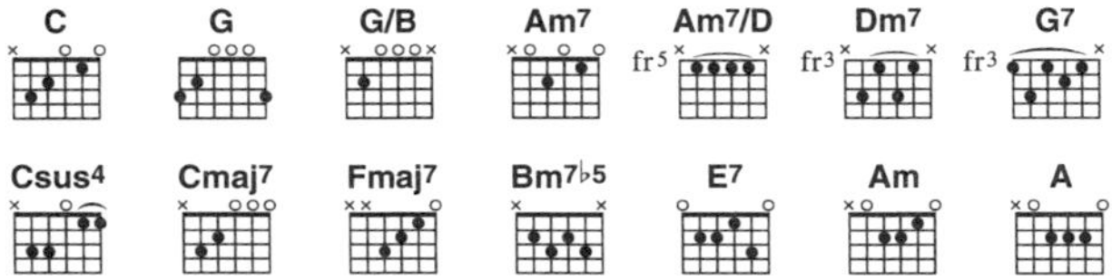


```
               C                  G
*Chorus 1*     Boy, you're gonna carry that weight,
                                      C
               Carry that weight a long time.
               C                  G
               Boy, you're gonna carry that weight,
                                      C          G/B
               Carry that weight a long time.


Link / Solo    | Am7        | Am7/D  Dm7 | G7         | Csus4  C   Cmaj7 |

               | Fmaj7      | Bm7♭5  E7  | Am         ||


               Am7                        Am7/D   Dm7
Verse 1          I never give you my pil   -   low,
               G7                     Csus4  C      Cmaj7
                 I only send you my in   -   vi  -  tations,
               Fmaj7                        Bm7♭5  E7          Am7        G     C     G
                 And in the middle of the cele  -  brations I break down.


               C                  G
Chorus 2       Boy, you're gonna carry that weight,
                                      C
               Carry that weight a long time.
               C                  G
               Boy, you're gonna carry that weight,
                                      C          G/B  A
               Carry that weight a long time.

               | C    G/B | A        ||
```

Christmas Time (Is Here Again)

Words & Music by
George Harrison, John Lennon, Paul McCartney & Ringo Starr

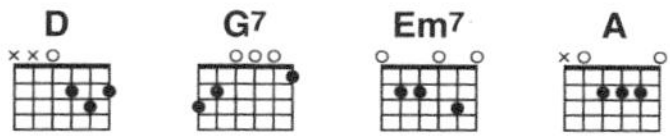

Spoken Inter-planetary mix - page four hundred and forty four.

```
            D
Verse 1     Christmas time is here again,

            Christmas time is here again,
            G7
            Christmas time is here again,
            D
            Christmas time is here again,
            Em7                   A
            Ain't been round since you know when,
            D
            Christmas time is here again,
                        A
            O-U-T spells 'out'.


Verse 2     As Verse 1

            D
Verse 3     Christmas time is here again,

            Christmas time is here again,
            G7
            Christmas time is here again,
            D
            Christmas time is here again,
            Em7                             A
            Ain't been round since you know when,
            D
            Christmas time is here again.   Fade out
```

Come Together

Words & Music by
John Lennon & Paul McCartney

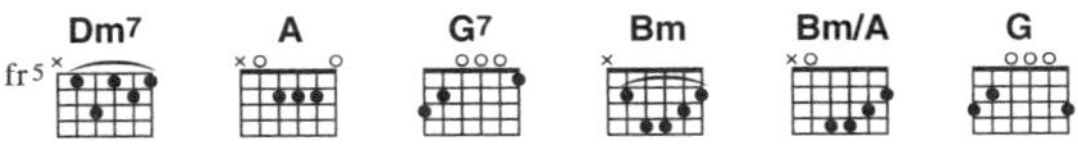

Intro ‖: Dm7 | Dm7 :‖
(Shoot me.) (Shoot me.)

Verse 1
Dm7
Here come old flat top, he come grooving up slowly,

He got joo joo eyeball, he one holy roller,

A
He got hair down to his knee,

G7 N.C.
Got to be a joker, he just do what he please.

Link | Dm7 | Dm7 | Dm7 | Dm7 ‖

Verse 2
Dm7
He wear no shoe shine, he got toe-jam football,

He got monkey finger, he shoot Coca-Cola,

A
He say, "I know you, you know me."

G7 N.C.
One thing I can tell you is you got to be free.

Chorus 1
Bm
Come together,

Bm/A G A
Right now,

N.C.
Over (me.)

Link | Dm7 | Dm7 | Dm7 | Dm7 ‖
me.

Verse 3

```
Dm7
   He Bag production, he got walrus gumboot,

He got Ono sideboard, he one spinal cracker,
          A
He got   feet down below his knee,
G7     N.C.
Hold you in his armchair, you can feel his disease.
```

Chorus 2

```
             Bm
Come together,
Bm/A   G      A
Right   now,
N.C.
Over (me.)
```

Link

```
| Dm7      | Dm7     || Dm7     | Dm7     | Dm7     | Dm7     |
  me.              (Right!)                          (Come.)

| A        | A       | A        | A       | Dm7     | Dm7     ||
 (Come.)
```

Verse 4

```
Dm7
   He roller coaster, he got early warning,

He got muddy water, he one Mojo filter,
            A
He say,   "One and one and one is three."
G7   N.C.
Got to be good looking 'cause he's so hard to see.
```

Chorus 3

```
             Bm
Come together,
Bm/A   G      A
Right   now,
N.C.
Over (me.)
```

Link

```
| Dm7     | Dm7     | Dm7     | Dm7     || Dm7     | Dm7     |
  me.                             Oh!
```

Coda

```
    Dm7
||:  Come together, yeah!  :||  Repeat to fade
```

The Continuing Story Of Bungalow Bill

Words & Music by
John Lennon & Paul McCartney

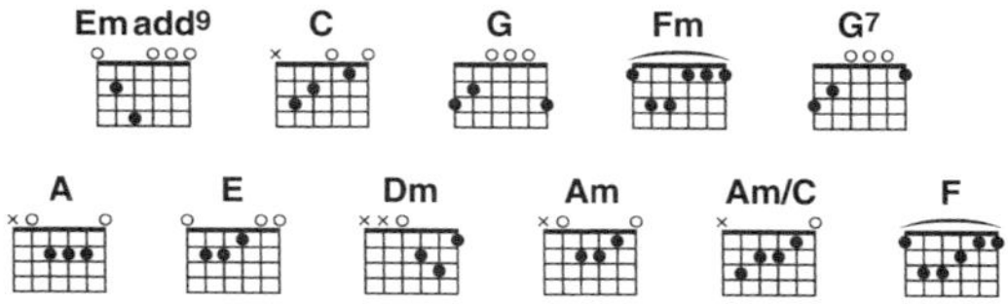

Intro | Emadd9 | (Emadd9) | (Emadd9) | (Emadd9) ||

Chorus 1

C   G   C
Hey, Bungalow Bill,
Fm   C
What did you kill,
Fm   G
Bungalow Bill?
A   E   A
Hey, Bungalow Bill,
Dm   A
What did you kill,
Dm   E
Bungalow Bill?

Verse 1

      Am   Am/C   F   G
He went out tiger hunting, with his elephant and gun.
Am   Am/C   F   G
   In case of accidents, he always took his mom.
            E   G   Am   Fm
He's the all-American, bullet-headed, Saxon mother's son.
N.C.
(All the children sing!)

Chorus 2 As Chorus 1

```
            Am              Am/C             F                 G
Verse 2       Deep in the jungle, where the mighty tiger lies,
            Am              Am/C           F               G
              Bill and his elephants were taken by surprise.
            E               G                  Am                Fm
              So Captain Marvel zapped him right between the eyes.
            N.C.
            (All the children sing!)

            C   G          C
Chorus 3    Hey, Bungalow Bill,
            Fm             C
            What did you kill,
            Fm         G
            Bungalow Bill?
            A   E          A
            Hey, Bungalow Bill,
            Dm             A
            What did you kill,
            Dm         E
            Bungalow Bill?

            Am               Am/C           F                  G
Verse 3       The children asked him if to kill was not a sin:
            Am                Am/C              F                    G
              "Not when he looks so fierce." his mommy butted in.
            E                   G                      Am           Fm
              If looks could kill, it would have been us instead of him.
            N.C.
            (All the children sing!)

Chorus 4    |: As Chorus 1 :|   Repeat to fade
```

Cry Baby Cry

Words & Music by
John Lennon & Paul McCartney

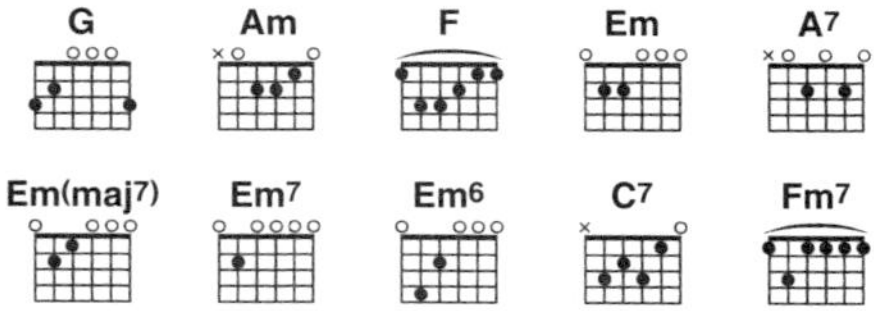

Intro

```
G            Am  F                         G
Cry baby cry,       make your mother sigh,
     Em                        A7      F
She's old enough to know better.
```

Verse 1

```
    Em               Em(maj7)
The King of Marigold
                 Em7
Was in the kitchen
               Em6             C7    G
Cooking breakfast for the Queen.
    Em                 Em(maj7)
The Queen was in the parlour,
        Em7
Playing piano
        Em6              C7
For the children of the King.
```

Chorus 1

```
G          Am  F                        G
Cry baby cry,     make your mother sigh,
     Em                        A7        F          G
She's old enough to know better, so cry baby cry.
```

Verse 2

```
    Em                 Em(maj7)
The King was in the garden,
        Em7          Em6
Picking flowers for a friend
              C7    G
Who came to play.
    Em                 Em(maj7)
The Queen was in the playroom,
         Em7
Painting pictures
        Em6        C7
For the children's holiday.
```

Chorus 2 As Chorus 1

Verse 3

```
       Em                Em(maj7)
The Duchess of Kirkaldy,
           Em7
Always smiling,
          Em6              C7   G
And arriving late for tea.
      Em                 Em(maj7)
The Duke was having problems
             Em7
With a message
          Em6            C7
At the local Bird and Bee.
```

Chorus 3 As Chorus 1

Verse 4

```
        Em                 Em(maj7)
At twelve o'clock a meeting
              Em7
Round the table
        Em6             C7   G
For a seance in the dark.
        Em              Em(maj7)
With voices out of nowhere,
            Em7
Put on specially
             Em6           C7
By the children, for a lark.
```

Chorus 4 As Chorus 1

Coda

```
           Am       F                      G
Cry, cry, cry baby,   make your mother sigh,
      Em                        A7       F        G
She's old enough to know better, so cry baby cry.

           Am F                  G
Cry, cry, cry,   make your mother sigh,
      Em                        A7       F            Em
She's old enough to know better, so cry baby cry.

Fm7
Can you take me back where I came from

Can you take me back?

Can you take me back where I came from

Brother can you take me back ______

Can you take me back?       Fade out
```

A Day In The Life

Words & Music by
John Lennon & Paul McCartney

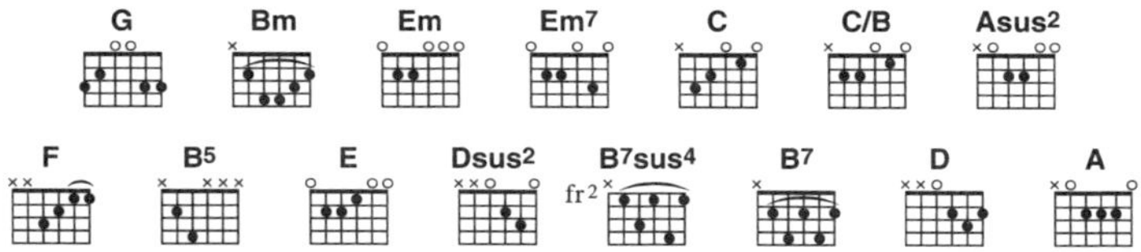


```
Intro       | G    Bm  | Em   Em7 | C        | C        ||

            G             Bm                  Em    Em7
Verse 1       I read the news today, oh boy,
            C          C/B                Asus2
              About a lucky man who made the grade.
            G                     Bm                 Em    Em7
              And though the news was rather sad,
            C            F             Em    Em7
              Well, I just had to laugh,
            C           F            Em    C
              I saw the photograph.

            G                Bm                  Em    Em7
Verse 2       He blew his mind out in a car,
            C             C/B                  Asus2
              He didn't notice that the lights had changed.
            G               Bm                   Em         Em7
              A crowd of people stood and stared,
            C                         F
              They'd seen his face before,
            Em
            Nobody was really sure
              Em7                             C
            If he was from the House of Lords.
```

Verse 3

```
G           Bm                 Em  Em7
  I saw a film today, oh boy,
C                C/B             Asus2
  The English army had just won the war.
G               Bm               Em    Em7
  A crowd of people turned away,
C              F            Em
  But I just had to look,
         Em7      C
Having read the book,
              N.C.(B5)
I'd love to turn you on.
```

Instrumental 1 𝄆 N.C. | N.C. | N.C. | N.C. | N.C. 𝄇 E | E ‖

Middle

```
(E)                                                    Dsus2
Woke up, got out of bed, dragged a comb across my head,
              E                       B7sus4
Found my way downstairs and drank a cup
      E              B7sus4           B7
And looking up I noticed I was late. Ha, ha, ha.
              E
Found my coat and grabbed my hat,
                          Dsus2
Made the bus in seconds flat,
              E                     B7sus4
Found my way upstairs and had a smoke
      E                               B7sus4
And somebody spoke and I went into a dream.
```

Interlude

```
C  G     D  A    E      C  G     D  A  | E D C D ‖
Ah,__    ah,__   ah,__  ah,__    ah.__
```

Verse 4

```
G             Bm                 Em  Em7
  I read the news today, oh boy,
C                  C/B                   Asus2
  Four thousand holes in Blackburn, Lancashire.
G                     Bm                 Em    Em7
  And though the holes were rather small,
C                F
  They had to count them all;
Em                                      Em7                    C
Now they know how many holes it takes to fill the Albert Hall.
              N.C.(B5)
I'd love to turn you on.
```

Instrumental 2 𝄆 N.C. | N.C. | N.C. | N.C. | N.C. 𝄇 E ‖

Day Tripper

Words & Music by
John Lennon & Paul McCartney

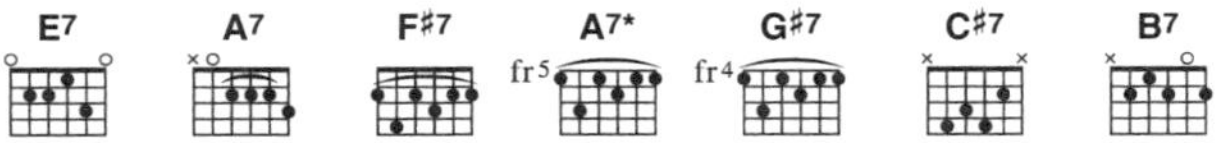

Intro | (E7) | (E7) |: E7 | E7 | E7 | E7 :|

Verse 1
E7
Got a good reason

For taking the easy way out.
A7
Got a good reason
E7
For taking the easy way out, now.
F♯7
She was a day tripper,

One way ticket, yeah.
A7* G♯7 C♯7
It took me so long to find out,
B7
And I found out.

Link | (E7) | (E7) | E7 | E7 ||

Verse 2
E7
She's a big teaser,

She took me half the way there,
A7
She's a big teaser,
E7
She took me half the way there, now.

cont.

```
                    F♯7
She was a day tripper,

One way ticket, yeah.
         A7* G♯7        C♯7
It took me so  long to find out,
           B7
And I found out.
```

Solo

```
|: B7     | B7     | B7     | B7     :|  Play three times
|  (E7)   | (E7)   | E7     | E7     ||
```

Verse 3

```
E7
Tried to please her,

She only played one night stands,
A7
Tried to please her,
E7
She only played one night stands, now.
          F♯7
She was a day tripper,

Sunday driver, yeah.
         A7* G♯7        C♯7
It took me so  long to find out,
           B7
And I found out.
```

Link 2

```
|: (E7)   | (E7)   | E7     | E7     :|
```

Coda

```
   E7
|: Day tripper, day tripper, yeah.

Day tripper, day tripper, yeah.  :|  Repeat to fade
```

Dear Prudence

Words & Music by
John Lennon & Paul McCartney

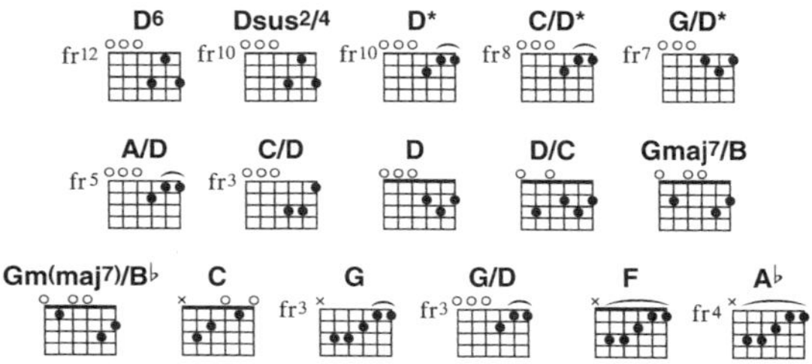

Tune bottom string down to D

Intro | D6 Dsus2/4 | D* C/D* | G/D* A/D | C/D ||
Fade In
| D D/C | Gmaj7/B Gm(maj7)/B♭ ||

Verse 1
```
        D               D/C  Gmaj7/B  Gm(maj7)/B♭
Dear  Prudence,
                              D  D/C  Gmaj7/B  Gm(maj7)/B♭
Won't you come out to play?
        D               D/C  Gmaj7/B  Gm(maj7)/B♭
Dear  Prudence,
                          D  D/C  Gmaj7/B  Gm(maj7)/B♭
Greet the brand new day. ______
      D             D/C
The sun is up, the sky is blue,
     Gmaj7/B       Gm(maj7)/B♭
It's beautiful and so are you,
       D        D/C
Dear Prudence,
C            G
Won't you come out to play.
```

Link 1 | D D/C | Gmaj7/B Gm(maj7)/B♭ ||
(play.)

Verse 2

D D/C Gmaj7/B Gm(maj7)/B♭
Dear Prudence,

D D/C Gmaj7/B Gm(maj7)/B♭
Open up your eyes.

D D/C Gmaj7/B Gm(maj7)/B♭
Dear Prudence,

D D/C Gmaj7/B Gm(maj7)/B♭
See the sunny skies. ________

D D/C
The wind is low, the birds will sing,

Gmaj7/B Gm(maj7)/B♭
That you are part of everything,

D D/C
Dear Prudence,

C G
Won't you open up your (eyes?)

Link 2

| D G/D | A/D G/D ||
(eyes?)

Bridge

D G/D
Look around round, (round round round

A/D G/D
Round round round, round round.)

D G/D
Look around, round round (round round

A/D G/D
Round round round, round round,)

F A♭ G
Look around, ah ______

Link 3

| D D/C | Gmaj7/B Gm(maj7)/B♭ ||

Verse 3

D D/C Gmaj7/B Gm(maj7)/B♭
Dear Prudence,

D D/C Gmaj7/B Gm(maj7)/B♭
Let me see you smile.

D D/C Gmaj7/B Gm(maj7)/B♭
Dear Prudence,

D D/C Gmaj7/B Gm(maj7)/B♭
Like a little child. ________

```
cont.       D                  D/C
            The clouds will be a daisy chain
               Gmaj7/B          Gm(maj7)/B♭
            So let me see you smile again,
                 D          D/C
            Dear   Prudence,
            C           G
            Won't you let me see you smile?


Link 4      | D   D/C       | Gmaj7/B   Gm(maj7)/B♭   ||
             (smile?)


                 D                D/C   Gmaj7/B   Gm(maj7)/B♭
Verse 4     Dear   Prudence,
                                          D  D/C   Gmaj7/B   Gm(maj7)/B♭
            Won't you come out to play?
                 D                D/C   Gmaj7/B   Gm(maj7)/B♭
            Dear   Prudence,
                                     D  D/C   Gmaj7/B   Gm(maj7)/B♭
            Greet the brand new day. _________
                D                D/C
            The sun is up, the sky is blue,
                 Gmaj7/B         Gm(maj7)/B♭
            It's beautiful and so are you,
                 D           D/C
            Dear Prudence,
            C            G              D
            Won't you come out to play.


Coda        | D6    Dsus2/4 | D*   C/D*   | G/D*   A/D   | C/D     | D      ||
                                                           Fade out
```

Dig It

Words & Music by
George Harrison, John Lennon, Paul McCartney & Ringo Starr

B♭
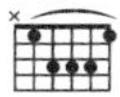
F

C

Verse

```
                 B♭       F         B♭   C
…Like a rolling stone,
              B♭           F       B♭    C
Like a rolling stone,
                B♭    F      B♭    C
Like the F. B. I.
                B♭    F      B♭    C
And the C. I.  A.
                B♭    F      B♭    C
And the B. B. C.
B♭             F   B♭    C
B. B. King,
                 B♭    F   B♭    C
And Doris Day,
         B♭
Matt Busby.
```

Coda

```
F        B♭
Dig it, dig it,
C        B♭
Dig it, dig it,
F        B♭
Dig it, dig it,
C        B♭
Dig it, dig it…
```
Fade out

Dig A Pony

Words & Music by
John Lennon & Paul McCartney

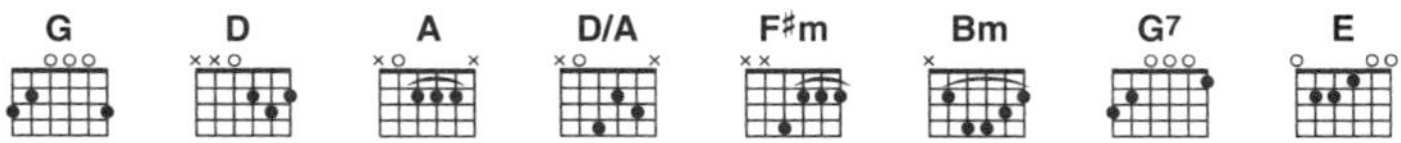


```
Intro       |: (G)      | (D)      | (A)      | (A)      :|

            A  D/A  A  D/A  A  D/A  A
Verse 1     I ______________________

                     F♯m
            Dig a pony,
                                Bm                     G7
            Well, you can celebrate anything you want,
                    Bm                          G7              E
            Yes,   you can celebrate anything you want, oh!

            A  D/A  A  D/A  A  D/A  A
Verse 2     I ______________________

                   F♯m
            Do a road hog,
                                Bm                     G7
            Well, you can penetrate any place you go,
                    Bm                        G7              E
            Yes,   you can penetrate any place you go, I told you so.

            G    D      A
Chorus 1    All I want is you,
            G                      D                            A
            Everything has got to be just like you want it to.
            N.C.
            Because…

            A  D/A  A  D/A  A  D/A  A
Verse 3     I ______________________

                      F♯m
            Pick a moondog,
                                Bm                      G7
            Well, you can radiate everything you are,
                    Bm                        G7          E
            Yes,   you can radiate everything you are, oh now.
```

Verse 4

```
A D/A A D/A A D/A A
I ____________________

      F#m
Roll a stoney,

                 Bm                    G7
Well,  you can imitate everyone you know,

      Bm                 G7          E
Yes,  you can imitate everyone you know, I told you so.
```

Chorus 2 As Chorus 1

Solo

```
| A  D/A  | A  D/A  | A  D/A  | A  D/A  |
| F#m     | F#m     | Bm      | G7      |
| G7      | Bm      | G7      | E       | E       ||
```

Verse 5

```
A D/A A D/A A D/A A
I ____________________

           F#m
Feel the wind blow.

                Bm                     G7
Well, you can indicate everything you see,

      Bm              G7           E
Yes,  you can indicate anything you see, oh now
```

Verse 6

```
A D/A A D/A A D/A A
I ____________________

             F#m
Cold and lonely.

                Bm           G7
Well, you can syndicate any boat you row.

       Bm               G7                 E
Yeah,  you can syndicate any boat you row, I told you so.
```

Chorus 3 As Chorus 1

Coda

```
|: G      | D      | A      | A      :| A      ||
```

Doctor Robert

Words & Music by
John Lennon & Paul McCartney

A7 Asus4 F♯7 E7 B E/B

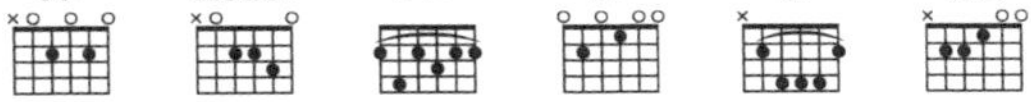

```
Intro       | A7  Asus4 | A7  Asus4 | A7  Asus4 | A7  Asus4 ||

            A7
Verse 1     Ring my friend, I said you'd call, Doctor Robert.

            Day or night, he'll be there any time at all, Doctor Robert.
                   F♯7
            Doctor Robert, you're a new and better man,

            He helps you to understand,
                    E7           F♯7        B
            He does everything he can, Doctor Robert.


            A7
Verse 2     If you're down, he'll pick you up, Doctor Robert.

            Take a drink from his special cup, Doctor Robert.
                   F♯7
            Doctor Robert, he's a man you must believe,

            Helping anyone in need,
            E7             F♯7           B
            No-one can succeed like Doctor Robert.


            B                       E/B    B
Bridge 1    Well, well, well, you're feeling fine,
                                  E/B
            Well, well, well, he'll make you,
                   A7
            Doctor Robert.
```

```
              A7
*Verse 3*     My friend works for the National Health, Doctor Robert.

              You'll pay money just to see yourself with Doctor Robert.
                    F♯7
              Doctor Robert, you're a new and better man,

              He helps you to understand,
                     E7             F♯7     B
              He does everything he can, Doc Robert.


              B                       E/B   B
*Bridge 2*    Well, well, well, you're feeling fine,
                                    E/B
              Well, well, well, he'll make you,
                    A7
              Doctor Robert.

              A7
*Coda*        Ring my friend, I said you'd call

              Doctor Robert.

              Ring my friend, I said you'd call

              Doc Robert.
                    F♯7      B
              Doctor Robert!  Fade out
```

Don't Bother Me

Words & Music by
George Harrison

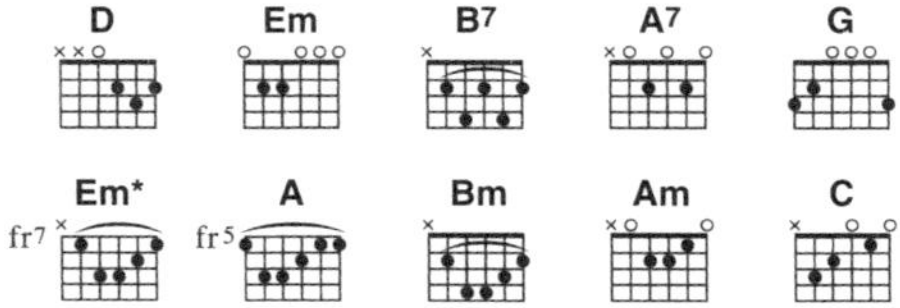

Intro | D | D | Em |

Verse 1

(Em) **B7** **A7** **G** **Em**
Since she's been gone, I want no-one to talk to me.
B7 **A7** **G**
It's not the same, but I'm to blame, it's plain to see.
Em* **A** **Em***
So go away, leave me alone, don't bother me.

Verse 2

B7 **A7** **G** **Em**
I can't believe that she would leave me on my own.
B7 **A7** **G**
It's just not right when every night I'm all alone.
Em* **A** **Em***
I've got no time for you right now, don't bother me.

Bridge 1

D **Em**
I know I'll never be the same
D **Em**
If I don't get her back again,
Bm **Am**
Because I know she'll always be
C **Em**
The only girl for me.

```
                      B7                                      A7                    G         Em
Verse 3        But till she's here, please don't come near, just stay away.
                   B7                                A7                G
               I'll let you know when she's come home, until that day,
                      Em*                       A                        Em*
               Don't come around, leave me alone, don't bother me.

Solo           | B7     | A7     | G      | Em     |

               | B7     | A7     | G      | G      ||

               N.C.         Em*                       A                        Em*
               I've got no time for you right now, don't bother me.

                        D                 Em
Bridge 2       I know I'll never be the same
                      D                  Em
               If I don't get her back again,
                          Bm                         Am
               Because I know she'll always be
                   C               Em
               The only girl for me.

               N.C.                B7                                     A7                    G         Em
Verse 4        But till she's here, please don't come near, just stay away.
                         B7                               A7                G
               I'll let you know when she's come home, until that day,
                          Em*                       A                        Em*
               Don't come around, leave me alone, don't bother me.
                  A                Em*
               |:    Don't bother me.    :|    Repeat to fade
```

Don't Let Me Down

Words & Music by
John Lennon & Paul McCartney

Intro | E Esus4 | E ||

Chorus 1

```
                F♯m
Don't let me down,
                E        Esus4  E
Don't let me down,
                F♯m
Don't let me down,
                E        Esus4  E
Don't let me down.
```

Verse 1

```
N.C.                             F♯m7
Nobody ever loved me like she does,
                       Emaj7  Esus4  E
Ooh she does, yes she does.
N.C.                                  F♯m7
And if somebody loved me like she do me,
                        Emaj7  Esus4  E
Ooh she do me, yes she does.
```

Chorus 2

```
                F♯m
Don't let me down,
                E        Esus4  E
Don't let me down,
                F♯m
Don't let me down,
                E        Esus4  E
Don't let me down.
```

Bridge

N.C. E
I'm in love for the first time,
B7
Don't you know it's going to last.

It's a love that lasts forever,
E Esus4 E
It's a love that has no past.

Chorus 3

F♯m
Don't let me down,
E Esus4 E
Don't let me down,
F♯m
Don't let me down,
E Esus4 E
Don't let me down.

Verse 2

N.C. F♯m7
And from the first time that she really done me,
Emaj7 Esus4 E
Ooh, she done me, she done me good.
N.C. F♯m7
I guess nobody ever really done me,
Emaj7 Esus4 E
Ooh she done me, she done me good.

Chorus 4

F♯m
Don't let me down, hey!
E Esus4 E
Don't let me down,
F♯m
Don't let me down,
E Esus4 E
Don't let me down.
F♯m E Esus4 E
Don't let me down,
F♯m
Don't let me down.

Can you dig it?
E Esus4 E
Don't let me down.

Don't Pass Me By

Words & Music by
Ringo Starr

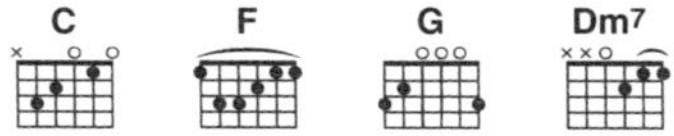

Intro | C | C ||

Verse 1
C
I listen for your footsteps coming up the drive,
F
Listen for your footsteps, but they don't arrive.
G
Waiting for your knock, dear, on my old front door,
F
I don't hear it,
C
Does it mean you don't love me anymore?

Verse 2
C
I hear the clock a-ticking on the mantelshelf,
F
See the hands a-moving, but I'm by myself.
G
I wonder where you are tonight and why I'm by myself,
F
I don't see you,
C
Does it mean you don't love me anymore?

Chorus 1
C
Don't pass me by, don't make me cry,
Don't make me blue,
F
'Cause you know, darling, I love only you.
C
You'll never know it hurt me so, I hate to see you go,
G F
Don't pass me by, don't make me cry. ____

Link | C | C ||

Verse 3
C
I'm sorry that I doubted you, I was so unfair,
F
You were in a car crash and you lost your hair.
G
You said that you would be late, about an hour or two,
F
I say that's all right,
C
I'm waiting here, just waiting to hear from you.

Chorus 2
C
Don't pass me by, don't make me cry,
Don't make me blue,
F
'Cause you know, darling, I love only you.
C
You'll never know it hurt me so, I hate to see you go,
G F
Don't pass me by, don't make me cry. ___

Link | C | C || *Drums for 2 bars* || C | C ||

Chorus 3
C
Don't pass me by, don't make me cry,
Don't make me blue,
F
'Cause you know, darling, I love only you.
C
You'll never know it hurt me so, I hate to see you go,
G F
Don't pass me by, don't make me cry. ___

Coda | C | C | F | G | Dm7 C | *Violin to fade* ||

Drive My Car

Words & Music by
John Lennon & Paul McCartney

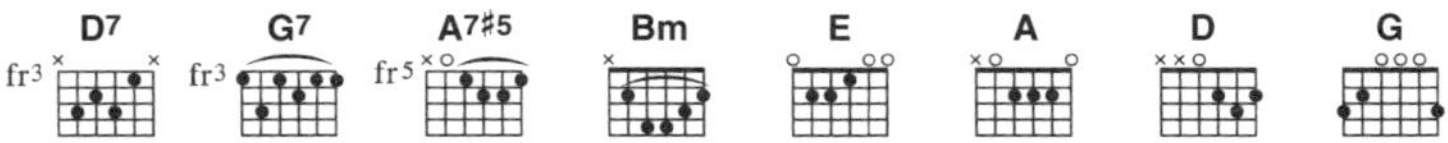

Intro | (D7) | (D7) ||

Verse 1

D7 G7
Asked a girl what she wanted to be,
D7 G7
She said, "Baby, can't you see?
D7 G7
I wanna be famous, a star of the screen,
A7♯5
But you can do something in between."

Chorus 1

Bm G7 Bm G7
Baby, you can drive my car, yes I'm gonna be a star,
Bm E A D G A
Baby, you can drive my car, and maybe I'll love you.

Verse 2

D7 G7
I told that girl that my prospects were good,
D7 G7
She said, "Baby, it's understood.
D7 G7
Working for peanuts is all very fine,
A7♯5
But I can show you a better time."

Chorus 2

Bm G7 Bm G7
Baby, you can drive my car, yes I'm gonna be a star,
Bm E A D G
Baby, you can drive my car, and maybe I'll love you.
A N.C.
Beep beep mm beep beep, yeah!

Guitar solo

| D7 | G7 | D7 | G7 |

| D7 | G7 | A | A ||

Chorus 3

Bm G7 Bm G7
Baby, you can drive my car, yes I'm gonna be a star,
Bm E A D G A
Baby, you can drive my car, and maybe I'll love you.

Verse 3

D7 G7
I told that girl I could start right away,
D7 G7
And she said, "Listen, babe, I've got something to say,
D7 G7
I've got no car, and it's breaking my heart,
A7♯5
But I've found a driver, and that's a start."

Chorus 4

Bm G7 Bm G7
Baby, you can drive my car, yes I'm gonna be a star,
Bm E A D G
Baby, you can drive my car, and maybe I'll love you.
A N.C. D G
Beep beep mm beep beep, yeah!
A D G
|: Beep beep mm beep beep, yeah! :| *Play 6 times to fade*

Do You Want To Know A Secret

Words & Music by
John Lennon & Paul McCartney

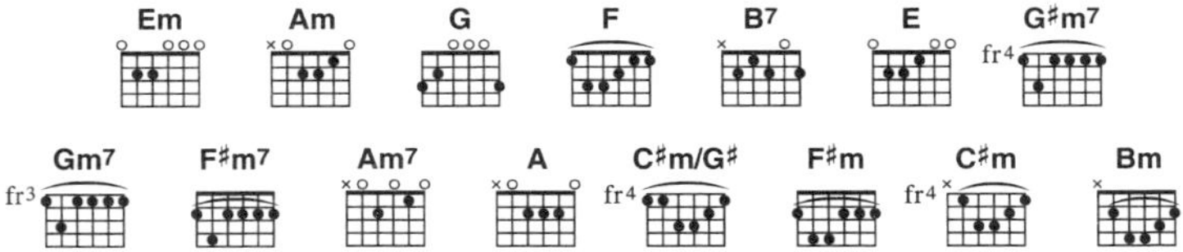

Intro

Em Am Em
You'll never know how much I really love you,
G F B7
You'll never know how much I really care.

Verse 1

E G♯m7 Gm7 F♯m7
Listen,
B7 E G♯m7 Gm7 F♯m7
Do you want to know a secret?
B7 E G♯m7 Gm7 F♯m7 Am7
Do you promise not to tell? Woh - oh - oh.
E G♯m7 Gm7 F♯m7
Closer,
B7 E G♯m7 Gm7 F♯m7
Let me whisper in your ear,
B7 A
Say the words you long to hear,
B7 C♯m/G♯ F♯m7 B7
I'm in love with you, woo - oo - oo - ooh.

Verse 2 As Verse 1

Bridge

A F♯m C♯m Bm
I've known the secret for a week or two,
A F♯m C♯m Bm F♯m B7
Nobody knows, just we two. ___

Verse 3 As Verse 1

Outro

C♯m/G♯ F♯m7 B7
𝄆 Woo - oo - oo - ooh. 𝄇 *Repeat to fade*

The End

Words & Music by
John Lennon & Paul McCartney

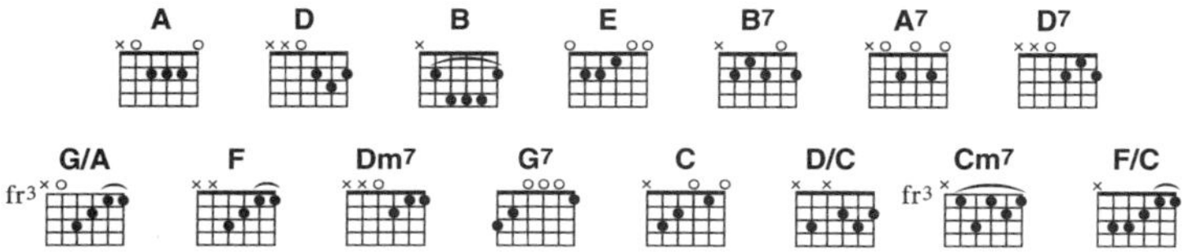

Intro | A | D B | E A | A B7 | B7 A | N.C. | *Drums* ||

A D B E
Oh yeah! All right!

A B7 A
Are you gonna be in my dreams tonight?

Link | *Drums for 8 bars* || A7 | D7 | A7 | D7 ||

Verse 1
A7 D7 A7 D7
Love you, love you, love you, love you,
A7 D7
Love you, love you.

Play 3 times

Solo ||: A7 | D7 | A7 | D7 | A7 | D7 :||
(Love you, love you, love you, love you, love you, love you.)

Piano link | A | A ||

Coda
A
And in the end,
G/A
The love you take
F Dm7 G7 C
Is equal to the love you make.
D/C Cm7 F/C C
Ahhh.

Eight Days A Week

Words & Music by
John Lennon & Paul McCartney

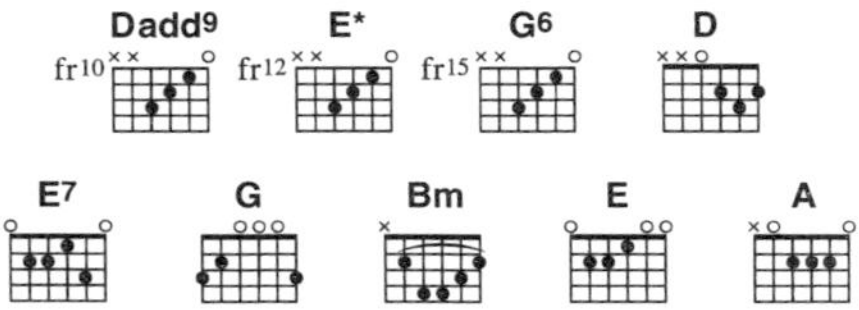

Intro | Dadd9 | E* | G6 | Dadd9 ||

Verse 1

D   E7
Ooh, I need your love, babe,
G   D
Guess you know it's true.
D   E7
Hope you need my love, babe,
G   D
Just like I need you.

Chorus 1

Bm   G
Hold me, love me,
Bm   E
Hold me, love me.
  D   E7
I ain't got nothing but love, babe,
G   D
  Eight days a week.

Verse 2

D   E7
Love you every day, girl,
              G   D
You're always on my mind.
D   E7
One thing I can say, girl,
G   D
Love you all the time.

Chorus 2

Bm **G**
Hold me, love me,
Bm **E**
Hold me, love me.
D **E7**
I ain't got nothing but love, girl,
G **D**
Eight days a week.

Middle 1

A
Eight days a week,
Bm
I love ___ you.
E
Eight days a week
G **A**
Is not enough to show I care.

Verse 3 As Verse 1

Chorus 3 As Chorus 1

Middle 2 As Middle 1

Verse 4 As Verse 2

Chorus 4

Bm **G**
Hold me, love me,
Bm **E**
Hold me, love me,
D **E7**
I ain't got nothing but love, girl,
G **D**
Eight days a week.
G **D**
Eight days a week.
G **D**
Eight days a week.

Outro | **Dadd9** | **E*** | **G6** | **Dadd9** ||

Eleanor Rigby

Words & Music by
John Lennon & Paul McCartney

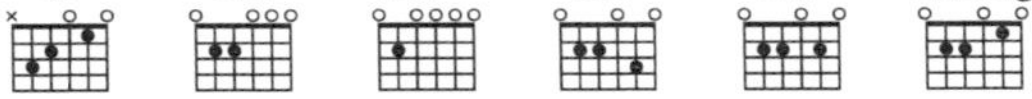

Intro

```
C                         Em
Ah, look at all the lonely people!
C                         Em
Ah, look at all the lonely people!
```

Verse 1

```
Em
Eleanor Rigby,
                                                         C
Picks up the rice in the church where a wedding has been,
                 Em
Lives in a dream.

Waits at the window,
                                        Em7*      C
Wearing a face that she keeps in a jar by the door,
              Em
Who is it for?
```

Chorus 1

```
Em7            Em6             Em aug            Em
All the lonely people, where do they all come from?
Em7            Em6             Em aug       Em
All the lonely people, where do they all belong?
```

Verse 2

```
Em
Father McKenzie,
                                                   C
Writing the words of a sermon that no-one will hear,
                Em
No-one comes near.

Look at him working,
                                                         C
Darning his socks in the night when there's nobody there,
                Em
What does he care?
```

```
            Em7          Em6          Emaug        Em
Chorus 2    All the lonely people, where do they all come from?
            Em7          Em6          Emaug     Em
            All the lonely people, where do they all belong?

            C                      Em
Bridge      Ah, look at all the lonely people!
            C                      Em
            Ah, look at all the lonely people!

            Em
Verse 3     Eleanor Rigby
                                                        C
            Died in the church and was buried along with her name,
                         Em
            Nobody came.

            Father McKenzie,
                                                           C
            Wiping the dirt from his hands as he walks from the grave,
                           Em
            No-one was saved.

            Em7          Em6          Emaug        Em
Chorus 3    All the lonely people, where do they all come from?
            Em7          Em6          Emaug     Em
            All the lonely people, where do they all belong?
```

Every Little Thing

Words & Music by
John Lennon & Paul McCartney

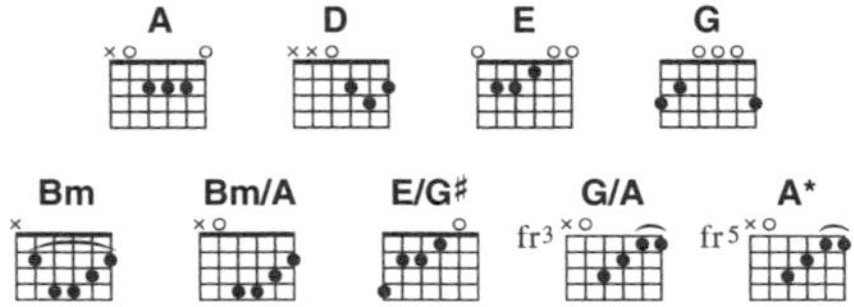

Intro | (A) | (D) (E) ||

Verse 1

A   D   E
  When I'm walking beside her,
A   G   D
  People tell me I'm luck-y,
Bm   Bm/A   E/G♯ A
  Yes, I know I'm a lucky guy.
                        D   E
I remember the first time
A   G   D
  I was lonely without her,
Bm   Bm/A   E/G♯   A
  Yes, I'm thinking about her now.

Chorus 1

A   G
  Every little thing she does,
                    G/A A* G/A   A*
She does for me,   yeah, ___
                              G
And you know the things she does,
                    G/A A* G/A   A*
She does for me,   ooh. ___

Verse 2

```
A                          D    E
   When I'm with her I'm hap-py,
A                        G     D
   Just to know that she loves me,
Bm       Bm/A            E/G#      A
   Yes I know that she loves me now.
                           D    E
There is one thing I'm sure of,
A                    G  D
   I will love her forev-er,
Bm       Bm/A              E/G#  A
   For I know love will never die.
```

Chorus 2

```
A               G
   Every little thing she does,
               G/A  A*  G/A    A*
She does for me,        yeah, ___
                    G
And you know the things she does,
               G/A  A*  G/A  A*
She does for me,        ooh. ___
```

Solo

```
| A      | D    E | A      | G    D | Bm   Bm/A | E/G#   A ||
```

Chorus 3

```
A               G
   Every little thing she does,
               G/A  A*  G/A    A*
She does for me,        yeah, ___
                    G
And you know the things she does,
               G/A  A*  G/A  A*
She does for me,        ooh. ___
```

Coda

```
||:  A  D  E
              Every little thing.  :||   Repeat to fade
```

Everybody's Got Something To Hide Except Me And My Monkey

Words & Music by
John Lennon & Paul McCartney

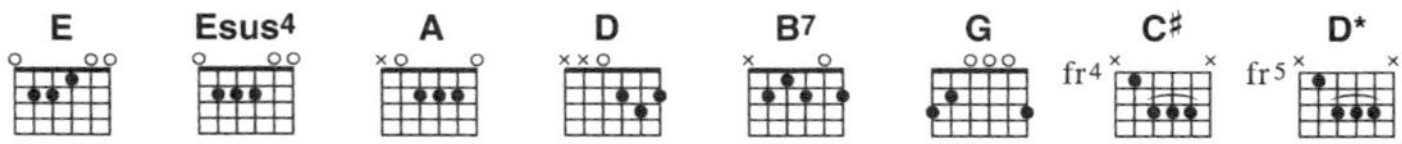

Intro ‖: E Esus4 A | E Esus4 A :‖

Verse 1
E
Come on, come on,

Come on, come on.

Come on is such a joy,

Come on is such a joy.

Come on is take it easy,

Come on is take it easy.

Chorus 1
A
Take it easy,
D
Take it easy.
B7
Everybody's got something to hide
E D G | E G | D ‖
Except for me and my monkey.

Verse 2
E
The deeper you go, the higher you fly,

The higher you fly, the deeper you go,

So come on, come on.

cont.

E
Come on is such a joy,

Come on is such a joy.

Come on is make it easy,

Come on is take it easy.

Chorus 2 As Chorus 1

Verse 3

    E
Your inside is out when your outside is in,

Your outside is in when your inside is out,

So come on, come on.

Come on is such a joy,

Come on is such a joy.

Come on is make it easy,

Come on is make it easy.

Chorus 3

         A
Make it easy,

         D
Make it easy.

     B7
Everybody's got something to hide

                           E   D G | E G | D ||
Except for me and my monkey.

Coda

N.C.
(Come on, come on, come on) *ad lib.*

| C# D* C# D* | C# D* C# D* | C# D* C# D* ||

||: E Esus4 A | E Esus4 A :|| *Repeat ad lib. to fade*
(Come on, come on, come on)

Fixing A Hole

Words & Music by
John Lennon & Paul McCartney

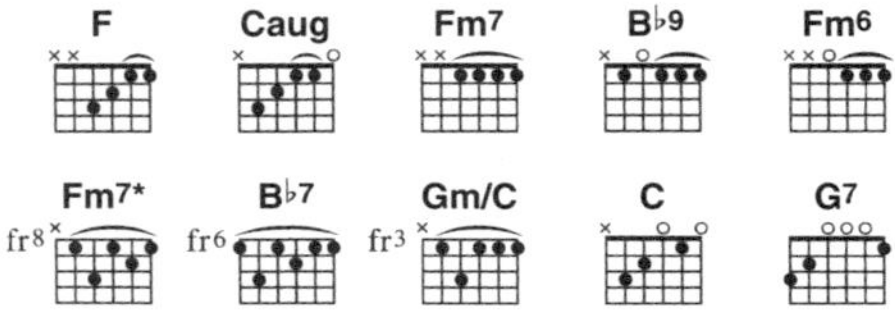

Intro | F | Caug | Fm7 | B♭9 ||

Verse 1
F Caug Fm7 Fm6
I'm fixing a hole where the rain gets in,
Fm7 B♭9
And stops my mind from wandering
Fm7 B♭9 Fm7* B♭7
Where it will go. ___

Verse 2
F Caug Fm7 Fm6
I'm filling the cracks that ran through the door,
Fm7 B♭9
And kept my mind from wandering
Fm7 B♭9 Fm7* B♭7
Where it will go. ___

Bridge 1
F Gm/C F
And it really doesn't matter if I'm wrong,
Gm/C F
I'm right where I belong,
Gm/C F
I'm right where I belong. __
C G7
See the people standing there
C G7
Who disagree and never win,
C G7 C
And wonder why they don't get in my door.

Verse 3

F Caug Fm7 Fm6
I'm painting the room in a colourful way,
Fm7 B♭9
And when my mind is wandering,
Fm7 B♭9
There I will go, ___
Fm7* B♭7
Ooh-ooh uh-uh, __ hey hey (hey.) __

Solo

| F Caug | Fm7 Fm6 | Fm7 | B♭9 |
hey.
| Fm7 | B♭9 | Fm7 | B♭9 ||

Bridge 2

F Gm/C F
And it really doesn't matter if I'm wrong,
Gm/C F
I'm right where I belong,
Gm/C F
I'm right where I belong. __
C G7
Silly people run around,
C G7
They worry me and never ask me
C G7 C
Why they don't get past my door.

Verse 4

F Caug Fm7 Fm6
I'm taking the time for a number of things
Fm7 B♭9
That weren't important yesterday,
Fm7 B♭9 Fm7* B♭7
And I still go, ___

Verse 5

F Caug Fm7 Fm6
||: I'm fixing a hole where the rain gets in,
Fm7 B♭9
And stops my mind from wandering
Fm7 B♭9
Where it will go. ___
Fm7* B♭7
Where it will go. ___ :|| *Repeat and fade*

The Fool On The Hill

Words & Music by
John Lennon & Paul McCartney

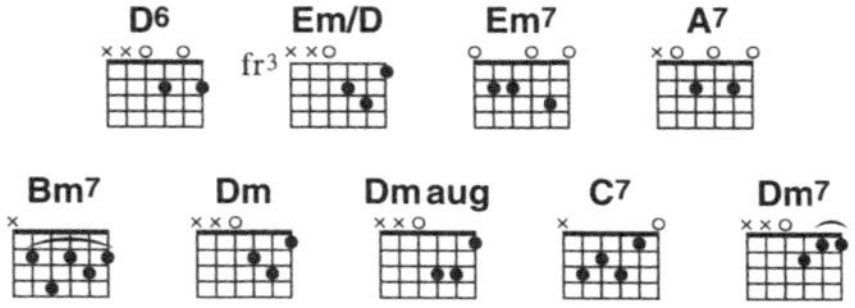

Intro | D6 | D6 ||

Verse 1

D6 Em/D
Day after day, alone on a hill,
D6 Em/D
The man with the foolish grin is keeping perfectly still.
Em7 A7
But nobody wants to know him,
D6 Bm7
They can see that he's just a fool.
Em7 A7
And he never gives an answer;

Chorus 1

Dm Dmaug Dm
But the fool on the hill
Dmaug
Sees the sun going down,
C7
And the eyes in his head
Dm Dm7 D6
See the world spinning round.

Verse 2

D6 Em/D
Well on the way, his head in a cloud,
D6 Em/D
The man of a thousand voices talking perfectly loud.
Em7 A7
But nobody ever hears him,
D6 Bm7
Or the sound he appears to make.
Em7 A7
And he never seems to notice;

Chorus 2 As Chorus 1

Solo 𝄆 D6 | D6 | Em/D | Em/D 𝄇

Verse 3

```
    Em7              A7
And nobody seems to like him,
          D6                    Bm7
They can tell what he wants to do.
    Em7                 A7
And he never shows his feelings;
```

Chorus 3

```
          Dm  Dmaug  Dm
But the fool  on  the  hill
         Dmaug
Sees the sun going down,
         C7
And the eyes in his head
           Dm             Dm7
See the world spinning round.
D6                Em/D
  (Oh, ______       oh, ______
D6                                Em/D
'Round, 'round, 'round, 'round, 'round.)
```

Verse 4

```
    Em7             A7
And he never listens to them,
   D6                      Bm7
He knows that they're the fool.
Em7            A7
  They don't like him;
```

Chorus 4

```
      Dm  Dmaug  Dm
The fool  on  the  hill
         Dmaug
Sees the sun going down,
         C7
And the eyes in his head
           Dm             Dm7
See the world spinning round.
   D6
𝄆   (Oh, ______
Em7/D
'Round, 'round, 'round,

'Round, and...)   𝄇  Repeat to fade
```

For No One

Words & Music by
John Lennon & Paul McCartney

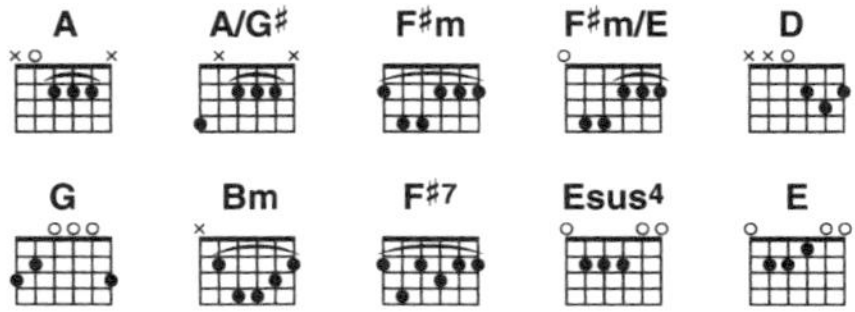

Capo second fret

Verse 1

A A/G♯
Your day breaks, your mind aches,
F♯m F♯m/E
You find that all her words
D G
Of kindness linger on
A
When she no longer needs you.

Verse 2

A A/G♯
She wakes up, she makes up,
F♯m F♯m/E
She takes her time
D G
And doesn't feel she has to hurry,
A
She no longer needs you.

Chorus 1

Bm F♯7
And in her eyes you see nothing,
Bm F♯7
No sign of love behind the tears cried for no-one,
Bm Esus4 E
A love that should have lasted years.

Verse 3

A A/G♯
You want her, you need her,

F♯m F♯m/E
And yet, you don't believe her

D G
When she says her love is dead,

A
You think she needs you.

Solo

| A A/G♯ | F♯m F♯m/E | D G | A ||

Chorus 2

Bm F♯7
And in her eyes you see nothing,

Bm F♯7
No sign of love behind the tears cried for no-one,

Bm Esus4 E
A love that should have lasted years.

Verse 4

A A/G♯
You stay home, she goes out,

F♯m F♯m/E D
She says that long ago she knew someone,

G
But now he's gone,

A
She doesn't need him.

Verse 5

A A/G♯
Your day breaks, your mind aches,

F♯m F♯m/E D
There will be times when all the things she said

G
Will fill your head,

A
You won't forget her.

Chorus 3

Bm F♯7
And in her eyes you see nothing,

Bm F♯7
No sign of love behind the tears cried for no-one,

Bm Esus4 E
A love that should have lasted years.

For You Blue

Words & Music by
George Harrison

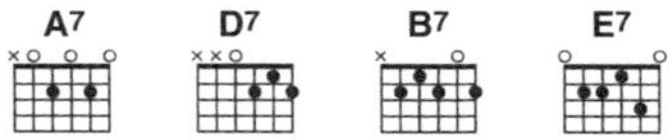

Capo fifth fret

Intro | A7 | D7 | B7 | E7 | E7 ||

Verse 1

```
  A7                      D7
Because you're sweet and lovely,
       A7
I love you.
  D7                                  A7
Because you're sweet and lovely, girl, it's true.
 E7                  D7         A7   E7
I love you more than ever, girl, I do.
```

Verse 2

```
 A7             D7
I want you in the morning, girl,
       A7
I love you.
 D7                              A7
I want you at the moment I feel blue,
    E7         D7                 A7   E7
I'm living every moment, girl, for you.
```

Solo break

| A7 | D7 | A7 | A7 | D7 | D7 |
(Bop) (Bop cat bop)

| A7 | A7 | E7 | D7 | A7 | E7 ||
(Go Johnny go) (Same old 12 bar blues)

| A7 | D7 | A7 | A7 |

| D7 | D7 | A7 | A7 |
(Elmore James got nothing on this baby)

| E7 | D7 | A7 | E7 ||

```
               A7                        D7       A7
*Verse 3*      I've loved you from the moment I saw you,
                D7                                      A7
               You looked at me, that's all you had to do.
                E7              D7                 A7     E7
               I feel it now, I hope you feel it too.

                 A7                        D7
*Verse 4*      Because you're sweet and lovely, girl,
                    A7
               I love you.
                 D7                                         A7
               Because you're sweet and lovely, girl, it's true.
                E7                        D7          A7
               I love you more than ever, girl, I do.
```

From Me To You

Words & Music by
John Lennon & Paul McCartney

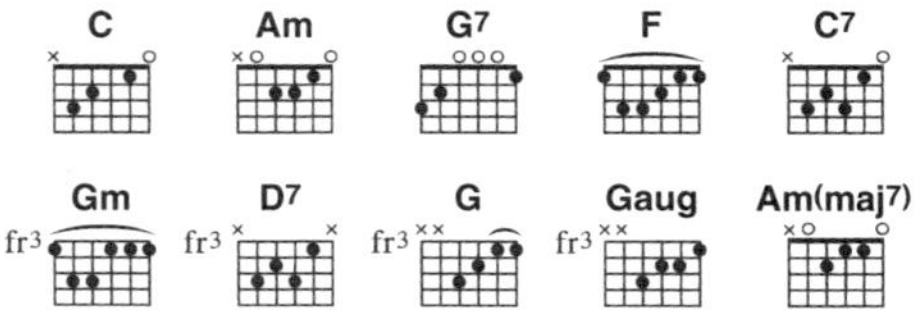

Intro

C Am
Da da da da-da dum dum da,
C Am
Da da da da-da dum dum da.

Verse 1

C Am
If there's anything that you want,
C G7
If there's anything I can do,
F Am
Just call on me and I'll send it along,
C G7 C Am
With love from me to you.

Verse 2

C Am
I've got everything that you want,
C G7
Like a heart that's oh so true,
F Am
Just call on me and I'll send it along,
C G7 C C7
With love from me to you.

Bridge 1

Gm C
I got arms that long to hold you,
F
And keep you by my side,
D7
I got lips that long to kiss you,
G Gaug
And keep you satisfied.

Verse 3

```
                C                       Am
If there's anything that you want,
                C                  G7
If there's anything I can do,
      F                      Am
Just call on me and I'll send it along,
     C          G7    C      Am
With love from me to you.
```

Solo

```
| C      | Am    From me.

| C      | G7    To you.
      F                      Am
Just call on me and I'll send it along,
     C          G7    C      C7
With love from me to you.
```

Bridge 2

```
      Gm                 C
I got arms that long to hold you,
      F
And keep you by my side,
      D7
I got lips that long to kiss you,
      G              Gaug
And keep you satisfied.
```

Verse 4

```
                C                       Am
If there's anything that you want,
                C                  G7
If there's anything I can do,
      F                      Am
Just call on me and I'll send it along,
     C          G7    C
With love from me to you.
   Am
To you,
   Am(maj7)
To you,
   C    Am
To you.
```

Get Back

Words & Music by
John Lennon & Paul McCartney

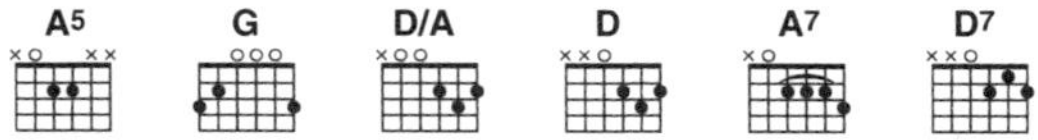

Intro | A5 | A5 | A5 | A5 G D/A ||

Verse 1

A5
Jojo was a man who thought he was a loner
D A5
But he knew it couldn't last.

Jojo left his home in Tucson, Arizona
D A5
For some California grass.

Chorus 1

A7
Get back, get back,
D7 A5 G D/A
Get back to where you once belonged.
A7
Get back, get back,
D7 A5
Get back to where you once belonged.

Get back Jojo.

Solo |: (A5) | A5 | D | A5 G D/A :|

Chorus 2

A7
Get back, get back,
D7 A5 G D/A
Get back to where you once belonged.
A7
Get back, get back,
A5 D
Get back to where you once belonged.
A5
Get back Jo.

Solo ‖: (A5) | A5 | D | A5 G D/A :‖

```
               A5
*Verse 2*      Sweet Loretta Martin thought she was a woman
               D                    A5
               But she was another man.

               All the girls around her say she's got it coming
               D                         A5
               But she gets it while she can.

                   A7
Chorus 3       Get back, get back,
                   D7                            A5          G  D/A
               Get back to where you once belonged.
                   A7
               Get back, get back,
                   D7                            A5
               Get back to where you once belonged.

               Get back Loretta.
```

Solo ‖: A5 | A5 | D | A5 G D/A :‖

```
                   A7
Chorus 4       Get back, get back,
                   D7                            A5          G  D/A
               Get back to where you once belonged.
                   A7
               Get back, get back,
                   D7                            D
               Get back to where you once belonged.  Ooh.

               ‖: A5   | A5       | D       | A5  G  D/A :‖  Repeat to fade
                          Get back.
```

Getting Better

Words & Music by
John Lennon & Paul McCartney

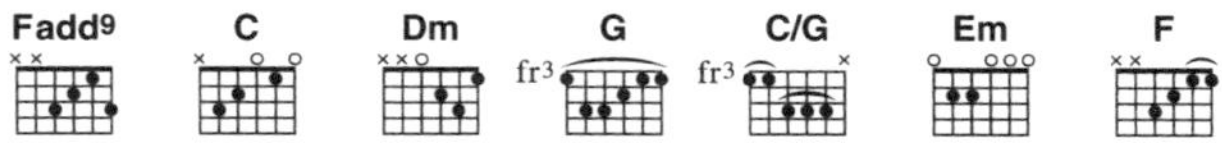

Intro | Fadd9 | Fadd9 ||

C   Dm7
It's getting better all the time.

Verse 1

G   C/G
I used to get mad at my school,
G   C/G
The teachers that taught me weren't cool.
G
You're holding me down, turning me round,
                                  C/G
Filling me up with your rules.

Chorus 1

C   Dm
I've got to admit, it's getting better,
Em   F
A little better all the time.
C   Dm
I have to admit, it's getting better,
Em   F
It's getting better since you've been mine.

Link 1 | G | G C/G ||

Verse 2

G   C/G   G   C/G
Me used to be angry young man,
G   C/G   G   C/G
Me hiding me head in the sand.
G   C/G
You gave me the word,
G   C/G
I finally heard
G   C/G   G   C/G
I'm doing the best that I can.

Chorus 2

```
     C                            Dm
I've got to admit, it's getting better,
         Em            F
A little better all the time.
 C                            Dm
I have to admit, it's getting better,
             Em             F
It's getting better since you've been mine.
F
Getting so much better all the time.
```

Chorus 3

```
   C                              Dm
|:    It's getting better all the time,
  Em              F
Better, better, better.  :|
```

Link 2

```
| G          | G          ||
```

Verse 3

```
 (G)
I used to be cruel to my woman,

I beat her and kept her apart

From the things that she loved.
G  C/G    G          C/G                   G               C/G
           Man, I was mean, but I'm changing my scene,
           G           C/G          G    C/G
And I'm doing the best that I can.
```

Chorus 4

```
C                         Dm
   I admit, it's getting better,
         Em            F
A little better all the time.
C                            Dm
Yes, I admit, it's getting better,
             Em             F
It's getting better since you've been mine.
F                                  C
Getting so much better all the time.
```

Coda

```
   C                              Dm
|:    It's getting better all the time,
  Em              F
Better, better, better.  :|
F                                  C
Getting so much better all the time.
```

Girl

Words & Music by
John Lennon & Paul McCartney

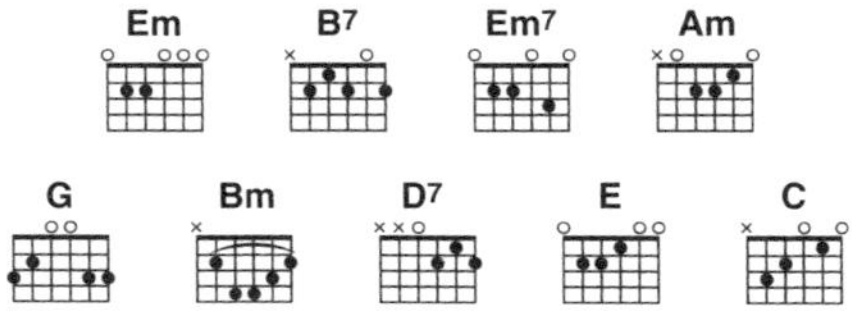

Capo eighth fret

Verse 1

Em B7 Em Em7
Is there anybody going to listen to my story,
Am G B7
All about the girl who came to stay?
Em B7 Em Em7
She's the kind of girl you want so much it makes you sorry,
Am Em
Still, you don't regret a single day.

Chorus 1

G Bm Am D7
Ah, girl ________
G Bm Am D7
Girl, girl.

Verse 2

Em B7 Em Em7
When I think of all the times I've tried so hard to leave her,
Am G B7
She will turn to me and start to cry.
Em B7 Em Em7
And she promises the earth to me and I be - lieve her,
Am Em
After all this time, I don't know why.

Chorus 2

G Bm Am D7
Ah, girl ________
G Bm Am D7
Girl, girl.

Bridge

```
Am
She's the kind of girl
                   E
Who puts you down when friends are there,
            Am    E
You feel a fool.
Am
When you say she's looking good,
    E
She acts as if it's understood,
     Am        C
She's cool, ooh, ooh, ooh.
```

Chorus 3

```
G    Bm  Am  D7
Girl ______
G    Bm  Am  D7
Girl, girl.
```

Verse 3

```
         Em                B7                    Em         Em7
Was she told when she was young that pain would lead to pleasure?
Am                           G        B7
Did she understand it when they said,
       Em                 B7              Em       Em7
That a man must break his back to earn his day of leisure?
Am                               Em
Will she still believe it when he's dead?
```

Chorus 4

```
    G    Bm  Am  D7
Ah, girl ______
G    Bm  Am  D7
Girl, girl.
```

Solo

```
| Em  B7 | Em  Em7 | Am      | G  B7   |
| Em  B7 | Em  Em7 | Am      | Em      ||
```

Chorus 5

```
    G    Bm  Am  D7
Ah, girl ______
G    Bm  Am  D7
Girl, girl.          Fade out
```

Glass Onion

Words & Music by
John Lennon & Paul McCartney

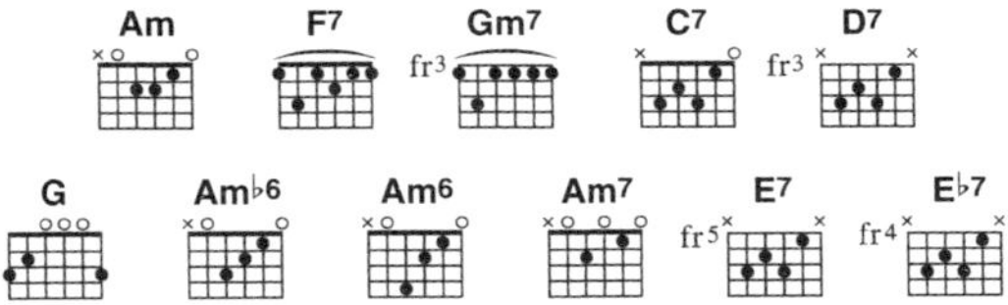

Verse 1

```
Am                     F7
   I told you 'bout Strawberry Fields,
Am                              F7
   You know the place where nothing is real.
Am                    Gm7              C7
   Well, here's another place you can go
      Gm7              C7
Where everything flows.
   F7                           D7
Looking through the bent-backed tulips
   F7                        D7
To see how the other half lives,
   F7                        G
Looking through a glass onion.
```

Verse 2

```
Am                     F7
   I told you 'bout the Walrus and me, man,
Am                            F7
   You know that we're as close as can be, man,
Am                    Gm7              C7
   Well, here's another clue for you all
      Gm7             C7
The Walrus was Paul.
   F7                           D7
Standing on a cast iron shore, yeah,
F7                                   D7
Lady Madonna trying to make ends meet, yeah,
F7                           G
Looking through a glass onion.
```

Instrumental | Am |

Am Am♭6 Am6 Am7
Oh yeah, oh yeah, oh yeah! ____

F7 G
Looking through a glass onion.

Verse 3

Am F7
I told you 'bout the Fool on the Hill,

Am F7
I tell you man, he's living there still,

Am Gm7 C7
Well here's another place you can be

Gm7 C7
Listen to me.

F7 D7
Fixing a hole in the ocean,

F7 D7
Trying to make a dovetail joint, yeah,

F7 G
Looking through a glass onion.

Coda ||: F7 | F7 E7 E♭7 | D7 E♭7 E7 | F7 :|| *Repeat and fade*

Good Day Sunshine

Words & Music by
John Lennon & Paul McCartney

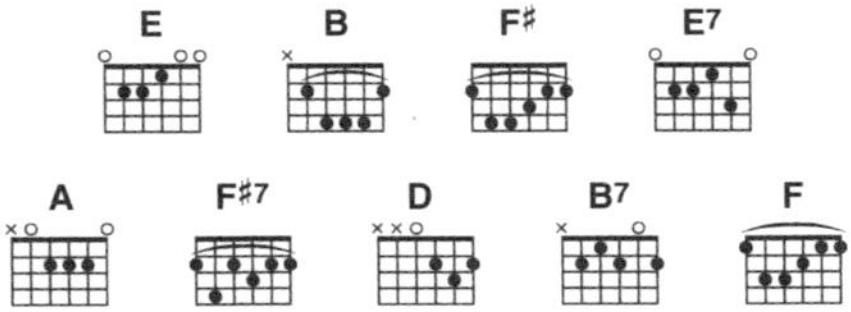

Intro | E | E | E | E ||

Chorus 1
B F♯ B F♯
Good day sunshine, good day sunshine,
E E7
Good day sunshine.

Verse 1
A F♯7 B7
I need to laugh, and when the sun is out,
E7 A
I've got something I can laugh about.
F♯7 B7
I feel good in a special way,
E7 A
I'm in love, and it's a sunny day.

Chorus 2
B F♯ B F♯
Good day sunshine, good day sunshine,
E E7
Good day sunshine.

Verse 2
A F♯7 B7
We take a walk, the sun is shining down,
E7 A
Burns my feet as they touch the ground.

Solo | D B7 | E7 | A7 | D ||

```
            B         F♯         B         F♯
Chorus 3    Good day sunshine, good day sunshine,
            E             E7
            Good day sunshine.

                     A  F♯7        B7
Verse 3     Then we lie  beneath a shady tree,
            E7                    A
            I love her and she's loving me.
                           F♯7                B7
            She feels good,  she knows she's looking fine,
            E7                           A
            I'm so proud to know that  she is mine.

            B         F♯         B         F♯
Chorus 4    Good day sunshine, good day sunshine,
            E             E7
            Good day sunshine.

            B         F♯         B         F♯
Chorus 5    Good day sunshine, good day sunshine,
            E             E7
            Good day sunshine.
               F
            ||: Good day, sunshine.  :||  Repeat to fade
```

Good Morning, Good Morning

Words & Music by
John Lennon & Paul McCartney

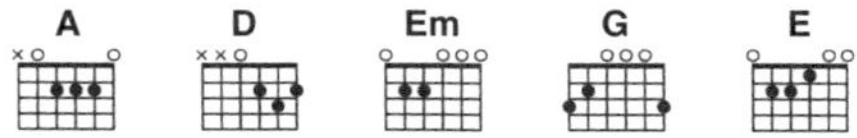

Intro

A D A D
Good morning, good morning,
A D
Good morning, good morning,
A
Good morning-ah!

Verse 1

A Em G A
Nothing to do to save his life, call his wife in.
Em G A
Nothing to say but "What a day, how's your boy been?"
D E
Nothing to do, it's up to you.
A Em G
I've got nothing to say, but it's O.K.
A D
(Good morning, good morning,
A
Good morning-ah!)

Verse 2

A Em G A
Going to work, don't want to go, feeling low down.
Em G A D
Heading for home you start to roam, then you're in town.

Bridge 1

A D A
Everybody knows there's nothing doing,
D A
Everything is closed, it's like a ruin,
D A
Everyone you see is half-asleep,
D A
And you're on your own, you're in the street.

Verse 3

```
A         Em          G                              A
After a while you start to smile, now you feel cool.
               Em      G                           A
Then you decide to take a walk by the old school.
D                                           E
Nothing has changed, it's still the same,
         A             Em      G
I've got nothing to say, but it's O.K.
        A                 D
(Good morning, good morning,
        A
Good morning-ah!)
```

Solo

```
| A  Em  G | G   A | A  Em  G | G   A | A   D ||
```

Bridge 2

```
A                         D               A
   People running round, it's five o'clock,
                   D                  A
Everywhere in town is getting dark,
                  D              A
Everyone you see is full of life,
               D                A
It's time for tea and meet the wife.
```

Verse 4

```
A              Em        G                               A
Somebody needs to know the time, glad that I'm here.
                Em         G                                A
Watching the skirt, you start to flirt, now you're in gear.
D                                    E
Go to a show, you hope she goes,
         A             Em      G
I've got nothing to say, but it's O.K.
        A                 D         A
(Good morning, good morning, good!)
             A                D          A          D
‖: (Good morning, good morning, good!)        :‖   Repeat to fade
```

Goodnight

Words & Music by
John Lennon & Paul McCartney

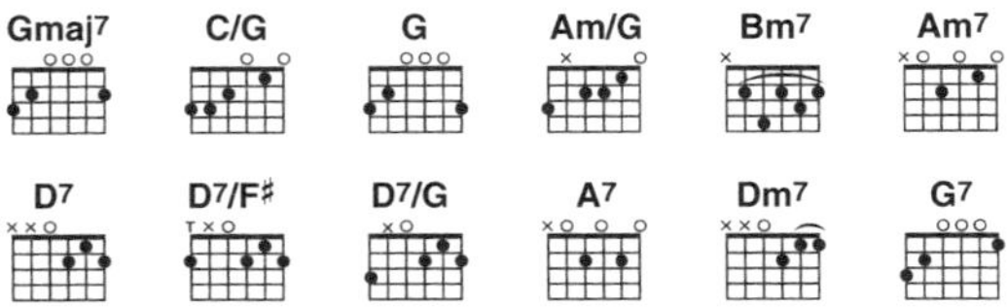

Intro

| Gmaj7 C/G | Gmaj7 C/G | G Am/G |
| G Am/G | G Bm7 | Am7 D7 ||

Verse 1

G Bm7 Am7
Now it's time to say good night,
Bm7 Am7 Am/G D7/F♯
Good night, sleep tight.
G Bm7 Am7
Now the sun turns out his light,
Bm7 Am7 Am/G D7/F♯
Good night, sleep tight.
Gmaj7 D7/G Gmaj7 D7/G
Dream sweet dreams for me,
G C/G G C/G
Dream sweet dreams for you.

Verse 2

G Bm7 Am7
Close your eyes and I'll close mine,
Bm7 Am7 Am/G D7/F♯
Good night, sleep tight.
G Bm7 Am7
Now the moon begins to shine,
Bm7 Am7 Am/G D7/F♯
Good night, sleep tight.
Gmaj7 D7/G Gmaj7 D7/G
Dream sweet dreams for me,
G C/G G C/G
Dream sweet dreams for you.

Bridge

```
| G       Am7 | A7    Dm7   | G7    C/G   | D7/F# Am7 D7 ||
Mm, ______    mm, ______    mm. ______
```

Verse 3

```
G              Bm7      Am7
Close your eyes and I'll close mine,
Bm7   Am7   Am/G  D7/F#
Good night, sleep   tight.
G           Bm7        Am7
Now the sun turns out his light,
Bm7   Am7   Am/G  D7/F#
Good night, sleep   tight.
Gmaj7          D7/G           Gmaj7     D7/G
Dream sweet dreams for me,
G              C/G          G      C/G
Dream sweet dreams for you.
```

Coda
(whispered)

```
| G       Bm7 | Am7  D7        |
                     Good night,
G                         Bm7
   Good night everybody,
Am7
Everybody everywhere,
D7                 G
   Good night.
```

Got To Get You Into My Life

Words & Music by
John Lennon & Paul McCartney

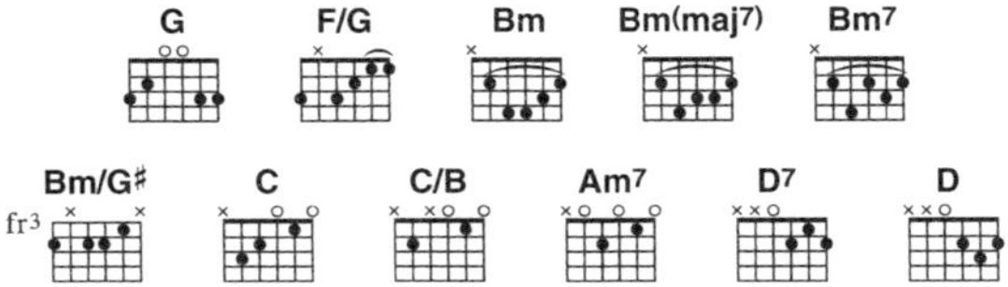

Brass intro | (G) | (G) | (G) | (G) ||

Verse 1

```
G
   I was alone, I took a ride,
                                     F/G
I didn't know what I would find there.
G
   Another road where maybe I
                                  F/G
Could see another kind of mind there.
```

Pre-chorus 1

```
Bm    Bm(maj7)   Bm7        Bm/G♯
Ooh,        then I suddenly see you,
Bm    Bm(maj7)  Bm7         Bm/G♯
Ooh,        did I tell you I need you
C       C/B     Am7  D7       G
Every single day   of my life?
```

Verse 2

```
G
   You didn't run, you didn't lie,
                                  F/G
You knew I wanted just to hold you.
G
   And had you gone, you knew in time
                                  F/G
We'd meet again, for I had told you.
```

Pre-chorus 2

Bm Bm(maj7) Bm7 Bm/G♯
Ooh, you were meant to be near me,
Bm Bm(maj7) Bm7 Bm/G♯
Ooh, and I want you to hear me
C C/B Am7 D7 G
Say we'll be to - gether every day.

Chorus 1

G C D
Got to get you into my life!

| G | G ||

Verse 3

G
What can I do, what can I be?
F/G
When I'm with you, I want to stay there.
G
If I am true I'll never leave,
F/G
And if I do, I know the way there.

Pre-chorus 3

Bm Bm(maj7) Bm7 Bm/G♯
Ooh, then I suddenly see you,
Bm Bm(maj7) Bm7 Bm/G♯
Ooh, did I tell you I need you
C C/B Am7 D7 G
Every single day of my life?

Chorus 2

G C D
Got to get you into my life!

| G | G | G F/G | C G |

G C D
I've got to get you into my life!

Coda (ad lib.)

G
I was alone, I took a ride

I didn't know what I would find there.

Another road where maybe I

Could see another kind of mind there.

Then suddenly I see you,

Did I tell you I need you

Every single day… *Fade out*

Golden Slumbers

Words & Music by
John Lennon & Paul McCartney

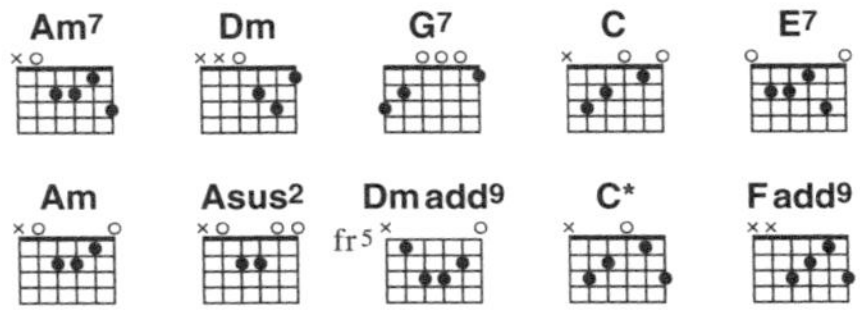

Intro | Am7 ||

Verse 1

Am7 Dm
Once there was a way to get back homeward,
G7 C
Once there was a way to get back home.
E7 Am Asus2 Dmadd9
Sleep pretty darling, do not cry,
G7 C
And I will sing a lullaby. __

Chorus

C* Fadd9 C*
Golden slumbers fill your eyes,
Fadd9 C*
Smiles awake you when you rise.
E7 Am Asus2 Dmadd9
Sleep pretty darling, do not cry,
G7 C
And I will sing a lullaby. __

Verse 2

Am7 Dm
Once there was a way to get back homeward,
G7 C
Once there was a way to get back home.
E7 Am Asus2 Dmadd9
Sleep pretty darling, do not cry,
G7 C
And I will sing a lullaby. __

Her Majesty

Words & Music by
John Lennon & Paul McCartney

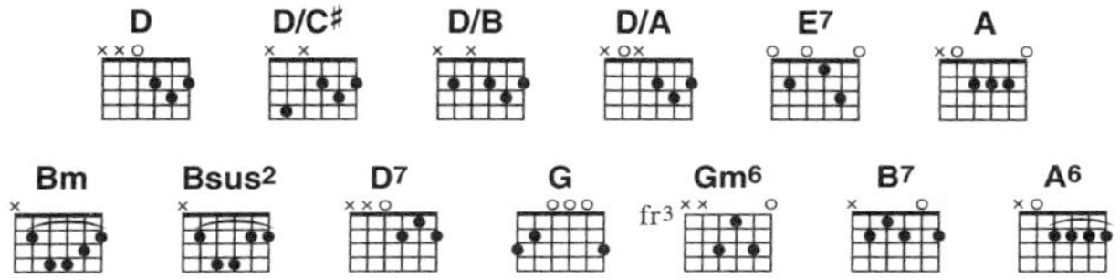

Intro | (D) ||

Verse 1

D D/C♯ D/B D/A
Her Majesty's a pretty nice girl,
E7 A D
But she doesn't have a lot to say.
D D/C♯ D/B D/A
Her Majesty's a pretty nice girl,
E7 A
But she changes from day to day.

Bm Bsus2
I wanna tell her that I love her a lot,
D7 G
But I gotta get a belly full of wine.

Gm6 D B7
Her Majesty's a pretty nice girl,
E7 A6 D
Some day I'm gonna make her mine,
B7
Oh yeah,
E7 A6 D
Some day I'm gonna make her mine.

Happiness Is A Warm Gun

Words & Music by
John Lennon & Paul McCartney

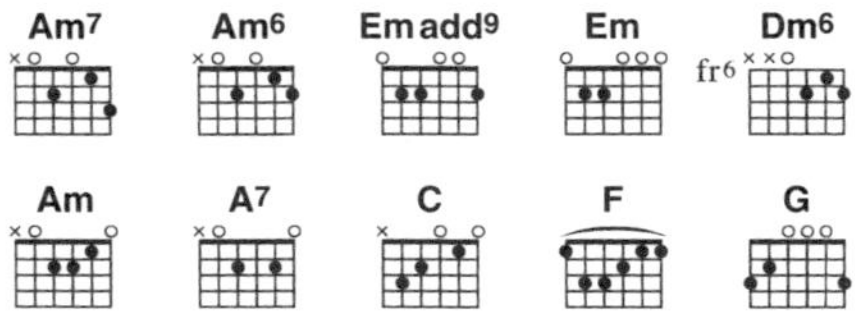

Intro

Am7 Am6 Em add9 Em
She's not a girl who misses much.
Am7 Am6 Em add9 Em
Do-do-do-do-do-do, oh yeah.

Verse 1

Dm6
She's well acquainted with the touch

Of the velvet hand,
Am
Like a lizard on a window pane.
Dm6
The man in the crowd,
Am
With the multicoloured mirrors on his hobnail boots.
Dm6
Lying with his eyes,
Am
While his hands are busy working overtime.
Dm6
A soap impression of his wife, which he ate,
Am
And donated to the National Trust.

Link

| A7 | A7 | C Am ||

A7
Verse 2 I need a fix, cause I'm going down,

Down to the bits that I left uptown,

C Am
I need a fix, cause I'm going down.

A7 C
Verse 3 𝄆 Mother Superior, jump the gun,

A7 G
Mother Superior, jump the gun. 𝄇 *Play 3 times*

C Am F
Verse 4 Happiness is a warm gun,
G C
(Bang, bang, shoot, shoot.)

Am F G
Happiness is a warm gun, momma.
C
(Bang, bang, shoot, shoot.)

Am F G
When I hold you in my arms,

C Am F G
And I feel my finger on your trigger,

C Am F G
I know nobody can do me no harm,

C
Because

Am F G
Happiness is a warm gun, momma.
C
(Bang, bang, shoot, shoot,)

C Am F G
Happiness is a warm gun, yes it is.
Fm
(Bang, bang, shoot, shoot)

(Fm) N.C.
Happiness is a warm, yes it is

C
Gun. ——— Well don't you know that
Am F G
(Happiness bang, bang, shoot, shoot)

C Am F G C
Happiness is a warm gun, momma.
(Happiness is a warm gun,yeah!)

A Hard Day's Night

Words & Music by
John Lennon & Paul McCartney

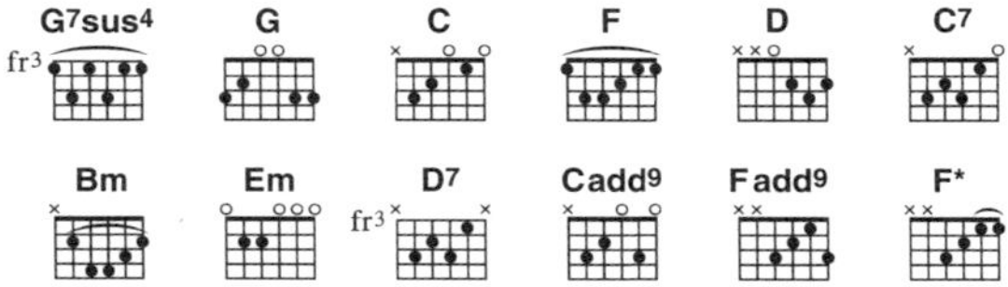

Verse 1

G7sus4 G C G
It's been a hard day's night,
F G
And I've been working like a dog.
C G
It's been a hard day's night,
F G
I should be sleeping like a log.
C
But when I get home to you,
D
I find the things that you do,
G C7 G
Will make me feel all right.

Verse 2

G C G
You know I work all day,
F G
To get you money to buy you things.
C G
And it's worth it just to hear you say,
F G
You're gonna give me everything.
C
So why on earth should I moan,
D
'Cause when I get you alone,
G C7 G
You know I feel O. K.

```
                      Bm
Middle 1      When I'm home
              Em                        Bm
              Ev'rything seems to be right.
                      G
              When I'm home,
              Em
              Feeling you holding me
              C7     D7
              Tight, tight, yeah.

Verse 3       As Verse 1

Instrumental  ||: G    C   | G        | F        | G       :||

                       C
              So why on earth should I moan,
                           D
              'Cause when I get you alone,
                         G   C7 G
              You know I feel O.  K

                      Bm
Middle 2      When I'm home
              Em                        Bm
              Ev'rything seems to be right.
                      G
              When I'm home,
              Em
              Feeling you holding me
              C7     D7
              Tight, tight, yeah.

Verse 4       As Verse 1

              C7              G   C7   G
Outro           You know I feel all   right,
              C7              G   Cadd9  Fadd9  F*
                You know I feel all      right.

              ||: Fadd9   F*   | Fadd9   F*   :||   Repeat to fade
```

Hello Goodbye

Words & Music by
John Lennon & Paul McCartney

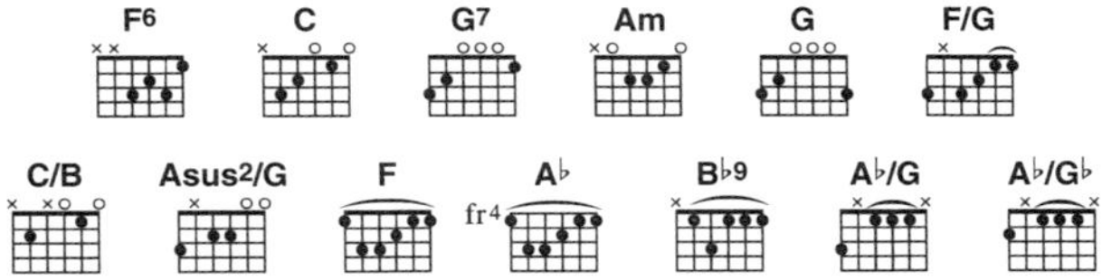

Verse 1

F6 C
You say yes, I say no,
G7 Am G7
You stay stop, but I say go, go, go.
Am G7
Oh no.
G G7 F/G
You say goodbye and I say;

Chorus 1

C C/B Am Asus2/G
Hello, hello, hello,
F A♭
I don't know why you say goodbye, I say hello,
C C/B Am Asus2/G
Hello, hello, hello,
F B♭9 C
I don't know why you say goodbye, I say hello.

Verse 2

F6 C
I say high, you say low,
G7 Am G7
You say why and I say I don't know.
Am G7
Oh no.
G G7 F/G
You say goodbye and I say hello.

Chorus 2

```
C                    C/B         Am
(Hello, goodbye, hello, goodbye,)
                        Hello, hello,

Asus2/G
(Hello, goodbye.)   F                  A♭          C
         I don't know why you say goodbye, I say hello.

C                    C/B         Am
(Hello, goodbye, hello, goodbye,)
                        Hello, hello,

Asus2/G
(Hello, goodbye,)   F                  B♭9         C
         I don't know why you say goodbye, I say hello.
                                   (Hello, goodbye.)
```

Link

```
F6  C                G7
      Why, why, why, why, why, why,
        Am              G7
Do you say goodbye, goodbye?
Am   G7
  Oh no.
G           G7     F/G
You say goodbye and I say;
```

Chorus 3 As Chorus 1

Verse 3

```
F6            C
You say yes,  I say no,
              (I say yes, but I may mean no,)
G7                   Am           G7
You say stop,        but I say go, go, go.
            (I can stay till it's time to go)
Am   G7
  Oh, no.
G           G7     F/G
You say goodbye and I say;
```

Chorus 4 As Chorus 1

Chorus 5

```
C/B           Am  Asus2/G
  Hello, hello,
             F                 A♭          A♭  A♭/G A♭/G♭ F
I don't know why you say goodbye, I say hello, ______
    C
Hello.
```

Coda

```
  C
|: Hela, heba, helloa. :|   Repeat to fade
```

Help!

Words & Music by
John Lennon & Paul McCartney

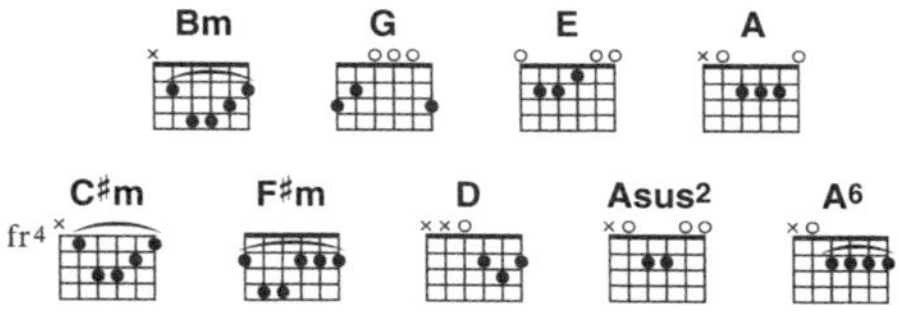

Intro

Bm
Help! I need somebody.
G
Help! Not just anybody.
E
Help! You know I need someone.
A
Help!

Verse 1

A C♯m
When I was younger, so much younger than today,
F♯m D G A
I never needed anybody's help in any way.
A C♯m
But now those days are gone I'm not so self-assured,
F♯m D G A
Now I find I've changed my mind, and opened up the doors.

Chorus 1

Bm
Help me if you can I'm feeling down,
G
And I do appreciate you being 'round,
E
Help me get my feet back on the ground,
A
Won't you please, please help me? | A Asus2 | A Asus2 A ||

```
               A                                   C♯m
*Verse 2*        And now my life has changed in oh, so many ways,
               F♯m                          D     G     A
                 My independence seems to vanish in the haze.
               A                            C♯m
                 But ev'ry now and then I feel so insecure,
               F♯m                                      D     G      A
                 I know that I just need you like I've never done before.

               Bm
*Chorus 2*     Help me if you can I'm feeling down,
                    G
               And I do appreciate you being 'round,
               E
               Help me get my feet back on the ground,
                         A                       | A   Asus2  | A   Asus2  A ||
               Won't you please, please help me?

               A                                 C♯m
*Verse 3*        When I was younger, so much younger than today,
               F♯m                         D      G   A
                 I never needed anybody's help in any way.
               A                                   C♯m
                 But now those days are gone I'm not so self-assured,
               F♯m                                        D      G      A
                 Now I find I've changed my mind, I've opened up the doors.

               Bm
*Chorus 3*     Help me if you can I'm feeling down,
                    G
               And I do appreciate you being around,
               E
               Help me get my feet back on the ground,
                         A                  F♯m
               Won't you please, please help me?
                          A   A6
               Help me, help me, ooh, mm.
```

Hello Little Girl

Words & Music by
John Lennon & Paul McCartney

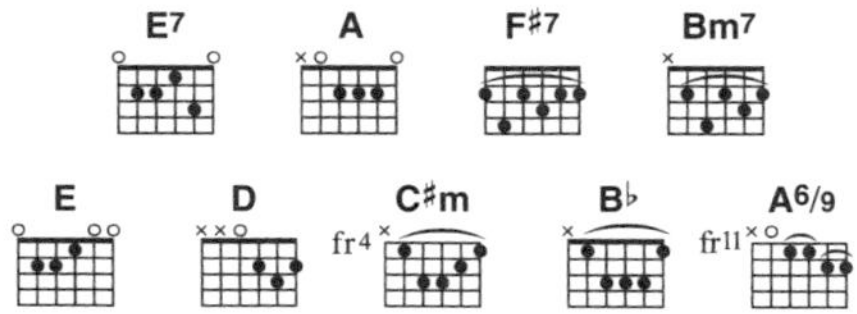

Intro

N.C. E7 A F♯7 Bm7
Hello little girl, ________
E7 A F♯7 Bm7
Hello little girl, ________
E7 A F♯7 Bm7 E7
Hello little girl. ________

Verse 1

A E
When I see you every day
D E7 D E A
I say, mm-mm, hello little girl.
A E
When youre passing on your way
D E7 D E A
I say, mm-mm, hello little girl.

Verse 2

A E
When I see you passing by
D E7 D E A
I cry, mm-mm, hello little girl.
A E
When I try to catch your eye
D E7 D E A
I cry, mm-mm, hello little girl.

Bridge 1

A F♯7 Bm7 E7
I send you flowers, but you don't care,

A F♯7 Bm7 E7
You never seem to see me standing there.

A F♯7 Bm7 E7
I often wonder what you're thinking of,

A F♯7 Bm7 E7
I hope it's me and love, love, love.

Verse 3

A E D
So I hope there'll come a day when you'll say

E7 D E A
Mm-mm, you're my little girl.

Solo

| A E | D E | D E | A ||

Bridge 2

A F♯7 Bm7 E7
It's not the first time that it's happened to me,

A F♯7 Bm7 E7
It's been a long, lonely time.

A F♯7 Bm7 E7
And it's so funny, so funny to see

A F♯7 Bm7 E7
That I'm about to lose my mi-mi-mind.

Verse 4

A E
So I hope there'll come a day when you'll say

D E7 D E A
Mm-mm, you're my little girl.

Coda

F♯7 Bm7 E A
Mm-mm, you're my little girl,

F♯7 Bm7 E A
Mm-mm, you're my little girl,

F♯7 Bm7 E A C♯m Bm7 B♭ A A6/9
Oh yeah, you're my little girl. ______

Helter Skelter

Words & Music by
John Lennon & Paul McCartney

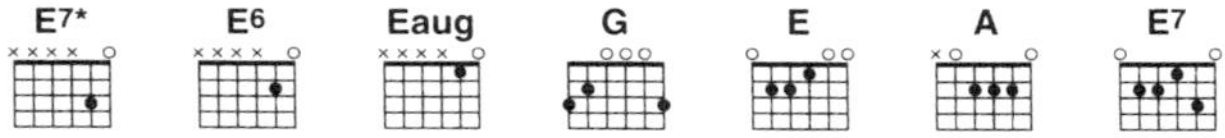

Intro | E7* ||

Verse 1

```
         E7*                                              E6
When I get to the bottom I go back to the top of the slide.
                                       Eaug
Where I stop and I turn and I go for a ride,
                                        G
Till I get to the bottom, and I see you again,
              E
Yeah, yeah, yeah!
```

Verse 2

```
E
Do you, don't you want me to love you?

I'm coming down fast, but I'm miles above you.

Tell me, tell me, tell me,
          G
Come on, tell me the answer,
          A                            E
Well, you may be a lover, but you ain't no dancer.
```

Chorus 1

```
A              E
Helter Skelter, Helter Skelter,
A              E
Helter Skelter, yeah!
```

Link | E | E ||

Verse 3

E
Will you, won't you want me to make you?

I'm coming down fast, but don't let me break you.

G
Tell me, tell me, tell me the answer,

     A   E
You may be a lover, but you ain't no dancer.

Look out!

Chorus 2

A   E
Helter Skelter, Helter Skelter,

A   E
Helter Skelter, yeah!

E
   Look out 'cause here she comes!

Solo

| A | E | A | E ||

Verse 4

As Verse 1

Verse 5

E
Well, do you, don't you want me to make you?

I'm coming down fast, but don't let me break you.

G
Tell me, tell me, tell me your answer,

            A   E
Well, you may be a lover, but you ain't no dancer.

Look out!

Chorus 3

A   E
Helter Skelter, Helter Skelter,

A
Helter Skelter.

Coda

E
   Look out! Helter Skelter!

She coming down fast!

Yes she is, yes she is, coming down fast…

Instrumental

|: E7 | E7 :| *Repeat ad lib. to fade*

Here Comes The Sun

Words & Music by
George Harrison

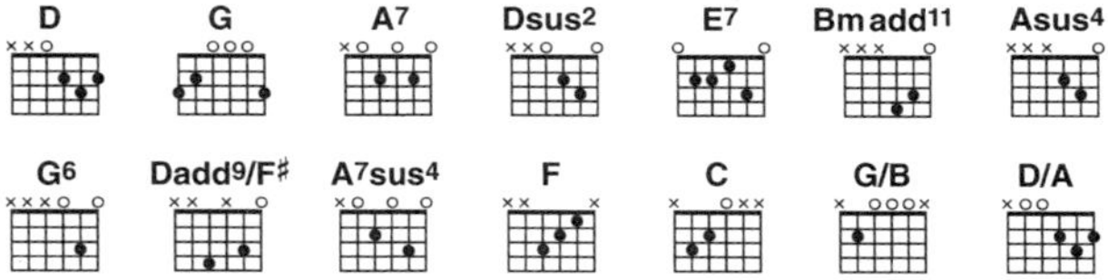

Capo seventh fret

Intro ||: D | D | G | A7 :||

Chorus 1

D Dsus2 D
Here comes the sun,
G E7
Here comes the sun,
D Dsus2 D
And I say, "It's all right."

| Bmadd11 Asus4 G6 | Dadd9/F♯ A7sus4 A7 ||

Verse 1

D Dsus2 D G A7 A7sus4
Little dar - ling, it's been a long, cold, lonely winter.
D Dsus2 D G A7 A7sus4
Little dar - ling, it feels like years since it's been here.

Chorus 2

D Dsus2 D
Here comes the sun,
G E7
Here comes the sun,
D Dsus2 D
And I say, "It's all right."

| Bmadd11 Asus4 G6 | Dadd9/F♯ A7sus4 A7 | D | A7 |

Verse 2

D Dsus2 D G A7 A7sus4
Little dar - ling, the smiles returning to their faces,
D Dsus2 D G A7 A7sus4
Little dar - ling, it seems like years since it's been here.

Chorus 3

```
D          Dsus2  D
   Here comes  the sun,
G                      E7
   Here comes the sun,
               D      Dsus2  D
And I say,  "It's all     right."

| Bmadd11  Asus4  G6 | Dadd9/F# A7sus4  A7 | D       | A7     ||
```

Bridge

```
| F        | C       | G/B     | G       | D       | A7      |

|: F       | C       | G/B     | G       | D       | A7     :|  Play 5 times
   Sun,      sun,      sun,      here it comes.

| A7         | A7sus4     | A7         | A7sus4  A   ||
```

Verse 3

```
D          Dsus2   D                   G                 A7       A7sus4
   Little dar  -   ling, I feel that ice is slowly melting,
D          Dsus2   D                      G                        A7      A7sus4
   Little dar  -   ling, it seems like years since it's been clear.
```

Chorus 4 As Chorus 1

Chorus 5

```
D          Dsus2  D
   Here comes  the sun,
G                      E7
   Here comes the sun,
              D    Dsus2  D
   It's all right.

| Bmadd11  Asus4  G6 | Dadd9/F# A7sus4  A7 |
D      Dsus2    D
   It's all       right.

| Bmadd11  Asus4  G6 | Dadd9/F# A7sus4  A7 |
```

Coda

```
| F     C     | G/B   G     | D/A        ||
```

Here, There And Everywhere

Words & Music by
John Lennon & Paul McCartney

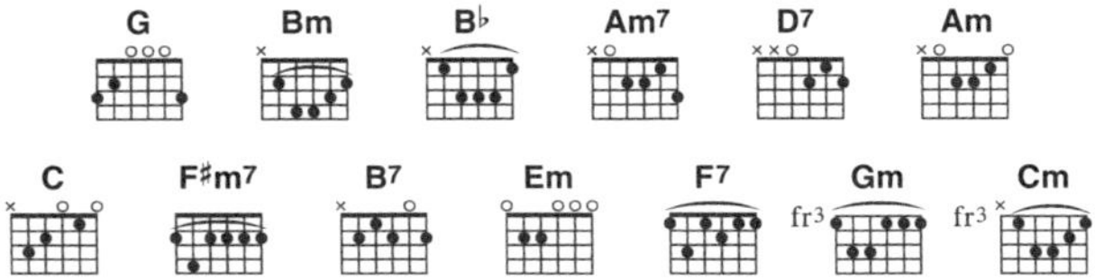

Intro

G Bm
To lead a better life,
B♭ Am7 D7
I need my love to be here.

Verse 1

G Am
Here,
Bm C G Am
Making each day of the year,
Bm C F♯m7 B7
Changing my life with a wave of her hand,
F♯m7 B7 Em Am Am7 D7
Nobody can deny that there's something there.

Verse 2

G Am
There,
Bm C G Am
Running my hands through her hair,
Bm C F♯m7 B7
Both of us thinking how good it can be,
F♯m7 B7 Em Am Am7 D7
Someone is speaking, but she doesn't know he's there.

Bridge 1

F7 B♭ Gm
I want her everywhere,
Cm D7 Gm
And if she's beside me, I know I need never care,
Cm D7
But to love her is to need her…

Verse 3

G   Am
Everywhere.

Bm   C   G   Am
Knowing that love is to share,

Bm   C   F#m7   B7
Each one believing that love never dies,

F#m7   B7   Em   Am   Am7   D7
Watching their eyes and hoping I'm always there.

Bridge 2

  F7   B♭   Gm
I want her everywhere,

           Cm   D7   Gm
And if she's beside me, I know I need never care,

Cm   D7
But to love her is to need her…

Verse 4

G   Am
Everywhere.

Bm   C   G   Am
Knowing that love is to share,

Bm   C   F#m7   B7
Each one believing that love never dies,

F#m7   B7   Em   Am   Am7   D7
Watching their eyes and hoping I'm always there.

Coda

            G   Am
I will be there

      Bm   C
And everywhere,

G   Am   Bm   C   G
Here, there and everywhere. ____

Hey Bulldog

Words & Music by
John Lennon & Paul McCartney

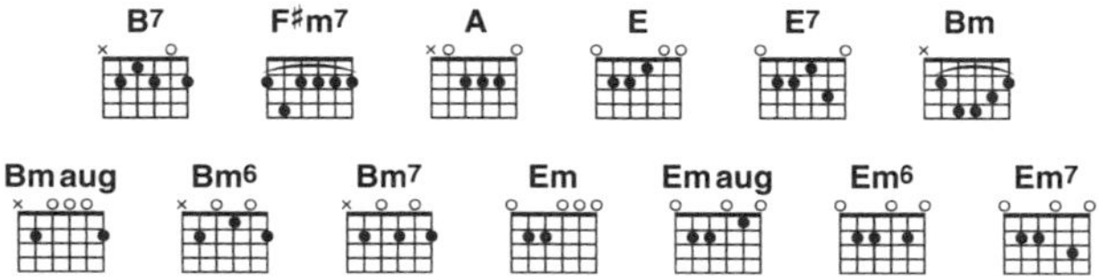

Intro ‖: B7 | B7 :‖ *Play 3 times*

Verse 1

B7 F♯m7
Sheepdog standing in the rain,
B7 F♯m7
Bullfrog, doing it again.
A F♯m7 E E7
Some kind of happiness is measured out in miles.
A F♯m7 B7
What makes you think you're something special when you smile?

Verse 2

B7 F♯m7
Child-like, no one understands,
B7 F♯m7
Jack-knife in your sweaty hands.
A F♯m7 E E7
Some kind of innocence is measured out in years,
A F♯m7 B7
You don't know what it's like to listen to your fears.

Chorus 1

Bm Bm aug Bm6
You can talk to me,
Bm7 Em Em aug
You can talk to me,
Em6 Em7
You can talk to me,
Bm Em
If you're lonely, you can talk to me.

Link ‖: B7 | B7 :‖
(me.)

Solo | B7 | F#m7 | B7 | F#m7 |
| A F#m7 | E E7 | A F#m7 | B7 ||

Verse 3

B7 F#m7
Big man, walking in the park,
B7 F#m7
Wigwam, frightened of the dark.
A F#m7 E E7
Some kind of solitude is measured out in you.
A F#m7 B7
You think you know me, but you haven't got a clue.

Chorus 2

Bm Bmaug Bm6
You can talk to me,
Bm7 Em Emaug
You can talk to me,
Em6 Em7
You can talk to me,
Bm Em
If you're lonely, you can talk to me.

Link |: B7 | B7 :|
(me.)

Coda | B7 |: F#m7 | B7 :| *Repeat to fade*
Hey, bull-dog.

Hey Jude

Words & Music by
John Lennon & Paul McCartney

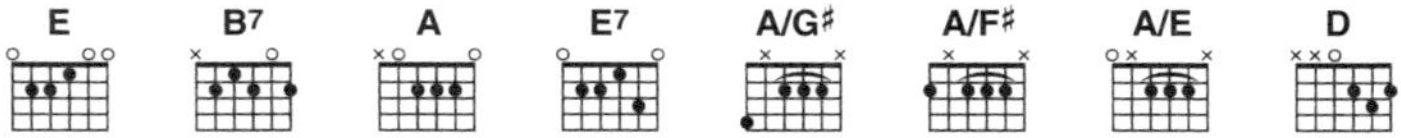

Capo first fret

Verse 1

```
     E                    B7
Hey Jude, don't make it bad,
                               E
Take a sad song and make it better.
   A                             E
Remember to let her into your heart,
                  B7              E
Then you can start to make it better.
```

Verse 2

```
     (E)              B7
Hey Jude, don't be afraid,
                                  E
You were made to go out and get her.
      A                               E
The minute you let her under your skin,
                B7               E    E7
Then you begin to make it better.
```

Bridge 1

```
                              A
And anytime you feel the pain,
       A/G♯     A/F♯
Hey Jude, refrain,
           A/E        B7                  E         E7
Don't carry the world upon your shoulders.
                                A
For well you know that it's a fool
         A/G♯     A/F♯
Who plays it cool
      A/E          B7           E
By making his world a little colder.
           E7     B7
Na na na na na, na na na na.
```

Verse 3

```
     E                 B7
Hey Jude, don't let me down,
                               E
You have found her, now go and get her.
  A                          E
Remember to let her into your heart,
                 B7             E   E7
Then you can start to make it better.
```

Bridge 2

```
                        A
So let it out and let it in,
     A/G♯    A/F♯
Hey Jude, begin,
           A/E          B7        E         E7
You're waiting for someone to perform with.
                               A
And don't you know that it's just you,
     A/G♯        A/F♯
Hey Jude, you'll do,
       A/E          B7             E
The movement you need is on your shoulder.
           E7    B7
Na na na na na, na na na na. Yeah.
```

Verse 4

```
     E                 B7
Hey Jude, don't make it bad,
                            E
Take a sad song and make it better.
  A                            E
Remember to let her under your skin,
               B7          E
Then you begin to make it better,

Better, better, better, better, better, oh.
```

Outro

```
   E          D
𝄆 Na __ na na, na na na na, __
A                E
Na na na na. __ Hey Jude. 𝄇   Repeat to fade
```

Hold Me Tight

Words & Music by
John Lennon & Paul McCartney

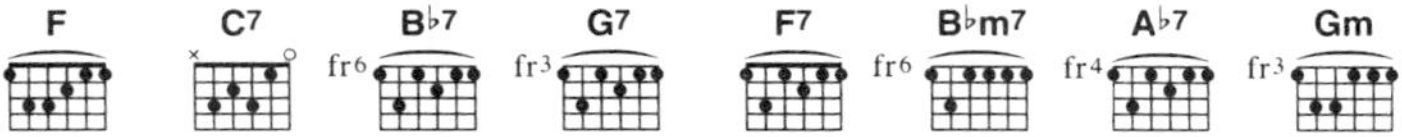

Intro

F C7
It feels so right now.

Verse 1

F B♭7
Hold me tight,
G7 C7
Tell me I'm the only one,
F B♭7
And then I might
G7 C7
Never be the lonely one.
F F7 B♭7 B♭m7
So hold me tight, tonight, tonight,
F B♭m7
It's you
F C7
You, you, you.

Verse 2

F B♭7
Hold me tight,
G7 C7
Let me go on loving you
F B♭7
Tonight, tonight,
G7 C7
Making love to only you.
F F7 B♭7 B♭m7
So hold me tight, tonight, tonight,
F B♭m7
It's you
F A♭7
You, you, you.

Bridge 1

(A♭7) F7 A♭7 F7
Don't know what it means to hold you tight,
B♭7 Gm G7
Being here alone tonight with you,
C7
It feels so right now.

Verse 3

F B♭7
Hold me tight,
G7 C7
Tell me I'm the only one,
F B♭7
And then I might
G7 C7
Never be the lonely one.
F F7 B♭7 B♭m7
So hold me tight, tonight, tonight,
F B♭m7
It's you
F A♭7
You, you, you.

Bridge 2

As Bridge 1

Verse 4

F B♭7
Hold me tight,
G7 C7
Let me go on loving you
F B♭7
Tonight, tonight,
G7 C7
Making love to only you.
F F7 B♭7 B♭m7
So hold me tight, tonight, tonight,
F B♭m7
It's you
F A♭7 F
You, you, you.
A♭7 F
You.

Honey Pie

Words & Music by
John Lennon & Paul McCartney

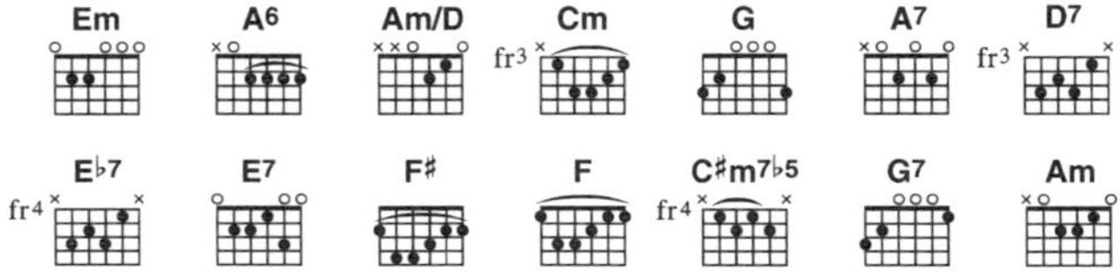

Intro

Em A6 Am/D
She was a working girl.
Cm G
North of England way.
Em A6 Am/D Cm G
Now she's hit the big time in the U. S. A.
A7
And if she could only hear me,
D7
This is what I'd say:

Verse 1

G E♭7
Honey Pie, you are making me crazy,
E7 A7
I'm in love, but I'm lazy,
D7 G E♭7 D7
So won't you please come home?

Verse 2

G E♭7
Oh, Honey Pie, my position is tragic,
E7 A7
Come and show me the magic
D7 G F♯ F
Of your Hollywood song.

Bridge 1

Em C♯m7♭5 G
You became a legend of the silver screen,
G7 C
And now the thought of meeting you
E7 Am D7
Makes me weak in the knee.

Verse 3

G E♭7
Oh, Honey Pie, you are driving me frantic,

E7 A7
Sail across the Atlantic

D7 G
To be where you belong.

E♭7 D7 G
Honey pie, come back to me.

Solo

| G | G | E♭7 | E7 | A7 | D7 ||
(me.)

G E♭7 D7
(I like it like that)

Verse 4

G E♭7
…I like this kind of, hot kind of music,

E7
Hot kind of music,

A7
Play it to me,

D7 G F♯ F
Play it to me, Hollywood blues.

Bridge 2

Em C♯m7♭5 G G7
Will the wind that blew her boat across the sea

C E7 Am D7
Kindly send her sailing back to me.

Verse 5

G E♭7
Now, Honey pie, you are making me crazy,

E7 A7
I'm in love, but I'm lazy,

D7 G
So won't you please come home?

E♭7 D7 G
(Come, come back to me Honey Pie,) ____

| G | E♭7 | E7 | A7 |

D7 G
(Honey Pie, Honey Pie.)

| E♭7 D7 | G

I Am The Walrus

Words & Music by
John Lennon & Paul McCartney

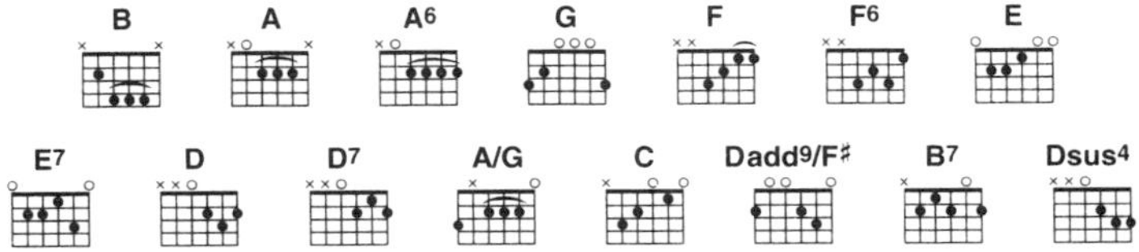

Intro | B | B A A6 | G F F6 | E | E7 | D | D7 ||

Verse 1

A A/G
I am he as you are he
C D A A/G
As you are me and we are all together.
C
See how they run like pigs from a gun,
D A
See how they fly, I'm crying.

Verse 2

A A/G Dadd9/F♯
Sitting on a cornflake,
F G A A/G
Waiting for the van to come.
F
Corporation T-shirt stupid bloody Tuesday,
B7
Man, you been a naughty boy, you let your face grow long.

Chorus 1

C D
I am the eggman, they are the eggmen,
E
I am the walrus,

Goo goo g'joob.

```
            A         A/G              C          D              A    A/G
Verse 3     Mr. City p'licemen sitting pretty little p'licemen in a row.
            C
            See how they fly like Lucy in the sky,
               D               A
            See how they run, I'm crying.
               Dsus4
            I'm cry   -   ing,
               A
            I'm crying,
               E        D    D7
            I'm cry   -   ing.

            A                     A/G     Dadd9/F♯
Verse 4     Yellow matter custard,
            F                G        A    A/G
            Dripping from a dead dog's eye.
            F
            Crabalocker fishwife, pornographic priestess,
            B7
            Boy, you been a naughty girl, you let your knickers down.

                     C                 D
Chorus 2    I am the eggman, they are the eggmen,
                     E
            I am the walrus,

            Goo goo g'joob.

Link        | B   A  | G   F  | E        ||

            B          A      G              F    E
Bridge      Sitting in an English garden, waiting for the sun.
            F                B7
              If the sun don't come, you get a tan

            From standing in the English rain.

                     C                 D
Chorus 3    I am the eggman, they are the eggmen,
                     E
            I am the walrus,

            Goo goo g'joob.
            D
            Goo goo goo g'joob.
```

Verse 5

A A/G
Expert texpert choking smokers,
C D A
Don't you think the joker laughs at you?
A/G
(Ha ha ha! Hee hee hee! Ha ha ha!)
C
See how they smile like pigs in the sty,
D A
See how they snied, I'm crying.

Verse 6

A A/G Dadd^9/F$\sharp$
Semolina pilchard,
F G A A/G
Climbing up the Eiffel Tower.
F
Elementary penguin singing Hare Krishna,
B^7
Man, you should have seen them

Kicking Edgar Allen Poe.

Chorus 4

C D
I am the eggman, they are the eggmen,
E
I am the walrus,

Goo goo g'joob,
D
Goo goo goo g'joob,
C
Goo goo g'joob,
B^7
Goo goo goo g'joob, goo.
(B^7)
Chooga, chooga, chooga.

Joob-a, joob-a, joob-a.

Coda

‖: A | G | F | E |
Joob-a, joob-a, etc.

| D | C | B^7 :‖ *Repeat to fade*

I Want You (She's So Heavy)

Words & Music by
John Lennon & Paul McCartney

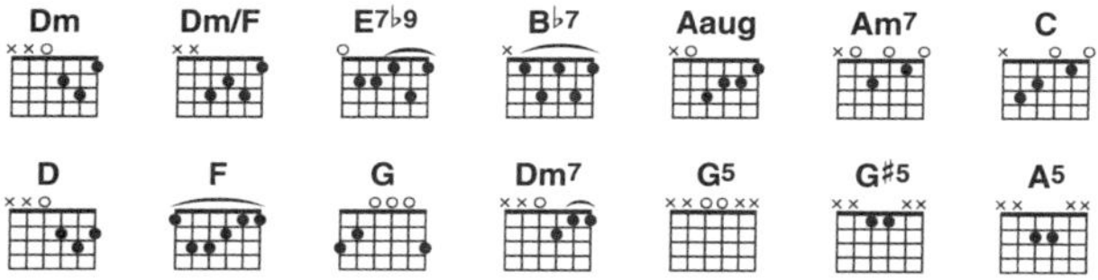

Intro	Dm	Dm/F	E7♭9	B♭7	Aaug	N.C.

Verse 1

(Am7)
I want you,

I want you so bad,

I want you,

Am7 C
I want you so bad, ___

D F
It's driving me mad,

G Am7
It's driving me mad.

Dm7
I want you,

I want you so bad, babe,

I want you,

F
I want you so bad, ___

C B♭7
It's driving me mad,

G5 G♯5 A5
It's dri-ving me mad.

Link	E7♭9	E7♭9 N.C.	E7♭9	E7♭9 N.C.	E7♭9	E7♭9 N.C.

(mad.)

Verse 2

Am7
I want you,

I want you so bad, babe,

I want you,

C
I want you so bad, ___

D F
It's driving me mad,

G Am7
It's driving me mad.

Dm7
I want you,

I want you so bad,

I want you,

F
I want you so bad, ___

C B♭7
It's driving me mad,

G5 G♯5 A5
It's dri - ving me...

Link

| E7♭9 | E7♭9 N.C. | E7♭9 | E7♭9 N.C. | E7♭9 | E7♭9 N.C. ||

Chorus 1

N.C. Dm Dm/F E7♭9
She's so...

B♭7 Aaug
Heavy. ______

Dm Dm/F E7♭9 B♭7 Aaug
Heavy, (heavy, heavy.) ______

Solo

| Am7 | Am7 | Am7 | Am7 | Am7 | Am7 |

| Am7 C | D F | G | Am7 | Am7 ||

| Dm7 | Dm7 | Dm7 | Dm7 | Dm7 | Dm7 |

| Dm7 F | C B♭ | G5 G♯5 A5 ||

Link

| E7♭9 | E7♭9 N.C. | E7♭9 | E7♭9 N.C. | E7♭9 | E7♭9 N.C. ||

Chorus 2

N.C. Dm Dm/F E7♭9
She's so...

B♭7 Aaug
Heavy. ______

Dm Dm/F E7♭9 B♭7 Aaug
She's so heavy, (heavy, heavy.) ______

Verse 3

(Am7)
I want you,

I want you so bad,

I want you,

Am7 C
I want you so bad, ____

D F
It's driving me mad,

G Am7
It's driving me mad.

Dm7
I want you,

You know I want you so bad, babe,

I want you,

F
You know I want you so bad, ____

C B♭7
It's driving me mad,

G5 G♯5 A5
It's dri-ving me mad.

Link

| E7♭9 | E7♭9 N.C. | E7♭9 | E7♭9 N.C. | E7♭9 | E7♭9 N.C. ||
She's so...

Coda

|: Dm | Dm/F | E7♭9 | B♭7 | Aaug :| *Repeat until sudden end*

I Call Your Name

Words & Music by
John Lennon & Paul McCartney

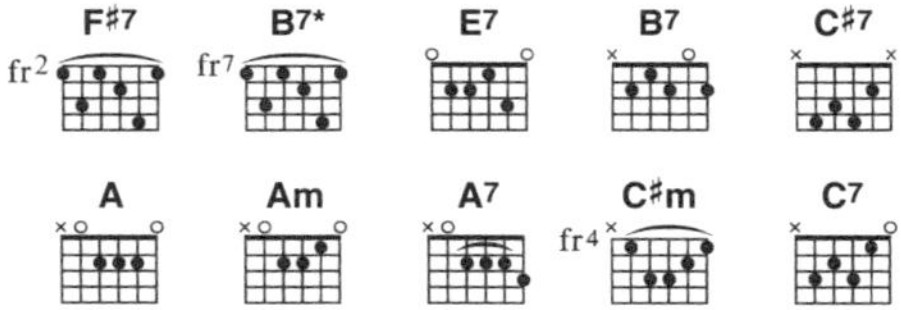

Intro | F♯7 | B7* | E7 | B7 ||

Verse 1

```
              E7
I call your name,
                  C♯7
But you're not there,
             F♯7
Was I to blame
                B7
For being unfair?
              E7
Oh, I can't sleep at night
                        C♯7
Since you've been gone.
           F♯7
I never weep at night,
A     Am       E7
   I can't go on.
```

Bridge 1

```
                            A7
Don't you know I can't take it?
                          C♯m
I don't know who can.
                    F♯7
I'm not goin' to make it,
                          C7          B7
I'm not that kind of man. ______
```

Verse 2

```
                 E7
Oh, I can't sleep at night,
                  C#7
But just the same
           F#7
I never weep at night,
A   Am         E7
  I call your name.
```

Solo

E7	E7	C#7	C#7
F#7	A Am	E7	E7 ‖

Bridge 2

```
                             A7
Don't you know I can't take it?
                           C#m
I don't know who can.
                    F#7
I'm not goin' to make it,
                          C7          B7
I'm not that kind of man. ______
```

Verse 3

```
                 E7
Oh, I can't sleep at night,
                  C#7
But just the same,
           F#7
I never weep at night,
A   Am         E7
  I call your name.
   A7            E7
‖:    I call your name,
A7             E7
  I call your name. :‖   Repeat to fade
```

I Don't Want To Spoil The Party

Words & Music by
John Lennon & Paul McCartney

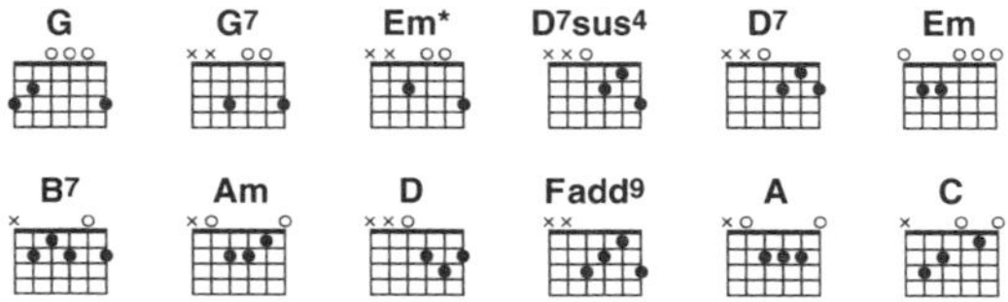

Intro | G | G7 Em* | D7sus4 | D7sus4 |
| D7 | D7 | G | G ||

Verse 1
G
I don't want to spoil the party so I'll go,
D7
I would hate my disappointment to show.
Em B7 Am D
There's nothing for me here, so I will disappear,
G Fadd9 G
If she turns up while I'm gone, please let me know.

Verse 2
G
I've had a drink or two and I don't care,
D7
There's no fun in what I do if she's not there.
Em B7 Am D
I wonder what went wrong, I've waited far too long,
G Fadd9 G
I think I'll take a walk and look for her.

Bridge 1
G
Though tonight she's made me sad,
Em A C D7
I still love her.
G
If I find her I'll be glad,
Em A C D7
I still love her.

```
               G
Verse 3     I don't want to spoil the party so I'll go,
                                           D7
            I would hate my disappointment to show.
                  Em              B7      Am        D
            There's nothing for me here, so I will disappear,
                 G                  Fadd9           G
            If she turns up while I'm gone, please let me know.


Solo        | G     | G     | G     | G     | G     | G     |

            | D7    | D7    | Em    | B7    | Am    | D     |

            | G     | Fadd9 | G     ||


                    G
Bridge 2    Though tonight she's made me sad,
            Em  A   C   D7
            I     still love her.
                G
            If I find her I'll be glad,
            Em  A   C   D7
            I     still love her.


                    G
Verse 4     So, I've had a drink or two and I don't care,
                                                  D7
            There's no fun in what I do if she's not there.
              Em                   B7          Am           D
            I wonder what went wrong, I've waited far too long,
              G               Fadd9           G
            I think I'll take a walk and look for her.


Coda        | G          | G7   Em* | D7sus4   | D7sus4   |

            | D7    | D7    | G     ||
```

I Feel Fine

Words & Music by
John Lennon & Paul McCartney

D7 C7 G7 G Bm C Am

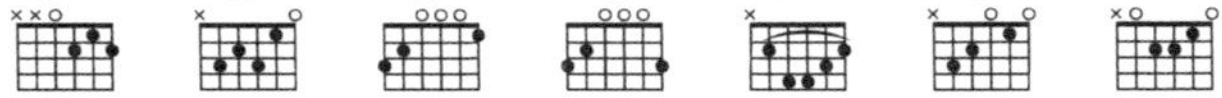

Intro

| (D7) | (D7) | (C7) | (C7) |
Feedback
| (G7) | (G7) | (G7) | (G7) ||

Verse 1

G7
Baby's good to me, you know,

She's happy as can be, you know
D7
She said so.
C7 G7
I'm in love with her and I feel fine.

Verse 2

G7
Baby says she's mine, you know,

She tells me all the time, you know
D7
She said so.
C7 G7
I'm in love with her and I feel fine.

Bridge 1

G Bm
I'm so glad
C D7
That she's my little girl,
G Bm
She's so glad,
Am D7
She's telling all the world;

Verse 3

G7
That her baby buys her things, you know,

He buys her diamond rings, you know
D7
She said so.
C7 G7
She's in love with me and I feel fine.

Solo

| G7 | G7 | G7 | G7 | D7 | D7 ||

| (D7) | (D7) | (C7) | (C7) |

| (G7) | (G7) | (G7) | (G7) ||

Verse 4

G7
Baby says she's mine, you know,

She tells me all the time, you know
D7
She said so.
C7 G7
I'm in love with her and I feel fine.

Bridge 2

G Bm
I'm so glad
C D7
That she's my little girl,
G Bm
She's so glad,
Am D7
She's telling all the world;

Verse 5

G7
That her baby buys her things, you know,

He buys her diamond rings, you know
D7
She said so.
C7 G7
She's in love with me and I feel fine.

Coda

D7 C7 G7
She's in love with me and I feel fine.

||: G7 | G7 | G7 | G7 :|| *Repeat to fade*

I Me Mine

Words & Music by
George Harrison

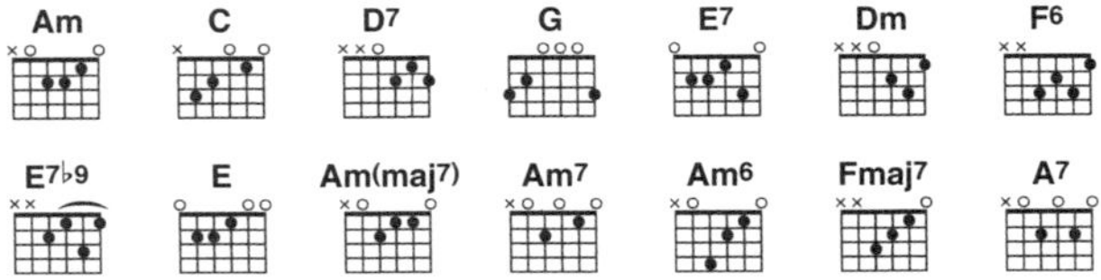

Intro | Am C | D7 | G E7 ||

Verse 1

Am C D7
All ___ through the day,
G E7 Am
I me mine, I me mine, I me mine.
C D7
All ___ through the night,
G E7 Am
I me mine, I me mine, I me mine.
Dm
Never frightened of leaving it,
F6
Everyone's weaving it,
E7♭9 E
Coming on strong all the time.
Am Am(maj7) Am7 Am6
All ___ through the day,
Fmaj7
I me mine.

Chorus 1

A7
I me-me mine,

I me-me mine,
D7
I me-me mine,
A7 E7 | E7 ||
I me-me mine.

```
           Am   C              D7
Verse 2    All ___ I can hear,
                G              E7           Am
           I me mine, I me mine, I me mine.
             C            D7
           Even those tears,
                G              E7           Am
           I me mine, I me mine, I me mine.
                         Dm
           No-one's frightened of playing it,
           F6
           Everyone's saying it,
           E7♭9                            E
           Flowing more freely than wine.
           Am  Am(maj7)            Am7   Am6
           All ___ through the day,
                 Fmaj7
           I me mine.

           A7
Chorus 2   I me-me mine,

           I me-me mine,
           D7
              I me-me mine,
           A7                      E7 | E7            ||
              I me-me mine.

           Am   C              D7
Verse 3    All ___ I can hear,
                G              E7           Am
           I me mine, I me mine, I me mine.
             C            D7
           Even those tears,
                G              E7           Am
           I me mine, I me mine, I me mine.
                         Dm
           No-one's frightened of playing it,
           F6
           Everyone's saying it,
           E7♭9                            E
           Flowing more freely than wine.
           Am  Am(maj7)            Am7   Am6
           All ___ through your life,
                 Fmaj7
           I me mine.
```

I Need You

Words & Music by
George Harrison

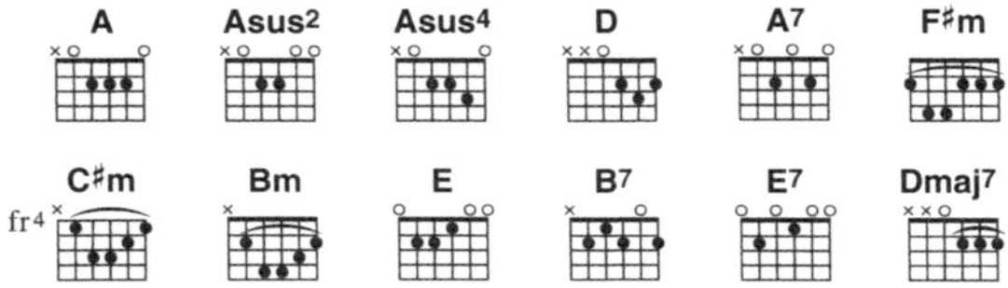


```
Intro        | A  Asus2  | Asus4  A  ||

             A                D                 A    Asus2  Asus4  A
Verse 1      You don't realise how much I need you,
             A                  D                A    A7  Asus4  A
             Love you all the time and never leave you,
                  F♯m              C♯m      F♯m           Bm
             Please come on back to me, I'm lonely as can be,
               A    Asus2  Asus4  A
             I need you.

             A                  D                A   Asus2  Asus4  A
Verse 2      Said you had a thing or two to tell me,
             A              D                      A   A7  Asus4  A
             How was I to know you would upset me?
               F♯m      C♯m     F♯m              Bm
             I didn't realise as I looked in your eyes,
                 A    Asus2  Asus4  A
             You told me.

                            D
Bridge 1     Oh yes, you told me
                  E                       A
             You don't want my lovin' anymore.
                             D           E
             That's when it hurt me, and feeling like this
               B7              E7
             I just can't go on anymore.
```

Verse 3

```
A                  D          A    Asus2  Asus4  A
Please remember how I feel about you,
A             D             A  A7  Asus4  A
I could never really live without you.
   F#m              C#m
So, come on back and see
    F#m               Bm
Just what you mean to me,
 A    Asus2  Asus4  A
I need you.
```

Bridge 2

```
                D
But when you told me
   E                   A
You don't want my lovin' anymore,
                D           E
That's when it hurt me, and feeling like this
 B7                 E7
I just can't go on anymore.
```

Verse 4

```
A                  D          A    Asus2  Asus4  A
Please remember how I feel about you,
A             D             A  A7  Asus4  A
I could never really live without you.
   F#m              C#m
So, come on back and see
    F#m               Bm
Just what you mean to me,
 A    Asus2  Asus4  A
I need you.
```

Coda

```
 F#m         Dmaj7
I need you, I need you.

| A  Asus2 | Asus4  A  ||
```

I Saw Her Standing There

Words & Music by
John Lennon & Paul McCartney

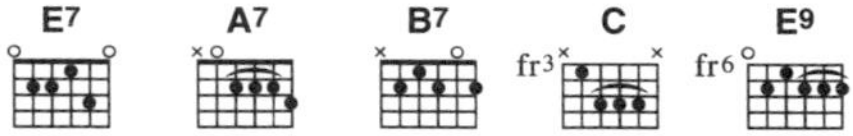

Intro | E7 | E7 | E7 | E7 ||

Verse 1

```
                      E7
Well, she was just seventeen,
        A7           E7
You know what I mean,
                                                                       B7
And the way she looked was way beyond compare.
    E7                                        A7
So how could I dance with another,
C               E7          B7           E7
Oh, when I saw her standing there.
```

Verse 2

```
              E7
Well, she looked at me,
        A7        E7
And I, I could see,
                                                                  B7
That before too long, I'd fall in love with her.
E7                                          A7
She wouldn't dance with another,
C               E7          B7           E7
Oh, when I saw her standing there.
```

Bridge 1

```
                  A7
Well, my heart went boom
When I crossed that room,
                                    B7          A7
And I held her hand in mine. ____
```

Verse 3

```
         E7
Well, we danced through the night,
          A7               E7
And we held each other tight,
                                              B7
And before too long I fell in love with her.
      E7                          A7
Now I'll never dance with another,
C             E7       B7        E7
Oh, when I saw her standing there.
```

Solo

```
| E7  | E7  | E7  | E7  | E7  | E7  |
| B7  | B7  | E7  | E7  | A7  | A7  |
| E7  | B7  | E7  | E7  ||
```

Bridge 2

```
          A7
Well, my heart went boom
When I crossed that room,
                             B7       A7
And I held her hand in mine. ____
```

Verse 4

```
        E7
Oh, we danced through the night,
          A7               E7
And we held each other tight,
                                              B7
And before too long I fell in love with her.
      E7                          A7
Now I'll never dance with another,
C            E7       B7        E7
Oh, since I saw her standing there,
                      B7        E7
Oh, since I saw her standing there,
                              B7        A7      E7   E9
Yeah, well since I saw her standing there.
```

I Should Have Known Better

Words & Music by
John Lennon & Paul McCartney

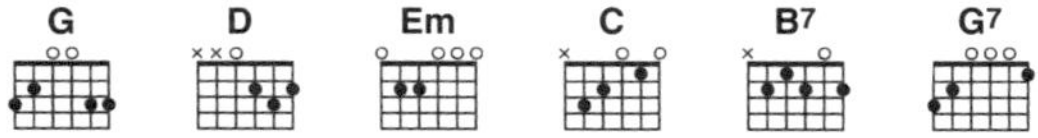


```
Intro       | G   D  | G   D  | G   D  | G   D  ||

            G D G D                      G          D       G    D
Verse 1     I _____ should have known better with a girl like you,
                           G         D                Em
            That I would love everything that you do,
                      C            D           G D G
            And I do, hey hey hey, and I do.

            D         G D G  D            G           D          G   D
Verse 2     Woh woh, I _____ never realised what a kiss could be,
                             G     D          Em
            This could only happen to me.
                           C              B7
            Can't you see, can't you see?

            Em                 C               G          B7
Bridge 1      That when I tell you that I love you, oh,
            Em                                  G    G7
              You're gonna say you love me too, __ oh,
            C                 D              G     Em
              And when I ask you to be mine __
            C                   D              G    D    G
              You're gonna say you love me too.

            D        G D G  D              G             D        G     D
Verse 3     So, oh, I _____ should have realised a lot of things before.
                         G                     D       Em
            If this is love, you've got to give me more,
                           C              D               G      D  G  D
            Give me more, hey hey hey, give me more.
```

```
Solo      | G   D  | G   D  | G   D  | G   D  |

          | G   D  | Em     | C      | D      ||

          | G   D  | G   D      ||
                    Woh woh,

          G D G  D        G            D          G   D
Verse 4   I _____ never realised what a kiss could be,
                    G   D         Em
          This could only happen to me.
                    C            B7
          Can't you see, can't you see?

          Em             C              G          B7
Bridge 2    That when I tell you that I love you, oh,
          Em                                G       G7
            You're gonna say you love me too, ___ oh,
          C              D            G     Em
            And when I ask you to be mine ___
          C                D                G     D    G
            You're gonna say you love me too.
                D       G   D   G
Outro     You love me too.
                 D      G   D   G
          |: You love me too.         :|  Repeat to fade
```

I Wanna Be Your Man

Words & Music by
John Lennon & Paul McCartney

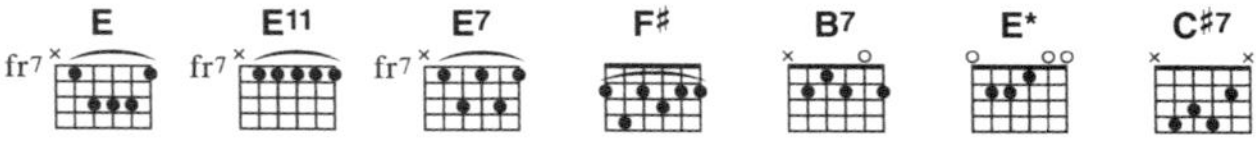

Verse 1

E E11 E E11
I wanna be your lover, baby,
E E11 E E11
I wanna be your man,
E E11 E E11
I wanna be your lover, baby,
E E11 E7
I wanna be your man.

Verse 2

E E11 E E11
Love you like no other, baby,
E E11 E E11
Like no other can,
E E11 E E11
Love you like no other, baby,
E E11 E7
Like no other can.

Chorus 1

N.C. F♯7 B7
I wanna be your man,
E* C♯7
I wanna be your man,
F♯7 B7
I wanna be your man,
E E11
I wanna be your ma - an.

Verse 3

E E11 E E11
Tell me that you love me, baby,
E E11 E E11
Let me understand,
E E11 E E11
Tell me that you love me, baby,
E E11 E7
I wanna be your man.

Verse 4

```
E          E11       E      E11
I wanna be your lover, baby,
E          E11       E     E11
I wanna be your man,
E          E11       E      E11
I wanna be your lover, baby,
E          E11       E7
I wanna be your man.
```

Chorus 2

```
N.C.                 F#7   B7
I wanna be your man,
                     E*    C#7
I wanna be your man,
                     F#7   B7
I wanna be your man,
                     E     E11
I wanna be your ma  -  an.
```

Solo

𝄆 E E11 | E E11 | E E11 | E E11 𝄇 *Play 3 times*

Verse 5

```
E          E11       E      E11
I wanna be your lover, baby,
E          E11       E     E11
I wanna be your man,
E          E11       E      E11
I wanna be your lover, baby,
E          E11       E7
I wanna be your man.
```

Verse 6

```
E             E11      E      E11
Love you like no other, baby,
E          E11   E        E11
Like no other can,
E             E11      E      E11
Love you like no other, baby,
E          E11   E7
Like no other can.
```

Chorus 3 As Chorus 2

Coda

```
𝄆  E  E11  E          E11      E
                I wanna be your man.  𝄇
```
Repeat to fade

I Want To Hold Your Hand

Words & Music by
John Lennon & Paul McCartney

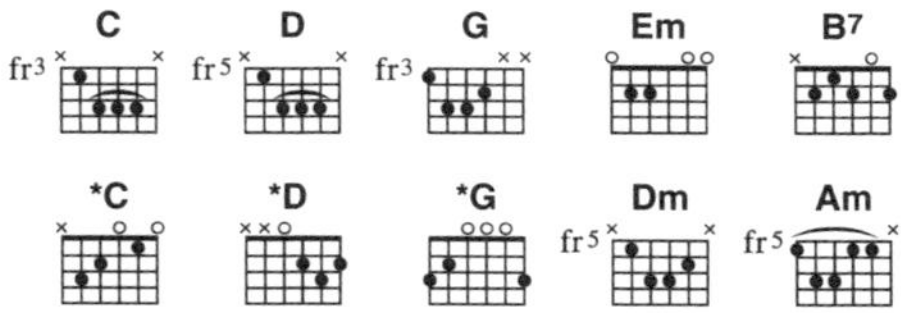

Intro C D | D C D | D C D | D | D ||

Verse 1
(D) G D
Oh yeah, I'll tell you something,
Em B7
I think you'll understand.
G D
When I say that something,
Em B7
I want to hold your hand.

Chorus 1
*C *D *G Em
I want to hold your hand,___
*C *D G
I want to hold your hand.

Verse 2
G D
Oh please say to me
Em B7
You'll let me be your man.
G D
And please say to me
Em B7
You'll let me hold your hand.

Chorus 2
*C *D *G Em
Now let me hold your hand, ___
*C *D G
I want to hold your hand.

```
               Dm          G
*Middle 1*       And when I touch you
                    C        Am
               I feel happy inside.
               Dm        G
                 It's such a feeling
                      C         D
               That my love I can't hide,
               C      D   C      D
               I can't hide, I can't hide.

                   G             D
*Verse 3*      Yeah, you got that something,
               Em                     B7
                 I think you'll understand.
                    G      D
               When I say that something,
               Em                     B7
                 I want to hold your hand.

               *C        *D        *G     Em
*Chorus 3*       I want to hold your hand,___
               *C        *D        G
                 I want to hold your hand.
```

Middle 2 As Middle 1

```
                   G             D
*Verse 4*      Yeah, you got that something,
               Em                     B7
                 I think you'll understand.
                    G       D
               When I feel that something,
               Em                     B7
                 I want to hold your hand.

               *C        *D        *G     Em
*Chorus 4*       I want to hold your hand,___
               *C        *D        B7
                 I want to hold your hand,
               *C        *D        *C     *G
                 I want to hold your hand.
```

I Want To Tell You

Words & Music by
George Harrison

A7 A7sus4 A B7 E7♭9 Bm Bdim Asus4

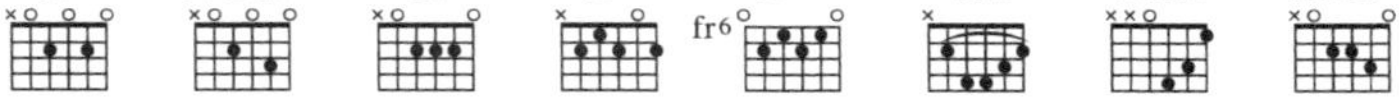

Intro | A7 | A7sus4 | A7 | A7sus4 ||

Verse 1

A
I want to tell you,
B7
My head is filled with things to say.
E7♭9
When you're here,
A7
All those words they seem to slip away.

Verse 2

A
When I get near you,
B7
The games begin to drag me down.
E7♭9
It's alright,
A7
I'll make you maybe next time around.

Bridge 1

Bm Bdim A
But if I seem to act unkind,
B7 Bm
It's only me, it's not my mind,
Bdim A Asus4
That is confusing things.

Verse 3

A
I want to tell you,
B7
I feel hung up and I don't know why.
E7♭9
I don't mind, I could wait forever,
A7
I've got time.

```
              Bm                 Bdim              A
Bridge 2        Sometimes I wish I knew you well,
                             B7                         Bm
              Then I could speak my mind and tell you,
              Bdim               A      Asus4
                Maybe you'd understand.

              A
Verse 4         I want to tell you,
                                  B7
              I feel hung up and I don't know why.
              E7♭9
                I don't mind, I could wait forever,
              A7
              I've got time, ______

              I've got time, ______

              I've got time. ______       Fade out
```

I Will

Words & Music by
John Lennon & Paul McCartney

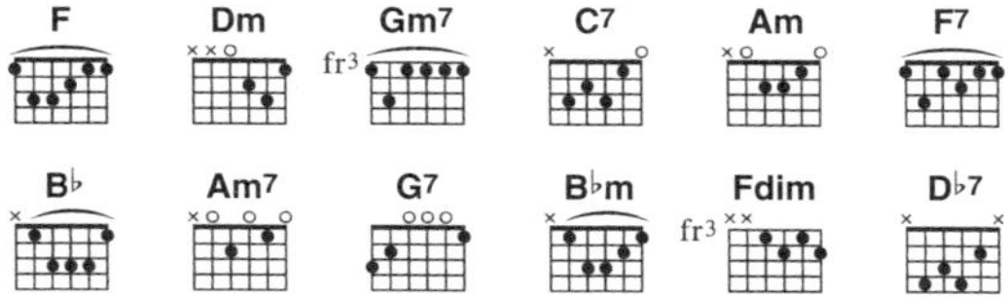

Verse 1

F Dm Gm7 C7
Who knows how long I've loved you?
F Dm Am
You know I love you still,
F7 B♭ C7 Dm F
Will I wait a lonely lifetime?
B♭ C7 F Dm Gm7 C7
If you want me to, I will.

Verse 2

F Dm Gm7 C7
For if I ever saw you,
F Dm Am
I didn't catch your name.
F7 B♭ C7 Dm F
But it never really mattered
B♭ C7 F F7
I will always feel the same.

Middle

B♭ Am7 Dm
Love you forever and forever,
Gm7 C7 F F7
Love you with all my heart,
B♭ Am7 Dm
Love you whenever we're together,
G7 C7
Love you when we're apart.

```
              F           Dm   Gm7       C7
Verse 3   And when at last I find you,
               F            Dm       Am
          Your song will fill the air.
          F7      B♭        C7   Dm         B♭m  F
          Sing it loud so I can hear you,
                  B♭    C7   Dm         B♭m  F
          Make it easy to be near you,
                  B♭          C7
          For the things you do
             Dm  B♭m  F     Fdim
          Endear you   to me
          Gm7    C7         D♭7
          Oh, you know I will,
               F     F7
          I will. ___

Coda      | B♭  Am | Dm      | Gm7  C7 | F        ||
            Ooo, __________     la. _______
```

If I Fell

Words & Music by
John Lennon & Paul McCartney

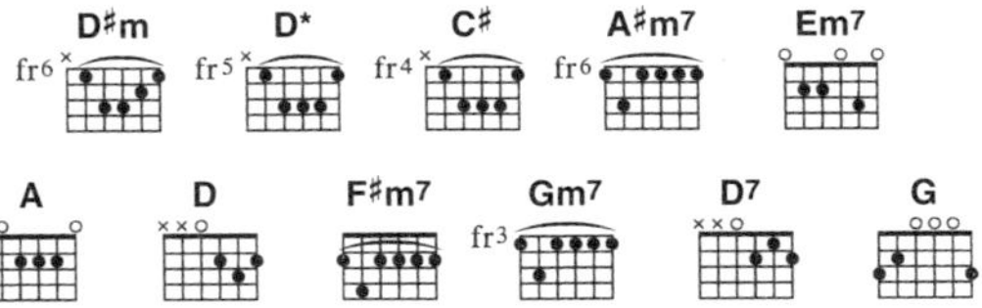

Intro

```
    D♯m
If I fell in love with you,
             D*
Would you promise to be true
     C♯          A♯m7
And help me understand?
             D♯m
'Cause I've been in love before,
       D*
And I found that love was more
       Em7          A
Than just holding hands.
```

Verse 1

```
    D    Em7  F♯m7    Em7
If I give my   heart to you,
  A
I  must be sure
             D  Em7  F♯m7      Em7
From the ve-ry    start, that you
        A                  D               Gm7  A
Would love me more than her.
```

Verse 2

```
    D    Em7  F♯m7    Em7
If I trust in    you, oh please,
      A
Don't run and hide.
    D    Em7   F♯m7   Em7
If I love you   too, oh please
      A             D7
Don't hurt my pride like her.
```

Bridge 1

(D7) G
'Cause I couldn't stand the pain
Gm7 D
And I, would be sad if our new love
A
Was in vain.

Verse 3

D Em7 F♯m7 Em7
So I hope you see that I
A
Would love to love you,
D Em7 F♯m7 Em7
And that she will cry
A D7
When she learns we are two.

Bridge 2

(D7) G
'Cause I couldn't stand the pain
Gm7 D
And I, would be sad if our new love
A
Was in vain.

Verse 4

D Em7 F♯m7 Em7
So I hope you see that I
A
Would love to love you,
D Em7 F♯m7 Em7
And that she will cry
A D
When she learns we are two.
Gm7 D Gm7 D
If I fell in love with you.

If I Needed Someone

Words & Music by
George Harrison

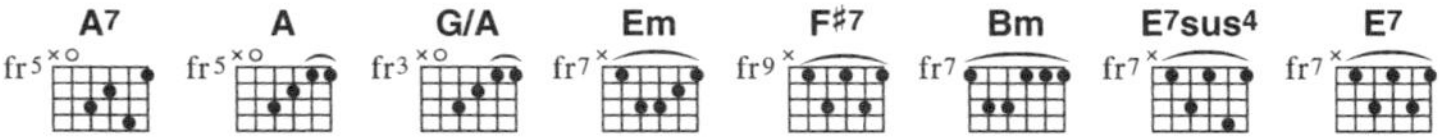

Intro | A7 | A7 | A7 | A7 ||

Verse 1
A
If I needed someone to love,
G/A
You're the one that I'd be thinking of,
A7
If I needed someone.

Verse 2
A
If I had more time to spend,
G/A
Then I guess I'd be with you, my friend,
A7
If I needed someone.

Bridge 1
Em F♯7
Had you come some other day,
Bm
Then it might not have been like this,
Em F♯7 Bm E7sus4 E7
But you see now I'm too much in love.

Verse 3
A
Carve your number on my wall,
G/A
And maybe you will get a call from me,
A7
If I needed someone.

Solo | A | A | A | A |
| G/A | G/A | A7 | A7 ||

Verse 4

A
If I had more time to spend,

G/A
Then I guess I'd be with you, my friend,

A7
If I needed someone.

Bridge 2

Em F#7
Had you come some other day,

Bm
Then it might not have been like this,

Em F#7 Bm E7sus4 E7
But you see now I'm too much in love.

Verse 5

A
Carve your number on my wall,

G/A
And maybe you will get a call from me,

A7
If I needed someone.

Coda

A7 A
Ah, ______ ah. ______

If You've Got Trouble

Words & Music by
John Lennon & Paul McCartney

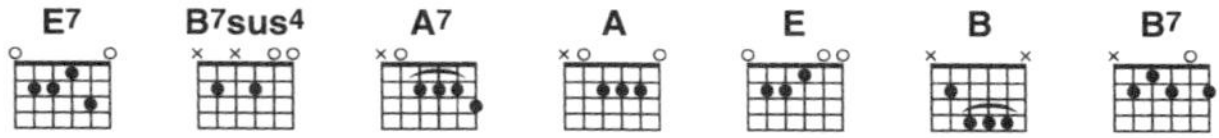

Intro | *Drums for 2 bars* || E7 | E7 ||

Verse 1

```
E7                            B7sus4                      E7
If you've got trouble then you've got less trouble than me.
                                B7sus4              E7
You say you're worried, you can't be as worried as me.
A7                             B7sus4
You're quite content to be bad,
A7                              B7sus4
With all the advantage you had over me,
E7                                     B7sus4                      E7
Just 'cause you're troubled, then don't bring your troubles to me.
```

Verse 2

```
         E7                        B7sus4                E7
I don't think it's funny when you ask for money and things.
                                       B7sus4                   E7
Especially when you're standing there wearing diamonds and rings.
A7                           B7sus4
You think I'm soft in the head
      A7                         B7sus4
Well try someone softer instead, pretty thing,
E7                          B7sus4                      E7
It's not so funny when you know what money can bring.
```

Bridge 1

```
A                             E
   You better leave me alone,
A        E        B            E
I don't need a thing from you,
A                                 E
   You better take yourself home,
A        E         B       E
Go and count a ring or two.
```

Verse 3

E7 B7sus4 E7
If you've got trouble then you've got less trouble than me.

B7sus4 E7
You say you're worried, you can't be as worried as me.

A7 B7sus4
You're quite content to be bad,

A7 B7sus4
With all the advantage you had over me,

E7 B7sus4 E7
Just 'cause you're troubled, then don't bring your troubles to me.

(Oh rock on, anybody!)

Solo

E	E	E	E	A7	A7
E	E	B7	A7	E	E

Bridge 2

A E
You better leave me alone,

A E B E
I don't need a thing from you,

A E
You better take yourself home,

A E B E
Go and count a ring or two.

Verse 4

E7 B7sus4 E7
If you've got trouble then you've got less trouble than me.

B7sus4 E7
You say you're worried, you can't be as worried as me.

A7 B7sus4
You're quite content to be bad,

A7 B7sus4
With all the advantage you had over me,

E7 B7sus4 E7
Just 'cause you're troubled, then don't bring your troubles to me,

E7 B7sus4 E7 E
Just 'cause you're troubled, then don't bring your troubles to me.

I'll Be Back

Words & Music by
John Lennon & Paul McCartney

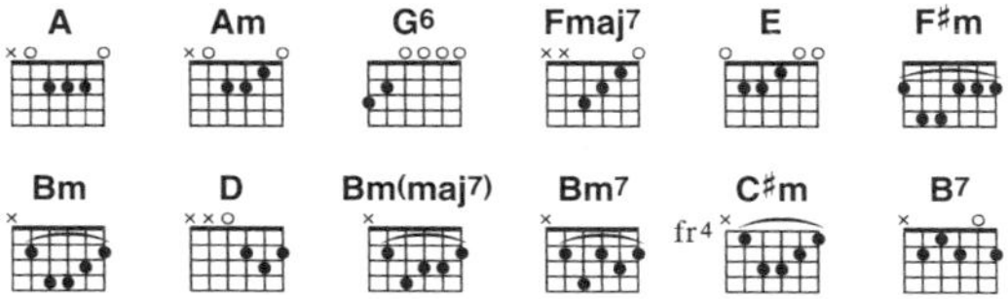

Intro | A | A ||

Verse 1
          Am   G6   Fmaj7
You know if you break my heart I'll go,
     E   A
But I'll be back again.
            Am   G6   Fmaj7
'Cause I told you once before goodbye,
     E   A
But I came back again.

Bridge 1
                F♯m
I love you so,
                        Bm
I'm the one who wants you,
                                E
Yes I'm the one who wants you,
D   E   D   E
Oh - ho, oh - ho.

Verse 2
Am   G6   Fmaj7
You could find better things to do,
           E   A
Than to break my heart again.
         Am   G6   Fmaj7
This time I will try to show you that I'm
     E   A
Not trying to pretend.

Bridge 2

Bm   Bm(maj7)   Bm7
I ________________

                                    C#m
Thought that you would realise,

          F#m
That if I ran away from you,

     B7
That you would want me too,

     D   E
But I got a big surprise,

D   E   D   E
Oh - ho, oh - ho.

Verse 3

Am   G6   Fmaj7
You could find better things to do,

         E   A
Than to break my heart again.

     Am   G6   Fmaj7
This time I will try to show you that I'm

    E   A
Not trying to pretend.

Bridge 3

           F#m
I wanna go,

                   Bm
But I hate to leave you,

                            E
You know I hate to leave you,

D   E   D   E
Oh - ho, oh - ho.

Coda

Am   G6   Fmaj7
You, if you break my heart I'll go,

    E   A
But I'll be back again.

|: A | A | Am | Am :| *Repeat to fade*

I'll Cry Instead

Words & Music by
John Lennon & Paul McCartney

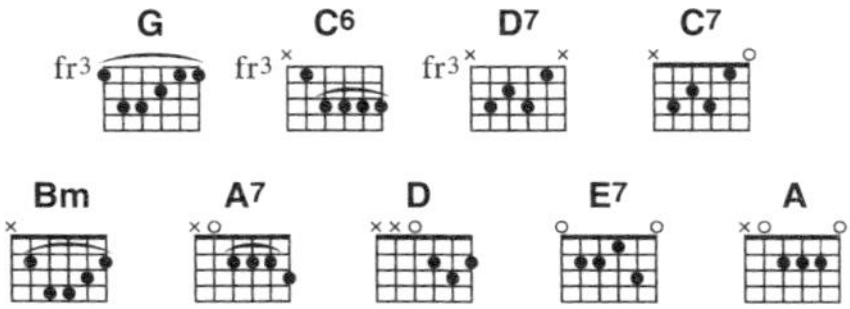

Intro | G C6 ||

Verse 1

```
G   C6          G       C6
          I've got every reason
     G        C6    G     C6   G   C6
On earth to be mad
            G             C6         G       C6    D7
'Cause I've just lost the only girl I had.
           C7
And if I could get my way,

I'd get myself locked up today,
          G     C6           D7        G       C6   G   C6
But I can't, _ so I'll cry instead.
```

Verse 2

```
                G                 C6
I've got a chip on my shoulder
          G          C6            G      C6   G   C6
That's bigger than my feet.
G        C6       G            C6       D7
I can't talk to people that I meet.
  C7
If I could see you now,

I'd try to make you sad somehow,
          G     C6           D7        G       C6   G   C6
But I can't, _ so I'll cry instead.
```

Bridge 1

```
                Bm
Don't want to cry when there's people there,
    A7
I get shy when they start to stare.
    D
I'm gonna lock myself away,
    E7            A        D
But I'll come back again some day.
```

Verse 3

```
              G
And when I do,
    C6   G   C6    G    C6  G  C6
You better hide all the girls,
G        C6        G        C6       D7
I'm gonna break their hearts all round the world.
    C7
Yes, I'm gonna break them in two,
N.C.
Show you what your lovin' man can do,
      G      D7   G    C6  G  C6
Until then I'll cry instead.
```

Bridge 2

```
                Bm
Don't want to cry when there's people there,
    A7
I get shy when they start to stare.
    D
I'm gonna hide myself away,
    E7            A        D
But I'll come back again some day.
```

Verse 4

```
              G
And when I do,
    C6   G   C6    G    C6  G  C6
You better hide all the girls,
G        C6        G        C6       D7
I'm gonna break their hearts all round the world.
    C7
Yes, I'm gonna break them in two,
N.C.
Show you what your lovin' man can do,
      G      D7   G    C6  G
Until then I'll cry instead.
```

I'll Follow The Sun

Words & Music by
John Lennon & Paul McCartney

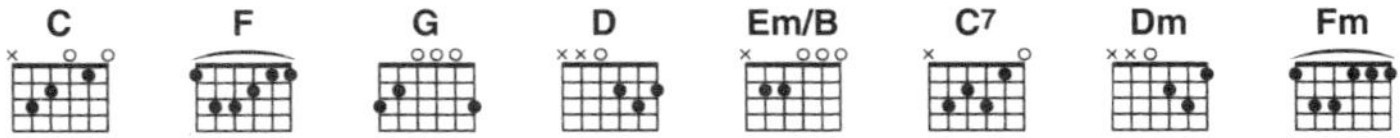


```
Intro        | C          | F    C    ||

             G          F
Verse 1      One day you'll look
             C               D
               To see I've gone,
                     C             Em/B     D
             For tomorrow may rain, so
                  G              C      F   C
             I'll follow the sun.

             G            F
Verse 2      Some day you'll know
             C              D
               I was the one,
                     C             Em/B     D
             But tomorrow may rain, so
                  G              C     C7
             I'll follow the sun.

                                Dm
Bridge 1     And now the time has come
                    Fm                  C     C7
             And so my love I must go.
                                 Dm
             And though I lose a friend
             Fm                  C      Dm
             In the end you will know, oh. ___
```

Verse 3

```
G        F
One day you'll find
C             D
  That I have gone,
      C           Em/B     D
But tomorrow may rain, so
   G         C    F   C
I'll follow the sun.
```

Solo

```
| G        | F        | C        | D        ||
      C           Em/B     D
Yes, tomorrow may rain, so
   G         C    C7
I'll follow the sun.
```

Bridge 2

```
            Dm
And now the time has come
    Fm                C   C7
And so my love I must go.
            Dm
And though I lose a friend
Fm                C     Dm
In the end you will know, oh. ___
```

Verse 4

```
G        F
One day you'll find
C             D
  That I have gone,
      C           Em/B     D
But tomorrow may rain, so
   G         C    F   C
I'll follow the sun.
```

I'll Get You

Words & Music by
John Lennon & Paul McCartney

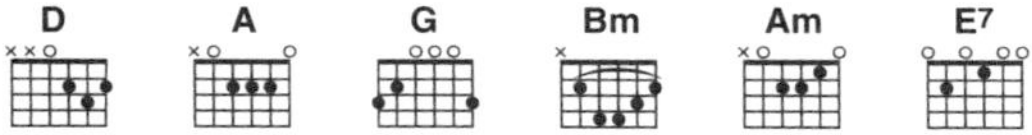

Intro

```
   D       A
Oh yeah, oh yeah,
   D       A
Oh yeah, oh yeah.
```

Verse 1

```
 D
Imagine I'm in love with you,
   G            A
It's easy 'cause I know.
     D              Bm
I've imagined I'm in love with you
G                           A
Many, many, many times before.
       D           Am
It's not like me to pretend,
       D                        Bm
But I'll get you, I'll get you in the end,
      G                     A
Yes I will, I'll get you in the end,
   D       A
Oh yeah, oh yeah.
```

Verse 2

```
 D
I think about you night and day,
  G              A
I need you and it's true,
        D              Bm
When I think about you, I can say,
   G                         A
I'm never, never, never, never blue.
       D              Am
So I'm telling you, my friend,
        D                        Bm
That I'll get you, I'll get you in the end,
```

cont.

```
    G                         A
Yes I will, I'll get you in the end,
  D       A
Oh yeah, oh yeah.
```

Bridge 1

```
                 G
Well there's gonna be a time,
            D
When I'm gonna change your mind,
       E7                             A
So you might as well resign yourself to me,

Oh yeah.
```

Verse 3

```
 D
Imagine I'm in love with you,
   G          A
It's easy 'cause I know.
     D              Bm
I've imagined I'm in love with you
G                          A
Many, many, many times before.
       D            Am
It's not like me to pretend,
       D                           Bm
But I'll get you, I'll get you in the end,
    G                         A
Yes I will, I'll get you in the end,
  D       A
Oh yeah, oh yeah,
  D       A       D
Oh yeah, oh yeah, oh yeah.
```

I'm A Loser

Words & Music by
John Lennon & Paul McCartney

Am D Fmaj7 G Fadd9 Em

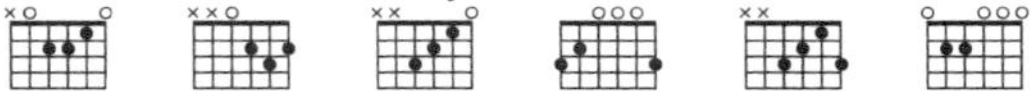

Intro

```
       Am  D
I'm a lo - ser,
       Am  D
I'm a lo - ser,
            Am              Fmaj7  D
And I'm not what I appear to be.
```

Verse 1

```
G             D              Fadd9        G
   Of all the love I have won or have lost,
                D                 Fadd9        G
There is one love I should never have crossed.
              D          Fadd9           G
She was a girl in a million, my friend,
                D                    Fadd9      G
I should have known she would win in the end.
```

Chorus 1

```
       Am  D
I'm a lo - ser,
       Am                       D
And I lost someone who's near to me,
       G    Em
I'm a lo - ser,
            Am              Fmaj7  D
And I'm not what I appear to be.
```

Verse 2

```
G               D               Fadd9      G
   Although I laugh and I act like a clown,
                D             Fadd9       G
Beneath this mask I am wearing a frown.
                D            Fadd9           G
My tears are falling like rain from the sky,
           D       Fadd9           G
Is it for her or myself that I cry?
```

Chorus 2

```
         Am   D
I'm a lo  -  ser,
         Am                    D
And I lost someone who's near to me,
         G    Em
I'm a lo  -  ser,
            Am              Fmaj7  D
And I'm not what I appear to be.
```

Solo

```
|: G       | D        | Fadd9    | G       :|
| Am       | D        | Am       | D        |
| G        | Em       | Am       | Fmaj7  D ||
```

Verse 3

```
G               D          Fadd9          G
   What have I done to deserve such a fate?
     D            Fadd9    G
I realise I have left it too late.
             D                  Fadd9    G
And so it's true, pride comes before a fall,
             D          Fadd9           G
I'm telling you so that you won't lose all.
```

Chorus 3

```
         Am   D
I'm a lo  -  ser,
         Am                    D
And I lost someone who's near to me,
         G    Em
I'm a lo  -  ser,
            Am              Fmaj7  D
And I'm not what I appear to be.
```

Solo

```
|: G       | D        | Fadd9    | G       :|
| Am       | D        | Am       | D        |
| G        | Em       |   Fade out
```

I'm Down

Words & Music by
John Lennon & Paul McCartney

G C7 D7

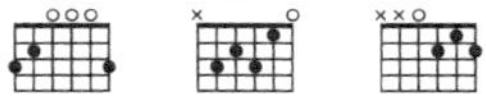

Verse 1

N.C.
You tell lies thinkin' I can't see,
G N.C.
You can't cry 'cause you're laughing at me.

Chorus 1

C7
I'm down, (I'm really down,)
G
I'm down, (down on the ground,)
C7
I'm down, (I'm really down,)
D7 G N.C.
How can you laugh when you know I'm down?
D7 G N.C.
(How can you laugh) when you know I'm down?

Verse 2

G N.C.
Man buys ring, woman throws it away,
G N.C.
Same old thing happen every day.

Chorus 2

C7
I'm down, (I'm really down,)
G
I'm down, (down on the ground,)
C7
I'm down, (I'm really down,)
D7 G N.C.
How can you laugh when you know I'm down?
D7 G N.C.
(How can you laugh) when you know I'm down?

Solo

| (G) | (G) | (G) | (G) | C7 | C7 |
| G | G | D7 | D7 | G | G ||

Verse 3

```
G      N.C.
We're all alone and there's nobody else,
G    N.C.
You still moan, keep your hands to yourself.
```

Chorus 3

```
    C7
I'm down, (I'm really down,)
    G
I'm down, (down on the ground,)
    C7
I'm down, (I'm really down,)
D7             G     N.C.
How can you laugh when you know I'm down?
D7              G     N.C.
(How can you laugh) when you know I'm down?
```

Solo 2

```
| G  | G  | G  | G  | C7 | C7 |
| G  | G  | D7 | C7 | G  | D7 ||
```

Coda

```
                            G
|: Oh babe, you know I'm down, (I'm really down,)

Oh yes I'm down, (I'm really down,)
                 C7
I'm down on the ground, (I'm really down,)
    G
I'm down, (I'm really down,)
                     D7       C7
Ah, baby, I'm upside   down.
          G          D7
Oh yeah, yeah, yeah, yeah, yeah.   :|   Repeat ad lib. to fade
```

I'm Happy Just To Dance With You

Words & Music by
John Lennon & Paul McCartney

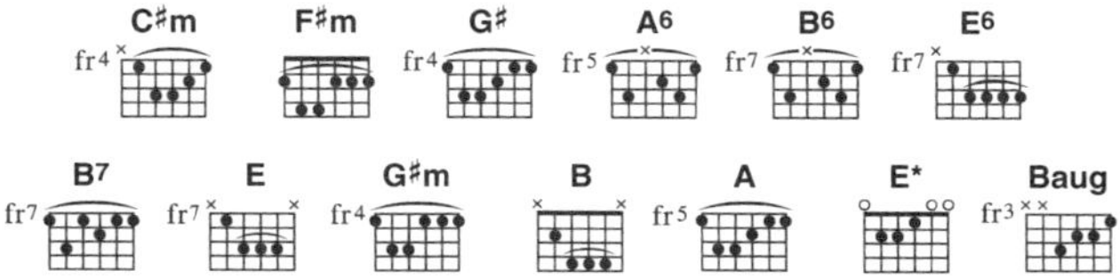

Intro | C♯m | F♯m G♯ | C♯m | F♯m G♯ ||

Chorus 1

C♯m
Before this dance is through,
F♯m G♯
I think I'll love you too,
A6 B6 E6 B7
I'm so happy when you dance with me.

Verse 1

E G♯m F♯m B
I don't wanna kiss or hold your hand,
E G♯m F♯m B
If it's funny, try and understand.
A F♯m E* C♯m
There is really nothing else I'd rather do,
A Baug E B7
'Cause I'm happy just to dance with you.

Verse 2

E G♯m F♯m B
I don't need to hug or hold you tight,
E G♯m F♯m B
I just wanna dance with you all night.
A F♯m E* C♯m
In this world there's nothing I would rather do,
A Baug E
'Cause I'm happy just to dance with you.

Bridge 1

C♯m F♯m G♯
Just to dance with you
C♯m F♯m G♯
Is everything I need.
C♯m
Before this dance is through,
F♯m G♯
I think I'll love you too,
A6 B6 E6 B7
I'm so happy when you dance with me.

Verse 3

E G♯m F♯m B
If somebody tries to take my place,
E G♯m F♯m B
Let's pretend we just can't see his face.
A F♯m E* C♯m
In this world there's nothing I would rather do,
A Baug E
'Cause I'm happy just to dance with you.

Bridge 2

As Bridge 1

Verse 4

E G♯m F♯m B
If somebody tries to take my place,
E G♯m F♯m B
Let's pretend we just can't see his face.
A F♯m E C♯m
In this world there's nothing I would rather do,
A Baug C♯m
I've discovered I'm in love with you.
F♯m G♯
Oh - oh,
A Baug C♯m
'Cause I'm happy just to dance with you.
F♯m G♯
Oh - oh,
A6 B6
Oh - oh,
E6
Oh!

I'm Looking Through You

Words & Music by
John Lennon & Paul McCartney

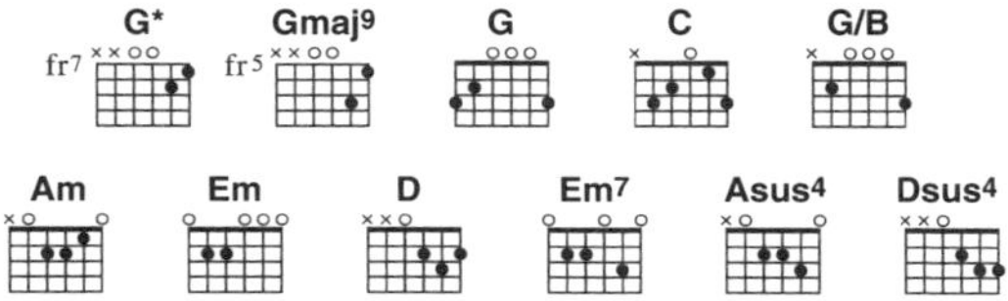

Capo first fret

Intro | G* | Gmaj9 | G C | G C | G C ‖

Verse 1

```
G        C    G/B  Am            Em               D
  I'm look-ing through you,   where did you go?
G   C        G/B   Am          Em            D
  I thought I      knew you,   what did I know?
Em7                    Asus4  Am       G    C    D
  You don't look differ - ent, but you have changed,
G        C     G/B  Am              C                  G        C
  I'm look-ing   through you,   you're not the same.
```

| G C | G C |

Verse 2

```
G          C     G/B    Am        Em          D
  Your lips are    moving,   I cannot hear,
G            C      G/B  Am          Em                    D
  Your voice is      soothing,   but the words aren't clear.
Em7                      Asus4  Am       G       C   D
  You don't sound differ - ent, I've learnt the game,
G        C     G/B  Am              C                  G        C
  I'm look-ing   through you,   you're not the same.
```

| G C | G C | G ‖

Bridge 1

```
C                                   G
Why, tell me why did you not treat me right?
C                               Dsus4          D
Love has a nasty habit of disappearing overnight.
```

Verse 3

```
G        C      G/B  Am    Em          D
  You're think - ing  of me  the same old way,
G     C    G/B  Am       Em        D
  You were a  -  bove me,  but not today.
Em7          Asus4 Am    G     C    D
  The only differ - ence is you're down there,
G    C    G/B  Am         C                G    C
  I'm look - ing  through you  and you're nowhere.

| G  C | G  C | G      ||
```

Bridge 2

```
C                                  G
Why, tell me why did you not treat me right?
C                          Dsus4      D
Love has a nasty habit of disappearing overnight.
```

Verse 4

```
G    C    G/B    Am      Em             D
  I'm look - ing through you,  where did you go?
G  C       G/B  Am        Em        D
  I thought I    knew you,  what did I know?
Em7                Asus4 Am    G   C   D
  You don't look differ - ent, but you have changed,
G    C    G/B  Am          C              G    C
  I'm look - ing  through you,  you're not the same.
```

Outro

```
G           C          G       C
Yeah! Well, baby, you've changed.
G    C             G      C
  Ah,  I'm looking through you,
G    C             G           C   G   C
Yeah,  I'm looking through you.            Fade out
```

I'm Only Sleeping

Words & Music by
John Lennon & Paul McCartney

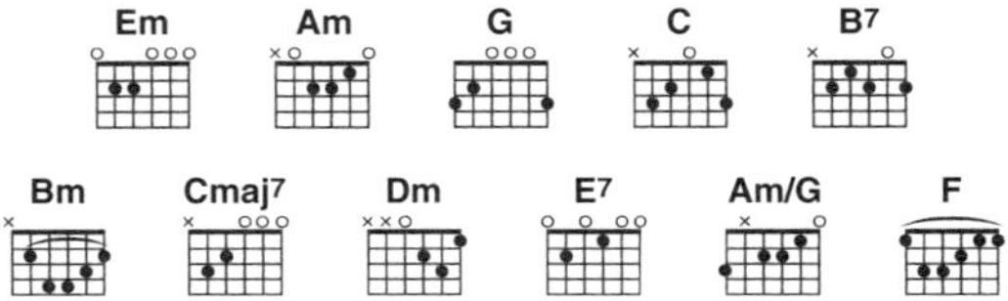

Tune guitar down one semitone

Verse 1

```
Em                                  Am
When I wake up early in the morning,
G         C     G         B7
Lift my head, I'm still yawning.
Em                                  Am
When I'm in the middle of a dream,
G         C    G        C
Stay in bed, float upstream.

(Float upstream.)
```

Chorus 1

```
G                           Am
Please don't wake me, no, don't shake me,
Bm                  Am             Cmaj7
Leave me where I am, I'm only sleeping.
```

Verse 2

```
Em                                 Am
Everybody seems to think I'm lazy,
G       C        G              B7
I don't mind, I think they're crazy.
Em                                 Am
Running everywhere at such a speed,
G            C    G          C
Till they find there's no need.

(There's no need.)
```

Chorus 2

```
G                          Am                  Bm
Please don't spoil my day, I'm miles away,
              Am             Cmaj7      Em
And after all, I'm only sleeping.
```

Bridge 1

Dm   E7   Am   Am/G
Keeping an eye on the world going by my window,
F
Taking my time,
E7   Am
Lying there and staring at the ceiling,
G   C   G   B7
Waiting for a sleepy feeling.

Solo

| Em | Am | G C | G C | C ||

Chorus 3

G   Am   Bm
Please don't spoil my day, I'm miles away,
          Am   Cmaj7   Em
And after all, I'm only sleeping.

Bridge 2

Dm   E7   Am   Am/G
Keeping an eye on the world going by my window,
F
Taking my time.

Verse 3

E7   Am
When I wake up early in the morning,
G   C   G   B7
Lift my head, I'm still yawning.
Em   Am
When I'm in the middle of a dream,
G   C   G   C
Stay in bed, float upstream.

(Float upstream.)

Chorus 4

G   Am
Please don't wake me, no, don't shake me,
Bm   Am   Cmaj7   Em
Leave me where I am, I'm only sleeping.

I'm So Tired

Words & Music by
John Lennon & Paul McCartney

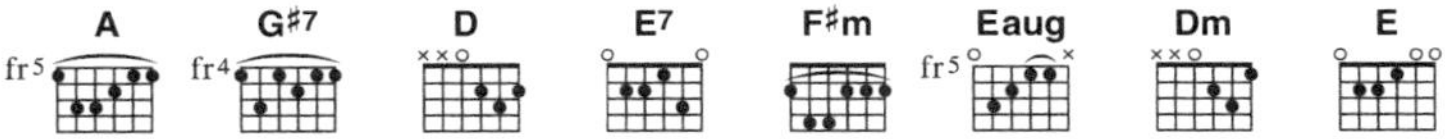

Verse 1

```
     A  G♯7    D               E7
I'm so tired, I haven't slept a wink,
     A  F♯m  D             E7
I'm so tired,   my mind is on the blink.
  A                 Eaug
I wonder should I get up
         F♯m           Dm
And fix myself a drink?

No, no, no.
```

Verse 2

```
     A    G♯7    D                   E7
I'm   so tired, I don't know what to do,
     A    F♯m    D                  E7
I'm   so   tired,   my mind is set on you.
  A                 Eaug
I wonder should I call you,
         F♯m                  Dm
But I know what you would do.
```

Chorus 1

```
A
You'd say I'm putting you on,

But it's no joke, it's doing me harm,
                 E
You know I can't sleep, I can't stop my brain,

You know it's three weeks, I'm going insane,
                    D
You know I'd give you everything I've got
                         A
For a little peace of mind.
```

```
              A  G#7        D               E7
Verse 3      I'm so tired, I'm feeling so upset,
               A        F#m         D                  E7
             Although  I'm so tired,  I'll have another cigarette,
                A              Eaug
             And  curse Sir Walter Raleigh,
                     F#m        Dm
             He was such a stupid git.

             A
Chorus 2     You'd say I'm putting you on,

             But it's no joke, it's doing me harm,
                         E
             You know I can't sleep, I can't stop my brain,

             You know it's three weeks, I'm going insane,
                           D
             You know I'd give you everything I've got
                                  A
             For a little peace of mind.

                D
Coda         I'd give you everything I've got
                                  A
             For a little peace of mind.
                D
             I'd give you everything I've got
                                  A
             For a little peace of mind.
```

In My Life

Words & Music by
John Lennon & Paul McCartney

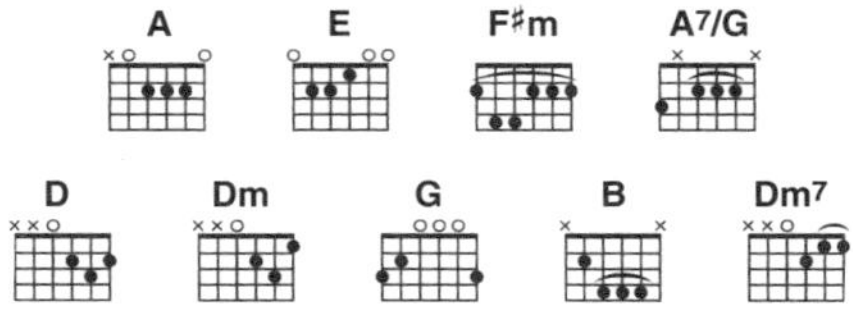

Intro

```
| A    | E    | A    | E    ||
```

Verse 1

```
              A      E   F♯m     A7/G
There are places I remember
           D     Dm         A
All my life, ___ though some have changed,
          A     E        F♯m    A7/G
Some forever, not for better,
              D      Dm      A
Some have gone ___ and some remain.
```

Bridge 1

```
          F♯m            D
All these places had their moments,
      G                     A
With lovers and friends I still can recall,
          F♯m                 B
Some are dead and some are living,
   Dm7        A
In my life I've loved them all.
```

Link

```
| A    | E    ||
```

Verse 2

```
        A        E           F♯m     A7/G
But of all these friends and lovers,
            D  Dm      A
There is no-one compares with you,
             A        E         F♯m       A7/G
And these memories lose their meaning
         D       Dm     A
When I think of love as something new.
```

Bridge 2

F♯m D
Though I know I'll never lose affection
G A
For people and things that went before,
F♯m B
I know I'll often stop and think about them,
Dm7 A
In my __ life I love you more.

Solo

𝄆 A E | F♯m A7/G | D Dm | A 𝄇

Bridge 3

F♯m D
Though I know I'll never lose affection
G A
For people and things that went before,
F♯m B
I know I'll often stop and think about them,
Dm7 A
In my __ life I love you more.

Coda

| A | E | Dm7 N.C. A
In my __ life I love you more.

| E | A ‖

The Inner Light

Words & Music by
George Harrison

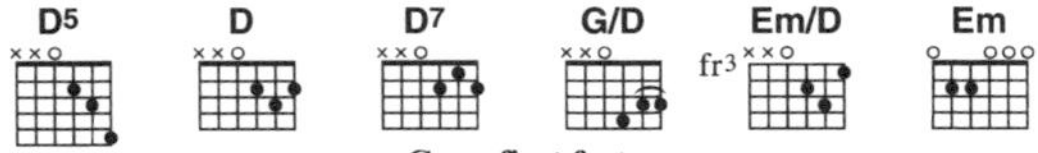

Capo first fret

Intro

```
|: (D5)  | (D5)  | (D5)  | (D5)  | (D5)  :|
```

Verse 1

```
      D          D7        G/D
Without going out of my door,
       D         D7         Em/D
I can know all things on earth.
      D             D7          Em
Without looking out of my window,
       D           D7      G/D
I can know the ways of heaven.
```

Chorus 1

```
     G/D                D                    D7
The farther one travels, the less one knows,
     D                 G/D        D
The less one really knows.
```

Link

```
|: D5  | D5  | D5  | D5  | D5  :|
```

Verse 2

```
      D          D7           Em/D
Without going out of your door,
           D         D7         G/D
You can know all things on earth.
      D             D7            Em
Without looking out of your window,
           D           D7      G/D
You can know the ways of heaven.
```

Chorus 2 As Chorus 1

Verse 3

```
D
Arrive without travelling

See all without looking,

Do all without doing.
```

Coda

```
| D  | D  | (D5)  | (D5)  | (D5)  | (D5)  ||
```

It's All Too Much

Words & Music by
George Harrison

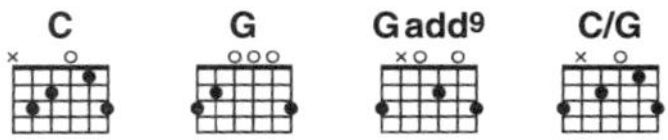

Intro

|: C G | Gadd9 G | C G Gadd9 | G :| *Play 3 times*

|: C/G G | Gadd9 G | C/G G Gadd9 | G :|
It's all too much. __

Verse 1

G
When I look into your eyes,

Your love is there for me.

And the more I go inside,

The more there is to see.

Chorus 1

C/G G Gadd9 G
It's all too much for me to take,
C/G G Gadd9 G
The love that's shining all a - round you.
C/G G Gadd9 G
Everywhere, it's what you make,
C/G G
For us to take,
Gadd9 G
It's all too much.

Verse 2

G
Floating down the stream of time

From life to life with me.

Makes no difference where you are,

Or where you'd like to be.

```
            C/G     G            Gadd9   G
*Chorus 2*  It's all too much for me  to   take,
              C/G          G         Gadd9   G
            The love that's shining all    a - round here.
            C/G      G          Gadd9    G
            All the world is birthday cake,
                C/G   G
            So take a piece,
                Gadd9   G
            But not too  much.
```

Play 4 times

Solo ‖: C/G G | Gadd9 G | C/G G Gadd9 | G :‖ G |

```
          G
*Verse 3* Sail me on a silver sun

          Where I know that I'm free.

          Show me that I'm everywhere,

          And get me home for tea.
```

```
            C/G     G            Gadd9   G
*Chorus 3*  It's all too much for me  to   see,
              C/G          G         Gadd9   G
            The love that's shining all    a - round here.
              C/G      G           Gadd9    G
            The more I learn, the less   I   know,
              C/G     G
            And what I do,
             Gadd9   G
            Is all too   much.
```

```
            C/G     G            Gadd9   G
*Chorus 4*  It's all too much for me  to   take,
              C/G          G         Gadd9   G
            The love that's shining all    a - round you.
            C/G    G             Gadd9        G
            Everywhere, it's what you make,
                C/G  G
            For us to take,
               Gadd9    G
            It's all too   much.
```

Outro

| **C/G G** | **Gadd9 G** | **C/G G Gadd9** | **G** |
It's too much, Ah, ___

| **C/G G** | **Gadd9 G** | **C/G G Gadd9** | **G** ||
It's too much,

|: **C/G G** | **Gadd9 G** | **C/G G Gadd9** | **G** :|

C/G G
With your long blonde hair
Gadd9 G
And your eyes of blue…

| **C/G G Gadd9** | **G** |
C/G G
With your long blonde hair
Gadd9 G
And your eyes of blue…

| **C/G G Gadd9** | **G** |

| **C/G G** | **Gadd9 G** | **C/G G Gadd9** | **G** |
You're too much, ah. __

|: **C/G G** | **Gadd9 G** | **C/G G Gadd9** | **G** :|

|: **C/G G Gadd9 G** :| *Repeat ad lib. to fade*
Too much, too much.

In Spite Of All The Danger

Words & Music by
Paul McCartney & George Harrison

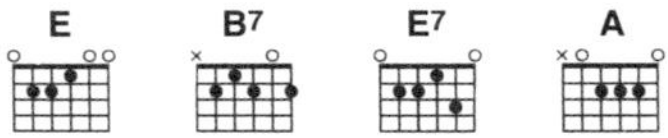


```
Intro      | (E)        ||

           B7                   E
Verse 1       In spite of all the danger,

           In spite of all that may be,
           E7                       A
              I'll do anything for you,
                                    B7
           Anything you want me to,
                                E   A   E
           If you'll be true to me.

                                E
Verse 2    In spite of all the heartache

           That you may cause me,
           E7                       A
              I'll do anything for you,
                                    B7
           Anything you want me to,
                                E   A   E   E7
           If you'll be true to me.

               A                      E              E7
Bridge     I'll look after you like I've never done before,
               A                       B7       N.C.
           I'll keep all the others from knocking at your door.
```

Verse 3

N.C. E
In spite of all the danger,

In spite of all that may be,
E7 A
I'll do anything for you,
B7
Anything you want me to,
E A E
If you'll be true to me.

Solo

| E | E | E | E7 | A | A |

| E | E | B7 | A | E | B7 ||

Verse 4

E
In spite of all the heartache

That you may cause me,
E7 A
I'll do anything for you,
B7
Anything you want me to,
E A E E7
If you'll be true to me.

Coda

A
I'll do anything for you,
B7
Anything you want me to,
E A E
If you'll be true to me.

It Won't Be Long

Words & Music by
John Lennon & Paul McCartney

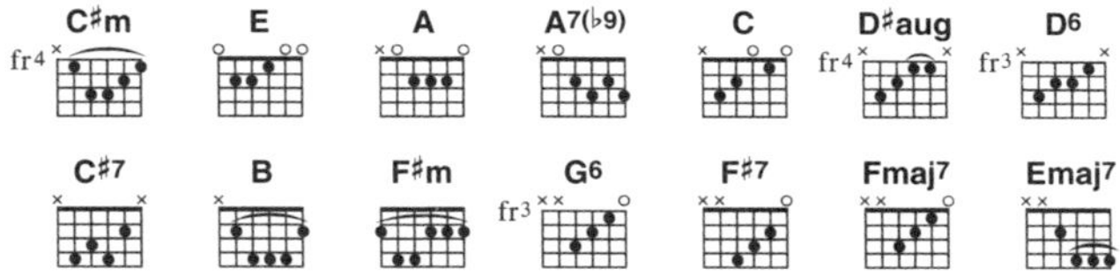

Chorus 1

C♯m
It won't be long, yeah, yeah, yeah,
E
It won't be long, yeah, yeah, yeah,
C♯m
It won't be long, yeah,
A A7(♭9) E
Till I belong to you.

Verse 1

(E) C E
Every night when everybody has fun,
C E
Here am I sitting all on my own.

Chorus 2

As Chorus 1

Bridge 1

E D♯aug
Since you left me I'm so alone,
D6 C♯7
Now you're coming, you're coming on home,
A B
I'll be good like I know I should,
F♯m B
You're coming home, you're coming home.

Verse 2

E C E
Every night the tears come down from my eyes,
C E
Every day I've done nothing but cry.

Chorus 3

```
                C♯m
It won't be long, yeah, yeah, yeah,
                E
It won't be long, yeah, yeah, yeah,
                C♯m
It won't be long, yeah,
    A   A7(♭9)  E
Till I belong to you.
```

Bridge 2

```
              E       D♯aug
Since you left me I'm so alone,
                 D6             C♯7
Now you're coming, you're coming on home,
A                B
I'll be good like I know I should,
                F♯m                B
You're coming home, you're coming home.
```

Verse 3

```
   E         C            E
So,  every day we'll be happy I know,
                    C                E
Now I know that you won't leave me no more.
```

Chorus 4

```
                C♯m
It won't be long, yeah, yeah, yeah,
                E
It won't be long, yeah, yeah, yeah,
                C♯m
It won't be long, yeah,
    A      N.C.   G6  F♯7  Fmaj7  Emaj7
Till I belong to you. ________________
```

It's Only Love

Words & Music by
John Lennon & Paul McCartney

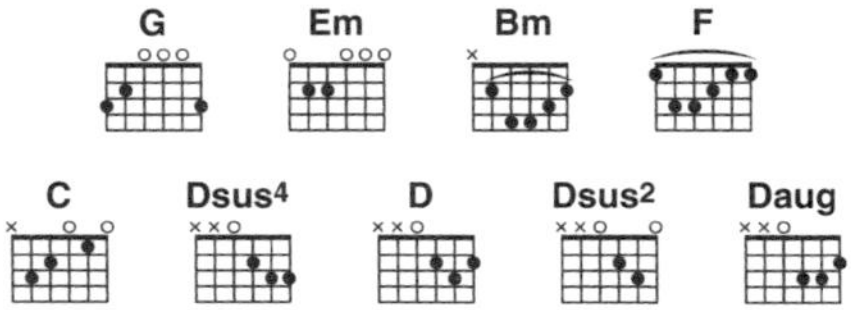

Capo fifth fret

Intro | G | Em | G | Em ||

Verse 1

```
G    Bm        F    C        Dsus4  D  Dsus2  D
I get high when I see you go by,
Daug
My oh my,
G          Bm       F    C          Dsus4  D  Dsus2  D
When you sigh my, my inside just flies,
Daug
Butterflies.
C           D              G          Em
Why am I so shy when I'm beside you?
```

Chorus 1

```
             F               D
It's only love and that is all,
               G              Em
Why should I feel the way I do?
             F               D
It's only love and that is all,
           C        D
But it's so hard loving you. ______
```

Verse 2

```
G    Bm        F         C           Dsus4  D  Dsus2  D
Is it right that you and I should fight
Daug
Every night?
G         Bm      F             C             Dsus4  D  Dsus2  D
Just the sight of you makes night time bright,
Daug
Very bright.
C                D                 G          Em
Haven't I the right to make it up, girl?
```

Chorus 2

```
          F                  D
It's only love and that is all,
                G                 Em
Why should I feel the way I do?
          F                  D
It's only love and that is all,
            C          D
But it's so hard loving you,
            C          D
Yes it's so hard loving you,
          G   Em  G    Em
Loving you. ______
```

Coda

```
| G      | Em      | G       ||
```

I've Got A Feeling

Words & Music by
John Lennon & Paul McCartney

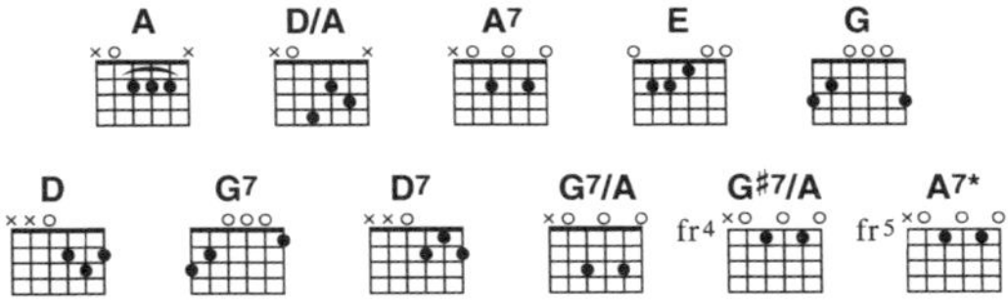

Intro | A D/A | A D/A ||

Verse 1

A D/A A D/A
I've got a feeling, a feeling deep inside,
A D/A A D/A
Oh yeah, oh yeah, that's right.
A D/A A D/A
I've got a feeling, a feeling I can't hide,
A D/A A D/A A
Oh no, no, oh no, oh no.
A7 E G D
Yeah, ___ yeah,
N.C. A D/A A D/A
I've got a feeling, yeah!

Verse 2

A D/A A D/A
Oh, please believe me, I'd hate to miss the train,
A D/A A D/A
Oh yeah, oh yeah.
A D/A A D/A
And if you leave me, I won't be late again,
A D/A A D/A
Oh no, oh no, oh no.
A7 E G D N.C. A D/A
Yeah, yeah! I've got a feeling, yeah!
A D/A
I've got a feeling.

Bridge

E
All these years I've been wandering around,
G7
Wondering how come nobody told me
D7
All that I've been looking for was
A7
Somebody who looked like you.

```
Link       | N.C.     | N.C.     ||

           A                D/A      A                 D/A
Verse 3       I've got a feeling that keeps me on my toes,
              A     D/A   A   D/A
           Oh yeah,   oh yeah.
           A              D/A                 A            D/A
              I've got a feeling, I think that everybody knows,
                  A   D/A      A     D/A    A7
           Oh yeah,           oh yeah,   oh yeah.
           (A7)    E  G  D  N.C.          A
              Yeah,yeah!     I've got a feeling, yeah!

Link       | (A)  D/A  | A   D/A  ||

           A                       D/A       A                D/A
Verse 4       Everybody had a hard year, everybody had a good time,
           A                    D/A        A                 D/A
           Everybody had a wet dream, everybody saw the sunshine,
              A                     D/A          A    D/A
           Oh yeah, (oh yeah,) oh yeah, oh yeah.

           A                    D/A      A                    D/A
Verse 5    Everybody had a good year, everybody let their hair down,
           A                         D/A      A                      D/A
           Everybody pulled their socks up, everybody put their foot down,

           Oh yeah.

Link       | A7   G7/A   G#7/A  | A7*  G#7/A   G7/A |
           (yeah.)

           | A   D/A  | A   D/A  ||

           A                       D/A       A                 D/A
Verse 6       Everybody had a good year, everybody had a hard time,
           A                    D/A      A                   D/A
           Everybody had a wet dream, everybody saw the sunshine.

Verse 7    As Verse 5

Coda       | A7  G7/A  G#7/A     | A7*  G#7/A  G7/A        |
           (yeah.)                     (I've got a feeling)

           |: A7   G7/A  G#7/A   | A7*  G#7/A   G7/A    :| A        ||
                          (I've got a feeling)
```

I've Just Seen A Face

Words & Music by
John Lennon & Paul McCartney

F♯m D E A F♯m7 E7

Intro

| F♯m | F♯m | F♯m | F♯m | D |

| D | D | D | E | E ||

Verse 1

A
I've just seen a face,
F♯m
I can't forget the time or place where we just met,
She's just the girl for me
F♯m7 D
And I want all the world to see we've met.
E A
Mm mm mm mm-mm mm.

Verse 2

A
Had it been another day
I might have looked the other way
F♯m
And I'd have never been aware,
F♯m7 D
But as it is I'll dream of her tonight,
E A
Da da da da-da da.

Chorus 1

E D
Falling, yes I am falling,
A D A
And she keeps calling me back again.

```
            A
Verse 3     I have never know the like of this,

            I've been alone and I have
            F#m
            Missed things and kept out of sight,
                                         F#m7     D
            But other girls were never quite like this,
                   E        A
            Da da da da-da da.


Chorus 2    As Chorus 1


Solo        | A    | A    | A    | A    | F#m  | F#m  |

            | F#m  | F#m F#m7 | D  | D    | E    | A    ||

            E7                   D
Chorus 3    Falling, yes I am falling,
                             A    D          A
            And she keeps calling   me back again.

            A
Verse 4     I've just seen a face,
                                                         F#m
            I can't forget the time or place where we just met,

            She's just the girl for me
                                            F#m7     D
            And I want all the world to see we've met.
                     E           A
            Mm mm mm, da-da da.


Chorus 4    As Chorus 1


Chorus 5    As Chorus 1

                E                D
Coda        Oh, falling, yes I am falling,
                             A    D                   E  A
            And she keeps calling   me back again.
```

Julia

Words & Music by
John Lennon & Paul McCartney

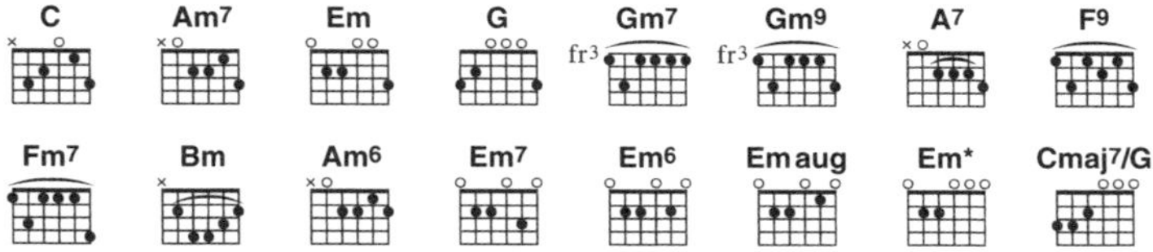

Capo second fret

Chorus 1

```
C                 Am7              Em
Half of what I say is meaningless,
C              Am7                 Em  G  C
But I say it just to reach you, Ju  -  lia.
```

Verse 1

```
C       Am7  Gm7   Gm9  A7           F9    Fm7
Ju  -  lia,  Ju  - lia,   ocean child, calls me,
C            Am7            Em  G   C
So I sing a song of love, Ju  -  lia.
```

Verse 2

```
C       Am7  Gm7        Gm9  A7           F9     Fm7
Ju  -  lia,  sea-shell eyes, windy smile, calls me,
C            Am7            Em  G   C
So I sing a song of love, Ju  -  lia.
```

Bridge

```
Bm                                 C
   Her hair of floating sky is shimmering,
Am7          Am6
Glimmering
Em7   Em6   Em aug   Em*
In the sun. ________
```

Verse 3

```
C       Am7  Gm7   Gm9  A7              F9      Fm7
Ju  -  lia,  Ju  - lia,   morning moon, touch me,
C            Am7            Em  G   C
So I sing a song of love, Ju  -  lia.
```

Chorus 2

```
C                 Am7              Em
When I cannot sing my heart,
C            Am7                Em  G  C
I can only speak my mind, Ju  -  lia.
```

Verse 4

```
C      Am7  Gm7     Gm9  A7           F9     Fm7
Ju  -  lia,  sleeping sand, silent cloud, touch me,
C            Am7           Em  G  C   Am7
So I sing a song of love, Ju  -  lia.
```

Coda

```
Gm7      Gm9    A7
Mm, ______
F9    Fm7
Calls me,
C            Am7
So I sing a song of love
    Em     C
For Ju  -  lia,
Em     C
Ju  -  lia,
Em  G   Cmaj7/G
Ju  -  lia.
```

Lady Madonna

Words & Music by
John Lennon & Paul McCartney

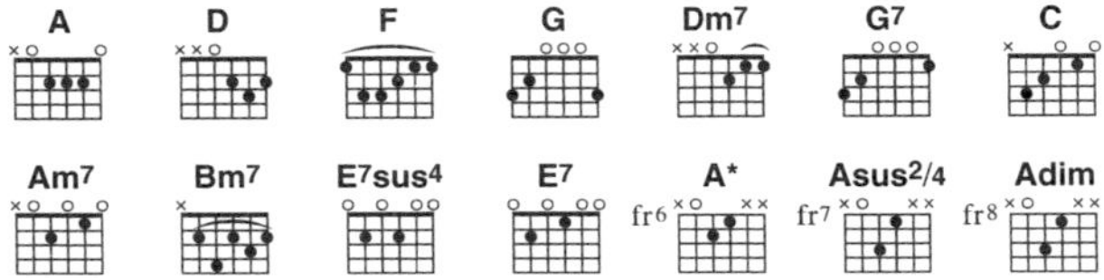

Intro | A D | A D | A D | F G A ||

Verse 1

```
A            D       A                   D
Lady Madonna, children at your feet,
A                         D                    F     G     A
Wonder how you manage to make ends meet.
                      D          A                         D
Who finds the money when you pay the rent?
A                         D                 F     G     A
Did you think that money was heaven sent?
```

Bridge 1

```
Dm7                                         G7
Friday night arrives without a suitcase,
C                                             Am7
Sunday morning, creeping like a nun.
Dm7                                                G7
Monday's child has learned to tie his bootlace.
C    Bm7          E7sus4   E7
See how they run. ____
```

Verse 2

```
A            D       A                 D
Lady Madonna, baby at your breast,
A                         D                 F     G     A
Wonder how you manage to feed the rest.
```

Link | A D | A D | A D | F G A ||

Solo

| Dm7 | G7 | C | Am7 | Dm7 | G7 ||

```
C    Bm7      E7sus4  E7
See how they run. ____
```

Verse 3

```
A          D       A              D
Lady Madonna, lying on the bed,
A                  D              F      G      A
Listen to the music playing in your head.
```

Link

| A D | A D | A D | F G A ||

Bridge 2

```
Dm7                                G7
Tuesday afternoon is never ending,
C                                          Am7
Wednesday morning papers didn't come.
Dm7                                              G7
Thursday night, your stockings needed mending:
C    Bm7      E7sus4  E7
See how they run. ____
```

Verse 4

```
A          D       A                  D
Lady Madonna, children at your feet,
A                       D                F      G      A*   Asus2/4   Adim   A*
Wonder how you manage to make ends meet. ____
```

Coda

| A* Asus2/4 | Adim Asus2/4 A ||

Let It Be

Words & Music by
John Lennon & Paul McCartney

Intro | C G | Am Fmaj7 F6 | C G | F C ||

Verse 1

```
            C                 G
When I find myself in times of trouble,
Am               Fmaj7           F6
Mother Mary comes to me,
C                       G            F   C
Speaking words of wisdom, let it be.
      C                 G
And in my hour of darkness
        Am                   Fmaj7         F6
She is standing right in front of me,
C                       G            F   C
Speaking words of wisdom, let it be.
```

Chorus 1

```
        Am        C/G       F         C
Let it be, let it be, let it be, let it be,
                      G            F   C
Whisper words of wisdom, let it be.
```

Verse 2

```
      C                    G
And when the broken hearted people
Am               Fmaj7          F6
Living in the world agree,
C                    G           F   C
There will be an answer, let it be.
     C                         G
For though they may be parted there is
Am                     Fmaj7          F6
Still a chance that they will see.
C                    G           F   C
There will be an answer, let it be.
```

```
                          Am       C/G        F         C
Chorus 2          Let it be, let it be, let it be, let it be,
                                                G         F   C
                  There will be an answer, let it be.
                          Am       C/G        F         C
                  Let it be, let it be, let it be, let it be,
                                              G              F   C
                  Whisper words of wisdom, let it be.


                  | F   C   | G F C     | F   C   | G F C    |

Solo              |: C   G  | Am   F    | C   G   | F    C  :|

                          Am       C/G        F         C
Chorus 3          Let it be, let it be, let it be, let it be,
                                            G                F   C
                  Whisper words of wisdom, let it be.

                        C                      G
Verse 3           And when the night is cloudy,
                            Am                  Fmaj7            F6
                  There is still a light that shines on me,
                  C              G                 F   C
                  Shine until tomorrow, let it be.
                    C              G
                  I wake up to the sound of music,
                  Am              Fmaj7          F6
                  Mother Mary comes to me,
                  C                        G               F   C
                  Speaking words of wisdom, let it be.

                          Am       C/G        F         C
Chorus 4          Let it be, let it be, let it be, let it be,
                                                G         F   C
                  There will be an answer, let it be.
                          Am       C/G        F         C
                  Let it be, let it be, let it be, let it be,
                                                G         F   C
                  There will be an answer, let it be.
                          Am       C/G        F         C
                  Let it be, let it be, let it be, let it be,
                                            G                F   C
                  Whisper words of wisdom, let it be.

                  | F   C   | G F C     ||
```

Like Dreamers Do

Words & Music by
John Lennon & Paul McCartney

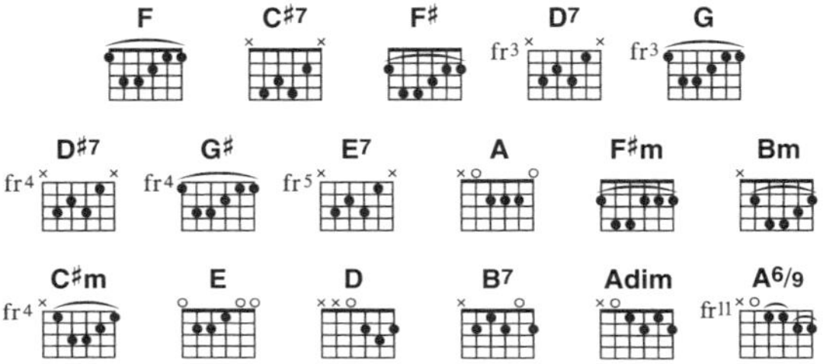

Intro | F C♯7 F♯ D7 | G D♯7 G♯ E7 ||

Verse 1

A F♯m
I, I saw a girl in my dreams,
Bm C♯m E
And so it seems that I will love her.
A F♯m
Oh you, you are that girl in my dreams,
Bm C♯m E
And so it seems that I will love you.

Chorus 1

A C♯7
And I waited for your kiss,
Bm E7
Waited for the bliss
N.C. A
Like dreamers do.

Bridge 1

D E
And I,
A
I, I, I, I, ___
Bm B7
Oh, I'll be there, yeah,
E7
Waiting for you, you, you, you, you, you.

Verse 2

A   F♯m
You, you came just one dream ago,
              Bm   C♯m E
And now I know that I will love you.
      A   F♯m
Oh, I knew when you first said hello,
              Bm   C♯m E
That's how I know that I will love you.

Chorus 2

      A   C♯7
And I waited for your kiss,
              Bm   E7
Waited for the bliss
N.C.   A
Like dreamers do.

Bridge 2

      D   E
And I,
       A
I, I, I, I, ___
              Bm   B7
Oh, I'll be there, yeah,
               E7
Waiting for you, you, you, you, you, you.

Verse 3

A   F♯m
You, you came just one dream ago,
              Bm   C♯m E
And now I know that I will love you.
      A   F♯m
Oh, I knew when you first said hello,
              Bm   C♯m E
That's how I know that I will love you.

Chorus 3

      A   C♯7
And I waited for your kiss,
              Bm   E7
Waited for the bliss
N.C.   A
Like dreamers do,
Adim   A
Oh, like dreamers do,
Adim   A
Like dreamers do.

Coda

| Adim | F C♯7 F♯ D7 | G D♯7 G♯ E7 | A | A6/9 ||

Little Child

Words & Music by
John Lennon & Paul McCartney

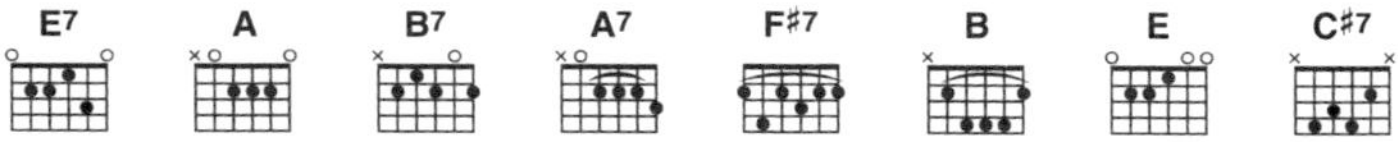

Harmonica | (E7) | (A) | E7 | E7 ||

```
           E7
Verse 1    Little child, little child,
                                     A          E7
           Little child, won't you dance with me?
           B7           A7
           I'm so sad and lonely.
           F♯7                      B
           Baby take a chance with me.

           E7
Verse 2    Little child, little child,
                                     A          E7
           Little child, won't you dance with me?
           B7           A7
           I'm so sad and lonely.
           F♯7         B7           E
           Baby take a chance with me.

             E                                  B7
Bridge 1   If you want someone to make you feel so fine,
                      E7
           Then we'll have some fun when you're mine, all mine,
                    F♯7                 B
           So come on, come on, come on!

           E7
Verse 3    Little child, little child,
                                     A          E7
           Little child, won't you dance with me?
           B7           A7
           I'm so sad and lonely.
           F♯7         B7           E
           Baby take a chance with me.
```

Solo

| E7 | E7 | E7 | E7 | A7 | A7 |

| E7 | E7 | B7 | A7 | F#7 | B7 ||

Bridge 2

```
                E                          B7
When you're by my side, you're the only one,
            E7
Don't you run and hide, just come on, come on,
              F#7                  B
Yeah, come on, come on, come on.
```

Verse 4

```
        E7
Little child, little child,
                              A          E7
Little child, won't you dance with me?
B7               A7
I'm so sad and lonely.
F#7              B7            E        C#7
Baby take a chance with me, oh yeah,
F#7              B7            E        C#7
Baby take a chance with me, oh yeah,
F#7              B7            E        C#7
Baby take a chance with me, oh yeah.
```
Fade out

The Long And Winding Road

Words & Music by
John Lennon & Paul McCartney

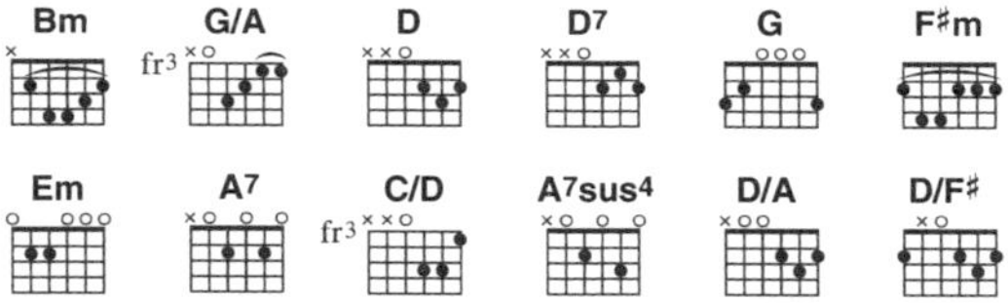

Capo first fret

Verse 1

Bm G/A
The long and winding road,
D D7 G
That leads to your door
F♯m Bm
Will never disappear.
Em A7 C/D
I've seen that road before.
G F♯m Bm
It always leads me here,
Em A7 A7sus4 D
Lead me to your door.

Verse 2

Bm G/A
The wild and windy night
D D7 G
That the rain washed away,
F♯m Bm
Has left a pool of tears
Em A7 C/D
Crying for the day.
G F♯m Bm
Why leave me standing here?
Em A7 A7sus4 D
Let me know the way.

Bridge 1

D/A G
Many times I've been alone,
D/F♯ Em A7
And many times I've cried.
D/A G
Anyway, you'll never know
D/F♯ Em A7
The many ways I've tried.

Verse 3

Bm G/A
And still they lead me back
D D7 G
To the long winding road.
F♯m Bm
You left me standing here
Em A7 C/D
A long, long time ago.
G F♯m Bm
Don't leave me waiting here,
Em A7 A7sus4 D
Lead me to your door.

Bridge 2

𝄆 D/A G | D/F♯ Em A7 𝄇

Verse 4

Bm G/A
But still they lead me back
D D7 G
To the long, winding road.
F♯m Bm
You left me standing here
Em A7 C/D
A long, long time ago.
G F♯m Bm
Don't keep me waiting here,
Em A7 D
Lead me to your door.
G/A D
(Yeah, yeah, yeah, yeah.)

Long Long Long

Words & Music by
George Harrison

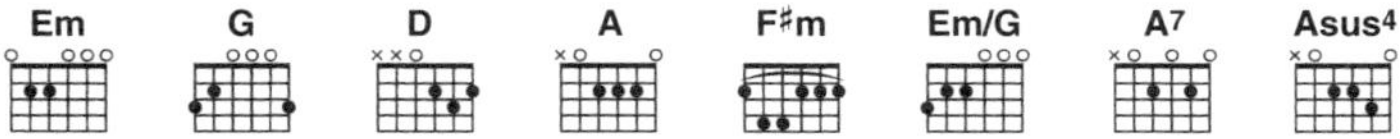

Capo third fret

Intro | Em G | Em D | A ||

Verse 1
G F#m Em D Em/G D
It's been a long, long, long time.
A Em D A
How could I ever have lost you,
Em D A
When I loved you?
G F#m Em D Em/G D
It took a long, long, long time.
A Em D A
Now I'm so happy I found you,
Em D A A7
How I love you.

Bridge 1
G D A Em
So many tears I was searching,
G D A Em G A
So many tears I was wasting, oh, oh!

Verse 2
G F#m Em D Em/G D
Now I can see you, be you.
A Em D A
How can I ever misplace you?
Em D A Em D A
How I want you, how I love you.
Em D A
You know that I need you.
Em D A
Oh, I love you.

Coda | (A) | (A) | (Asus4) | (Asus4) ||
Ah. ___________

Love Me Do

Words & Music by
John Lennon & Paul McCartney

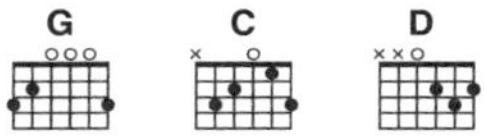

Intro | G | C | G | C | G | C | G | G ||

Chorus 1

G C
Love, love me do,
G C
You know I love you.
G C
I'll always be true,

So please ___
N.C. G C G C
Love me do, ___ oh, love me do.

Chorus 2

G C
As Chorus 1

Bridge

D
Someone to love,
C G
Somebody new.
D
Someone to love,
C G
Someone like you.

Chorus 3 As Chorus 1

Solo ||: D | D | C | G :||

| G | G | G | G (D) ||

Chorus 4 As Chorus 1

Outro

G C
||: Yeah, love me do,
G C
Oh, love me do. :|| *Repeat to fade*

Love You To

Words & Music by
George Harrison

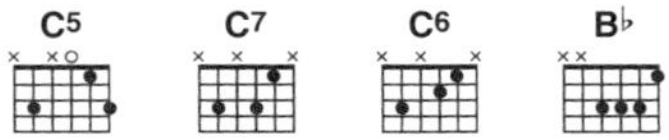

Sitar intro ‖: C5 | C5 | C5 | C5 :‖
ad lib.

Verse 1

```
C6                        C5
Each day just goes so fast,
C6                   C5
I turn around, it's past,
C6          C5        C7        C6       C7  C5
You don't get time to hang a sign on  me.
```

Chorus 1

```
B♭                        C5   B♭  C5
Love me while you can,
B♭                             C5    B♭  C5
Before I'm a dead old man.
```

Verse 2

```
C6              C5
A lifetime is so short,
C6                  C5
A new one can't be bought,
C6           C5            C7              C6    C7  C5
But what you've got means such a lot to   me.
```

Chorus 2

```
B♭                    C5    B♭  C5
Make love all day long,
B♭                     C5     B♭  C5
Make love singing songs.
```

Link ‖: C5 | C5 | C5 | C5 | C5 :‖
Ad lib. Sitar solo

Chorus 3

```
B♭                     C5     B♭  C5
Make love all day long,
B♭                     C5      B♭  C5
Make love singing songs.
```

Verse 3

```
C6                        C5
There's people standing round,
C6                         C5
Who'll screw you in the ground,
C6             C5      C7        C6
They'll fill you in with all their sins,
C7      C5
You'll see.
```

Chorus 4

```
B♭                    C5     B♭  C5
I'll make love to you,
B♭                 C5   B♭  C5
If you want me to.
```

Coda

```
||: C5    | C5    | C5    | C5    :||
```

Sitar ad lib. to fade

Lovely Rita

Words & Music by
John Lennon & Paul McCartney

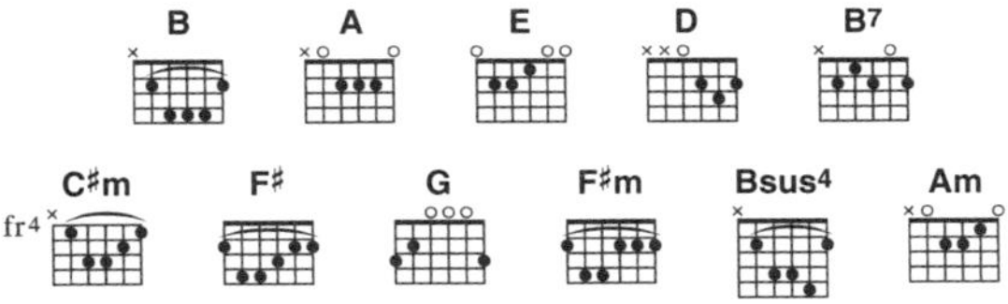

Tune guitar down one semitone

Intro | B | A | E | B ||

```
B              A
Lovely Rita meter maid,
E              B
Lovely Rita meter maid.
```

Chorus 1

```
E              D      A
Lovely Rita meter maid,
E                        B7
Nothing can come between us,
C♯m                   F♯                    B7
When it gets dark, I tow your heart away.
```

Verse 1

```
E                        A
   Standing by a parking meter,
D                           G
   When I caught a glimpse of Rita
E                                   B7
Filling in a ticket in her little white book.
```

Verse 2

```
E                      A
   In a cap, she looked much older,
D                    G
   And the bag across her shoulder
E                                      B7
Made her look a little like a military man.
```

Link 1 | E C♯m F♯m B ||

Chorus 2

E D A
Lovely Rita meter maid,
E B7
May I enquire discreetly,
C♯m F♯ B7
When are you free to take some tea with me?
Bsus4 B
Ah. ______

Solo

| E D A | E B7 | C♯m F♯ | B B7 ||
Rita!

Verse 3

E A
Took her out and tried to win her,
D G
Had a laugh, and over dinner
E B7
Told her I would really like to see her again.

Verse 4

E A
Got the bill and Rita paid it,
D G
Took her home, I nearly made it,
E B7
Sitting on a sofa with a sister or two.

Link 2

| E C♯m F♯m B ||
Oh. ____

Chorus 3

E D A
Lovely Rita meter maid,
E B7
Where would I be without you?
C♯m F♯ (B)
Give us a wink and make me think of you.

Outro

B A
||: Lovely Rita meter maid,
E B
Lovely Rita meter maid. :||

||: Am | Am | Am | Am :||

| Am | Am | A ||

Lucy In The Sky With Diamonds

Words & Music by
John Lennon & Paul McCartney

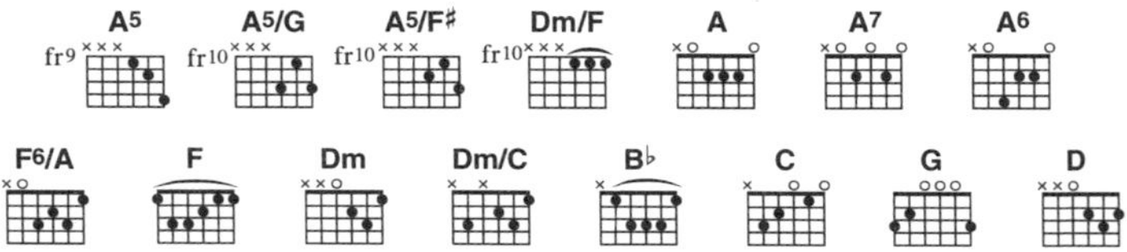

Intro | A5 | A5/G | A5/F♯ | Dm/F ||

Verse 1

A A7 A6 F6/A
Picture yourself in a boat on a river,
A A7 A6 F
With tangerine trees and marmalade skies.
A A7 A6 F6/A
Somebody calls you, you answer quite slowly,
A A7 A6 Dm Dm/C
A girl with kaleidoscope eyes. _____

Pre-chorus 1

B♭ C
Cellophane flowers of yellow and green,
F B♭
Towering over your head.
C G
Look for the girl with the sun in her eyes,
D
And she's gone.

Chorus 1

G C D
Lucy in the sky with diamonds,
G C D
Lucy in the sky with diamonds,
G C D
Lucy in the sky with diamonds,
D A
Ah - ah.

```
            (A)              A7          A6            F6/A
Verse 2     Follow her down to a bridge by a fountain,

                     A                A7         A6            F
            Where rocking horse people eat marshmallow pies.

            A           A7              A6             F6/A
            Everyone smiles as you drift past the flowers,

                  A          A7         A6      Dm     Dm/C
            That grow so incredibly high. ____


            B♭                        C
Pre-chorus 2 Newspaper taxis appear on the shore,

            F                           B♭
            Waiting to take you away.

            C                                 G
            Climb in the back with your head in the clouds,

                           D
            And you're gone.


            G             C          D
Chorus 2    Lucy in the sky with diamonds,

            G             C          D
            Lucy in the sky with diamonds,

            G             C          D
            Lucy in the sky with diamonds,

            D   A
            Ah - ah.


            (A)              A7          A6         F6/A
Verse 3     Picture yourself on a train in a station,

                  A           A7             A6           F
            With plasticine porters with looking glass ties.

            A           A7             A6            F6/A
            Suddenly someone is there at the turnstile,

                 A            A7          A6      Dm
            The girl with kaleidoscope eyes. ____


              G             C          D
Chorus 3    |: Lucy in the sky with diamonds,

            G             C          D
            Lucy in the sky with diamonds,

            G             C          D
            Lucy in the sky with diamonds,

            D   A
            Ah - ah.    :|  Repeat to fade
```

Magical Mystery Tour

Words & Music by
John Lennon & Paul McCartney

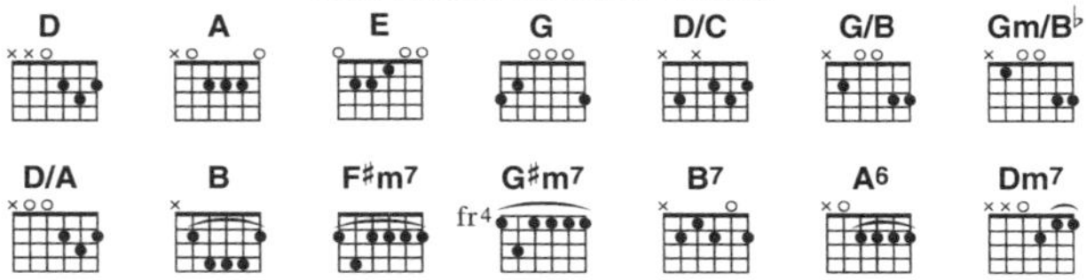

Intro | D | A ||

E *Spoken:*
(Roll up, roll up for the Magical Mystery Tour,

Step right this way!)

Verse 1

E G A
Roll up, ___ roll up for the Mystery Tour.
E G A
Roll up, ___ roll up for the Mystery Tour,
E
Roll up, ___ (and that's an invitation,)
G A
Roll up, ___ for the Mystery Tour.
E
Roll up, ___ (to make a reservation,)
G A
Roll up, ___ for the Mystery Tour.

Bridge 1

D D/C
The Magical Mystery Tour
G/B Gm/B♭
Is waiting to take you away,
D/A A
Waiting to take you away.

Verse 2

E G A
Roll up, ___ roll up for the Mystery Tour.
E G A
Roll up, ___ roll up for the Mystery Tour.
E
Roll up, ___ (we've got everything you need,)
G A
Roll up, ___ for the Mystery Tour.

cont.

```
E
   Roll up, ___ (satisfaction guaranteed,)
G                         A
   Roll up, ___ for the Mystery Tour.
```

Bridge 2

```
D                   D/C
   The Magical Mystery Tour
   G/B                   Gm/B♭
Is hoping to take you away,
D/A                   A
Hoping to take you away.
```

Link

```
| B        | B        | F♯m7      | F♯m7      |
                        (Mystery    trip.)

| B      | B      | F♯m7   | F♯m7  G♯m7 | A     | B7     ||
```

Verse 3

```
E   G                   A
Ah, ___ the Magical Mystery Tour.
E          G                   A
   Roll up, ___ roll up for the Mystery Tour,
E
   Roll up, ___ (and that's an invitation,)
G                       A
   Roll up, ___ for the Mystery Tour.
E
   Roll up, ___ (to make a reservation,)
G                       A
   Roll up, ___ for the Mystery Tour.
```

Bridge 3

```
D                   D/C
   The Magical Mystery Tour
   G/B                    Gm/B♭
Is coming to take you away,
D/A                    A6
Coming to take you away.
```

Bridge 4

```
D                   D/C
   The Magical Mystery Tour
   G/B                 Gm/B♭
Is dying to take you away,
D/A                  A6
Dying to take you away,
               D
Take you today. ___
```

Coda

```
| D      | D      ||

||: Dm7  | Dm7   | Dm7   | Dm7   :||   Repeat to fade
```

Martha My Dear

Words & Music by
John Lennon & Paul McCartney

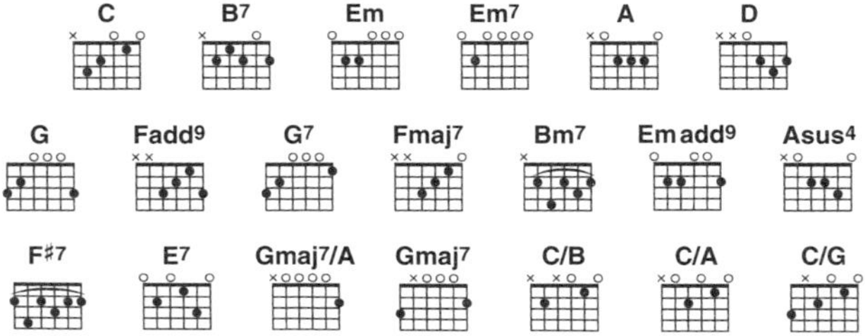

Capo third fret

Intro | C | C B7 | Em Em7 A | D |
| G Fadd9 | G7 Fmaj7 | G7 Fmaj7 | G G7 ||

Verse 1

```
C
Martha my dear,
                 B7      Em       Em7   A
Though I spend my days in conversation,
D                    G
Please remember me.
Fadd9          G7
Martha my love,
Fmaj7             G7
Don't forget me,
Fmaj7            G7
Martha my dear.
```

Verse 2

```
Bm7                           Em add9
Hold your head up, you silly girl,
D
Look what you've done.
             Asus4                 A
When you find yourself in the thick of it,
Asus4                  A                F♯7  Bm7
Help yourself to a bit of what is all around you,
       Em add9
Silly girl.
```

Verse 3

```
               Bm7         E7
Take a good look around you,
                Bm7                E7
Take a good look, you're bound to see
       Gmaj7/A
That you and me
       Gmaj7                    Bm7
Were meant to be for each other,
       Emadd9  C
Silly girl.
```

Link

```
| C      | C  B7  | Em   Em7  A | D       |
| G  Fadd9 | G7  Fmaj7 | G7  Fmaj7 | G  G7 ||
```

Verse 4

```
Bm7                           Emadd9
Hold your hand out, you silly girl,
D
See what you've done.
            Asus4                   A
When you find yourself in the thick of it,
Asus4                  A               F♯7      Bm7
Help yourself to a bit of what is all around you,
      Emadd9
Silly girl.

| C  G7  C ||
```

Verse 5

```
C
Martha my dear,
             B7       Em        Em7  A
You have always been my inspiration,
D                   G
Please be good to me.
Fadd9           G7
Martha my love,
Fmaj7               G7
Don't forget me,
Fmaj7              G7
Martha my dear.
```

Coda

```
| C  C/B  C/A  C/G | C       ||
```

Maxwell's Silver Hammer

Words & Music by
John Lennon & Paul McCartney

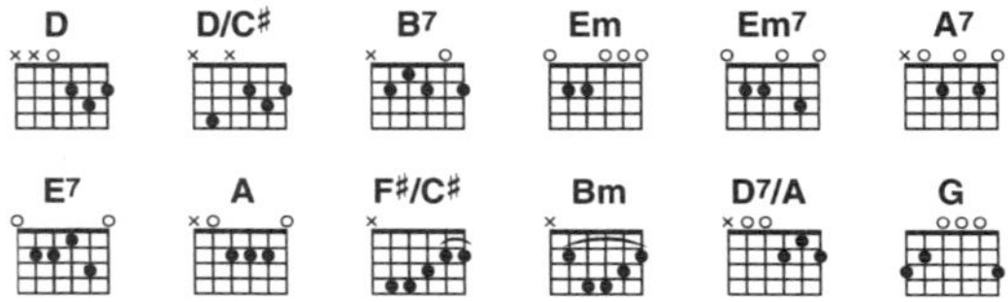

Verse 1

D D/C♯
Joan was quizzical,
B7 Em Em7
Studied pataphysical science in the home.
A7
Late nights all alone with a test-tube,
D A7
Oh, oh, oh oh.
D D/C♯ B7
Maxwell Edison, majoring in medicine,
Em Em7
Calls her on the phone:
A7 D A7
"Can I take you out to the pictures, Jo-o-o-an?"
E7
But as she's getting ready to go,
A7
A knock comes on the door.

Chorus 1

D
Bang, bang, Maxwell's silver hammer
E7
Came down upon her head,
A7
Clang, clang, Maxwell's silver hammer
Em A7 D A D
Made sure that she was dead.

Link

| D F♯/C♯ | Bm D7/A | G | D ||

Verse 2

```
D          D/C♯            B7
Back in school again, Maxwell plays the fool again,
Em                         Em7
Teacher gets annoyed.
A7                                     D       A7
Wishing to avoid an unpleasant sce-e-e-ene,
D           D/C♯         B7
She tells Max to stay when the class has gone away,
Em                    Em7
So he waits behind,
A7                                       D        A7
Writing fifty times, I must not be so-o-o-o.
      E7
But when she turns her back on the boy,
    A7
He creeps up from behind.
```

Chorus 2

```
D
Bang, bang, Maxwell's silver hammer
        E7
Came down upon her head,
A7
Clang, clang, Maxwell's silver hammer
        Em                  A7
Made sure that she was dead.
```

Solo

```
| D        | D        | E7       | E7       |
| A7       | A7       | Em7  A7  | D        ||
| D    F♯/C♯ | Bm  D7/A | G        | D        ||
```

Verse 3

```
D     D/C♯        B7
P.C. Thirty-One said,

"We've caught a dirty one."
Em                          Em7
Maxwell stands alone,
A7
Painting testimonial pictures,
D          A7
Oh, oh-oh oh.
```

cont.

D   D/C♯   B7
Rose and Valerie, screaming from the gallery,

Em   Em7
Say he must go free.

      A7   D   A7
The judge does not agree, and he tells them so-o-o-o.

             E7
But as the words are leaving his lips,

  A7
A noise comes from behind.

Chorus 3

D
Bang, bang, Maxwell's silver hammer

        E7
Came down upon his head,

A7
Clang, clang, Maxwell's silver hammer

        Em   A7
Made sure that he was dead.

Coda

              D
Wo-wo-wo-woh,

| D | E7 | E7 | A7 | A7 | Em7 A7 | D A D |

D   F♯/C♯   Bm   D7/A   G   D A D
Sil - ver   ham - mer   man.

Mean Mr Mustard

Words & Music by
John Lennon & Paul McCartney

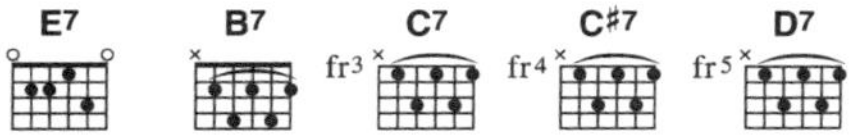

Verse 1

E7
Mean Mr. Mustard sleeps in the park,

Shaves in the dark

Trying to save paper.
B7   C7   C#7
Sleeps in a hole in the road.
D7   C#7   C7
   Saving up to buy some clothes.
B7
   Keeps a ten bob note up his nose,
          E7   C7 B7
Such a mean old man,
          E7   C7   B7
Such a mean old man.

Verse 2

E7
His sister Pam works in a shop,

She never stops,

She's a go-getter.
B7   C7   C#7
Takes him out to look at the Queen,
D7   C#7   C7
   Only place that he's ever been,
B7
   Always shouts out something obscene,
          E7   C7 B7
Such a dirty old man,
E7   C7   B7
Dirty old man.

Michelle

Words & Music by
John Lennon & Paul McCartney

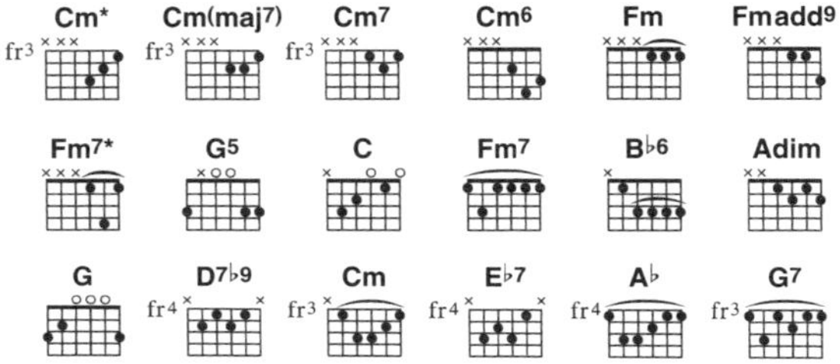

Capo fifth fret

Intro | Cm* Cm(maj7) | Cm7 Cm6 | Fm Fmadd9 Fm Fm7* | G5 ||

Verse 1

C Fm7
Michelle, ma belle,
B♭6 Adim G
These are words that go together well,
D7♭9 G
My Michelle.

Verse 2

C Fm7
Michelle, ma belle,
B♭6 Adim G
Sont les mots qui vont très bien ensemble
D7♭9 G
Très bien ensemble.

Bridge 1

Cm
I love you, I love you, I love you,
E♭7 A♭
That's all I want to say,
G7 Cm
Until I find a way,
Cm* Cm(maj7) Cm7 Cm6
I will say the only words I know
Fm Fmadd9 Fm Fm7* G5
That you'll ___ un - der - stand.

Verse 3 As Verse 2

Bridge 2

Cm
I need to, I need to, I need to,

E♭7 A♭
I need to make you see,

G7 Cm
Oh, what you mean to me.

Cm* Cm(maj7) Cm7 Cm6
Until I do I'm hoping you

Fm Fmadd9 Fm Fm7* G5
Will know ______ what I mean.

Solo

Cm Fm7
I love you. _____

| B♭6 | Adim | G D7♭9 | G ||

Bridge 3

Cm
I want you, I want you, I want you,

E♭7 A♭
I think you know by now,

G7 Cm
I'll get to you somehow.

Cm* Cm(maj7) Cm7 Cm6
Until I do I'm telling you,

Fm Fmadd9 Fm Fm7* G5
So you'll ______ un - der - stand.

Verse 4

C Fm7
Michelle, ma belle,

B♭6 Adim G
Sont les mots qui vont très bien ensemble

D7♭9 G
Très bien ensemble.

Cm* Cm(maj7) Cm7 Cm6
And I will say the only words I know

Fm Fmadd9 Fm Fm7* G5
That you'll ______ un - der - stand,

C
My Michelle.

Solo

| Fm7 | B♭6 | Adim | G D7♭9 |

| Fm7 | B♭6 | *Fade out*

Misery

Words & Music by
John Lennon & Paul McCartney

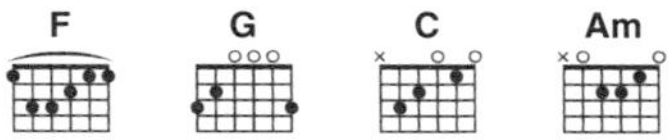


```
             F                           G
*Intro*         The world is treating me bad, __
             C          Am   G
             Misery.

             C               F
*Verse 1*    I'm the kind of guy
                 C             F
             Who never used to cry,
                                     G
             The world is treating me bad, ___
             C          Am
             Misery.

                C               F
*Verse 2*    I've lost her now for sure,
               C               F
             I won't see her no more,
                          G
             It's gonna be a drag, ___
             C
             Misery.

             Am                          C
*Bridge 1*   I'll remember all the little things we've done,
             Am                                G
             Can't she see she'll always be the only one,

             Only one.
```

Verse 3

C   F
Send her back to me,
            C   F
'Cause everyone can see,
                                   G
Without her I will be ___
    C
In misery.

Bridge 2

Am   C
I'll remember all the little things we've done,
Am   G
She'll remember and she'll miss her only one,

Lonely one.

Verse 4

C   F
Send her back to me,
            C   F
'Cause everyone can see,
                                   G
Without her I will be ___
    C
In misery,
Am   C   Am
Oh, in misery, ooh, ___
      C
My misery,
Am   C
La, la, la, la, la, la, misery.

Mother Nature's Son

Words & Music by
John Lennon & Paul McCartney

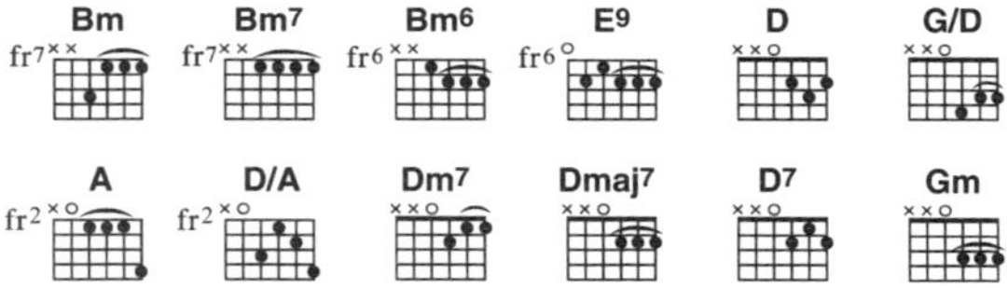

Intro | Bm Bm7 | Bm6 E9 || D | D | D | D ||

Verse 1

D G/D D
Born a poor young country boy,
Bm Bm7 Bm6 E9
Mother Nature's son.
A D/A A
All day long
D/A A D/A A D/A D Dm7 | G/D D ||
I'm sitting singing songs for everyone.

Link 1 | D Dm7 | G/D D ||

Verse 2

D G/D D
Sit beside a mountain stream,
Bm Bm7 Bm6 E9
See her waters rise.
A D/A A D/A A D/A
Lis-ten to the pretty sound
A D/A D Dm7 | G/D D ||
Of music as she flies.

Link 2

D G/D D
Do do, do do do do, do do do do, do.
G/D D Dmaj7
Do do do do, do do do do, do.
D7 G/D Gm | D ||
Do do do.

```
             D          G/D                  D
Verse 3      Find me in my field of grass,
             Bm       Bm7       Bm6   E9
             Mother Nature's son.
             A        D/A   A      D/A
             Sway - ing   dais - ies
             A       D/A  A          D/A           D   Dm7  | G/D   D  ||
             Sing a lazy song beneath the sun.

                     D                 G/D             D
Link 3       Do do, do do do do, do do do do, do.
                             G/D              D    Dmaj7
             Do do do do, do do do do, do.
             D7        G/D   Gm               D
             Do do do,            yeah, yeah, yeah.

Instrumental | D  G/D  | G/D  D  | Bm   Bm7  | Bm6  E9 |

             | A  D/A  A  D/A | A  D/A  A  D/A | D   Dm7 | G/D   D ||

             D   Dm7   G/D                   D7
Coda         Ah, _____ Mother Nature's son.
```

The Night Before

Words & Music by
John Lennon & Paul McCartney

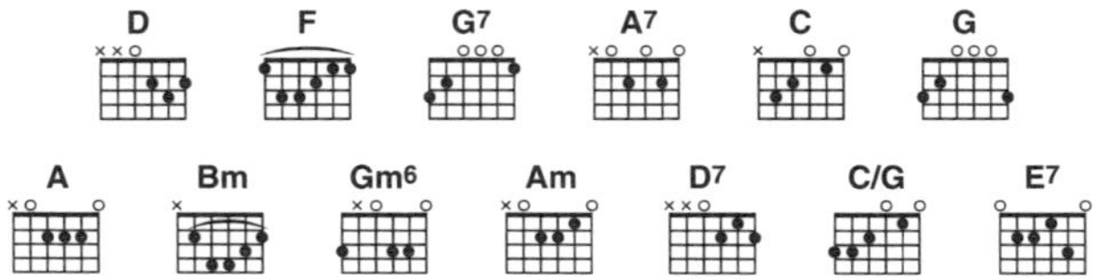

Intro | D | D | F | F | G7 | G7 | A7 | A7 ||

Verse 1

```
D                   C
We said our goodbyes,
G         A
(Ah, the night before,)
D                   C
Love was in your eyes,
G         A
(Ah, the night before,)
Bm             Gm6  Bm                      Gm6
Now today I find, you have changed your mind,
D                G7             D       F  G
Treat me like you did the night before.
```

Verse 2

```
D                 C
Were you telling lies?
G         A
(Ah, the night before.)
D            C
Was I so unwise?
G         A
(Ah, the night before.)
Bm                  Gm6  Bm              Gm6
When I held you near, you were so sincere,
D                G7             D
Treat me like you did the night before.
```

Bridge 1

```
Am               D7            G         C/G  G
Last night is the night I will remember you  by,
Bm               E7              A7
When I think of things we did, it makes me wanna cry.
```

Verse 3

D C
We said our goodbyes,

G A
(Ah, the night before,)

D C
Love was in your eyes,

G A
(Ah, the night before,)

Bm Gm6 Bm Gm6
Now today I find, you have changed your mind,

D G7 D F G
Treat me like you did the night before, yes…

Solo

|: D | C | G | A :|

Verse 4

Bm Gm6 Bm Gm6
When I held you near, you were so sincere,

D G7 D
Treat me like you did the night before.

Bridge 2

Am D7 G C/G G
Last night is the night I will remember you by,

Bm E7 A7
When I think of things we did, it makes me wanna cry.

Verse 5

D C
Were you telling lies?

G A
(Ah, the night before.)

D C
Was I so unwise?

G A
(Ah, the night before.)

Bm Gm6 Bm Gm6
When I held you near, you were so sincere,

D G7 D
Treat me like you did the night before.

F D
Like the night before.

No Reply

Words & Music by
John Lennon & Paul McCartney

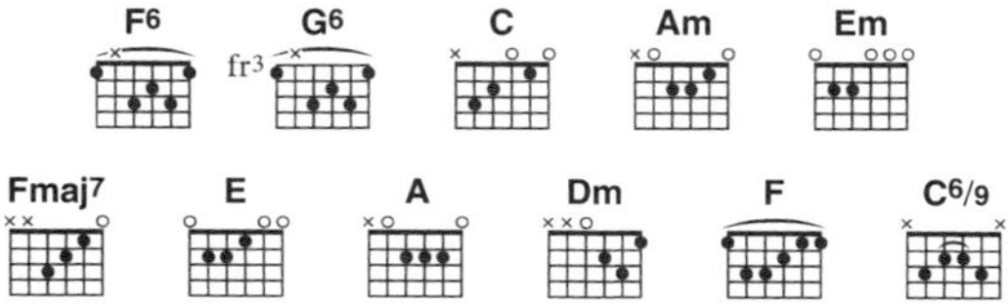

Verse 1

N.C. F6
This happened once before,
G6 C
When I came to your door, no reply.
F6
They said it wasn't you,
G6 C
But I saw you peep through your window.
Am Em Fmaj7 Em
I saw the light, I saw the light,
F6
I know that you saw me,
G6 C
'Cause I looked up to see your face.

Verse 2

F6
I tried to telephone,
G6 C
They said you were not home, that's a lie.
F6
'Cause I know where you've been,
G6 C
I saw you walk in your door.
Am Em Fmaj7 Em
I nearly died, I nearly died,
F6
'Cause you walked hand in hand
G6 C
With another man in my place.

Bridge

```
              C          E              A
If I were you, I'd realise that I
               Dm          F            C
Love you more than any other guy.
                                 E          A
And I'll forgive the lies that I
             Dm                  F                    C
Heard before, when you gave me no reply.
```

Verse 3

```
                  F6
I tried to telephone,
                                       G6                C
They said you were not home, that's a lie.
                                              F6
'Cause I know where you've been,
                                  G6        C
And I saw you walk in your door.
            Am    Em           Fmaj7   Em
I nearly died,   I nearly died,
                                           F6
'Cause you walked hand in hand
                   G6                 C
With another man in my place.
         Am  Em       Fmaj7  C6/9
No reply,   no reply.
```

Norwegian Wood

Words & Music by
John Lennon & Paul McCartney

Capo second fret

Intro ‖: D | D | D Cadd9 G/B | D :‖

Verse 1

D
I once had a girl,

Or should I say
Cadd9 G/B D
She once had me?
D
She showed me her room,

Isn't it good,
Cadd9 G/B D
Nor-wegian wood?

Middle 1

Dm G
She asked me to stay and she told me to sit anywhere.
Dm Em7 A
So I looked around and I noticed there wasn't a chair.

Verse 2

D
I sat on a rug

Biding my time,
Cadd9 G/B D
Drinking her wine.

cont.

```
D
We talked until two,

And then she said,
Cadd9    G/B  D
"It's time for   bed."
```

Instrumental ‖: D | D | D Cadd9 G/B | D :‖

Middle 2

```
     Dm                                                   G
She told me she worked in the morning and started to laugh.
  Dm                                                Em7    A
I told her I didn't and crawled off to sleep in the bath.
```

Verse 3

```
D
And when I awoke

I was alone,
Cadd9    G/B  D
This bird had   flown.
D
So I lit a fire,

Isn't it good,
Cadd9 G/B D
Nor-wegian wood?
```

Outro | D | D | D Cadd9 G/B | D ‖

Not A Second Time

Words & Music by
John Lennon & Paul McCartney

Verse 1

G E
You know you made me cry,
G E
I see no use in wondering why,
D G D7
I cried for you.

Verse 2

G E
And now you've changed your mind,
G E
I see no reason to change mine,
D Am D
My crying is through, oh.

Bridge 1

Am Bm
You're giving me the same old line,
G Em
I'm wondering why.
Am
You hurt me then, you're back again,
Bm D7 Em
No, no, no, not a second time.

Solo

Am	Bm	G	Em
Am	Am	Bm	D7
Em	Em	

```
             G                        E
Verse 3        You know you made me cry,
             G                          E
               I see no use in wondering why,
               D        G     D
             I cried for you, ___ yeah.

             G                                 E
Verse 4        And now you've changed your mind,
             G                          E
               I see no reason to change mine,
                  D         Am       D
             My crying is through, oh.

             Am                        Bm
Bridge 2       You're giving me the same old line,
             G                 Em
               I'm wondering why.
             Am
               You hurt me then, you're back again,
             Bm      D7                  Em
             No, no, no, not a second time.

             N.C.           G     E
Outro        Not a second time, ___
                            G     E
             Not a second time, ___
                              G     E
             No, no, no, no, no. ___ Fade out
```

Not Guilty

Words & Music by
George Harrison

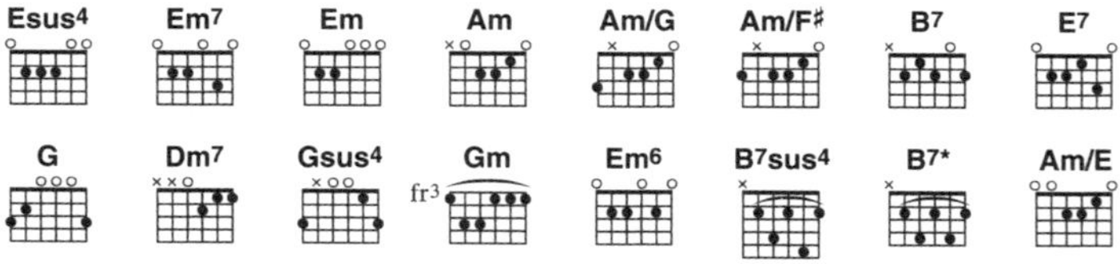

Intro | Esus4 Em7 Em | Em | Esus4 Em7 Em | Em ||

Verse 1

Am Am/G Am/F♯
Not guilty
B7 Em
Of getting in your way,
B7 E7
While you're trying to steal the day.
Am Am/G Am/F♯
Not guilty,
B7 Em
And I'm not before the rest,
B7 G Dm7
I'm not trying to steal your vest.

Bridge 1

E7
I am not trying to be smart,
Gsus4 Gm
I only want what I can get.
Em7 Em6
I'm really sorry for your ageing head,
B7sus4 B7*
But like you heard me said,

Verse 2

Am Am/G Am/F♯
Not guilty.
B7 Em
No use handing me a writ
B7 G Dm7
While I'm trying to do my bit.

Bridge 2

E7
I don't expect to take your heart,
Gsus4 Gm
I only want what I can get.
Em7 Em6
I'm really sorry that you're under-fed,
B7sus4 B7*
But like you heard me said,
Em Em7
Not guilty.

| Esus4 Em7 Em | Em ||

Solo

| Am Am/G | Am/F♯ | Em7 Em6 | Em7 Em6 |

| Am Am/G | Am/F♯ | Em7 Em6 | Em7 Em6 | Am/E Em ||

Verse 3

Am Am/G Am/F♯
Not guilty
B7 Em
For looking like a freak,
B7 E7
Making friends with every Sikh.
Am Am/G Am/F♯
Not guilty,
B7 Em
For leading you astray
B7 G Dm7
On the road to Mandalay.

Bridge 3

E7
I won't upset the apple cart,
Gsus4 Gm
I only want what I can get.
Em7 Em6
I'm really sorry that you've been misled,
B7sus4 B7* Am
But like you heard me said, not guilty.

Coda

||: Esus4 Em7 Em | Esus4 Em7 Em :|| Em | Em | Em |

| Em | Em | Em | Esus4 Em7 Em | Esus4 Em7 Em |

||: Em | Em | Em | Em :|| *Repeat ad lib. to fade*

Nowhere Man

Words & Music by
John Lennon & Paul McCartney

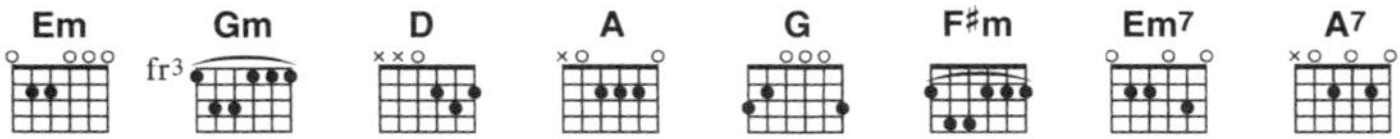

Capo second fret

Verse 1

N.C.
He's a real nowhere man,

Sitting in his nowhere land,

Em Gm D
Making all his nowhere plans for nobody.

Verse 2

D A
Doesn't have a point of view,
G D
Knows not where he's going to,
Em Gm D
Isn't he a bit like you and me?

Bridge 1

F♯m G
Nowhere man, please listen,
F♯m G
You don't know what you're missing,
F♯m Em7 A7
Nowhere man, the world is at your command.

Solo

| D | A | G | D |

| Em | Gm | D | D ||

Verse 3

D A
He's as blind as he can be,
G D
Just sees what he wants to see,
Em Gm D
Nowhere man, can you see me at all?

Bridge 2

```
        F#m         G
Nowhere man, don't worry,
          F#m         G
Take your time, don't hurry,
         F#m      Em7                              A7
Leave it all till somebody else lends you a hand.
```

Verse 4

```
D              A
Doesn't have a point of view,
G                   D
Knows not where he's going to,
Em         Gm                 D
Isn't he a bit like you and me?
```

Bridge 3

```
        F#m         G
Nowhere man, please listen,
          F#m                G
You don't know what you're missing,
        F#m      Em7                        A7
Nowhere man, the world is at your command.
```

Verse 5

```
D           A
He's a real nowhere man,
G              D
Sitting in his nowhere land,
Em             Gm                D
Making all his nowhere plans for nobody.
Em             Gm                D
Making all his nowhere plans for nobody.
Em             Gm                D
Making all his nowhere plans for nobody.
```

Ob-La-Di, Ob-La-Da

Words & Music by
John Lennon & Paul McCartney

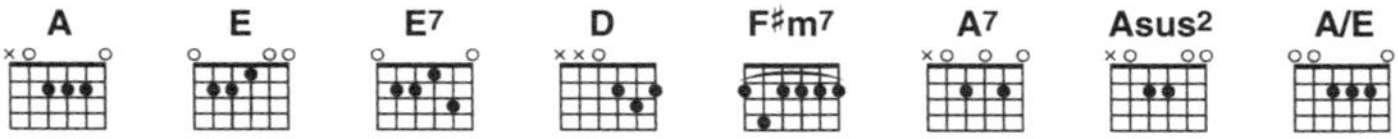

Capo first fret

Intro | A | A | A | A ||

Verse 1
```
A                           E
Desmond has a barrow in the market place,
E7                     A
Molly is a singer in a band.
                                D
Desmond says to Molly, "Girl, I like your face."
          A                E                 A
And Molly says this as she takes him by the hand:
```

Chorus 1
```
          A                   E   F♯m7
Ob-la-di, ob-la-da, life goes on, bra,
A             E         A
La-la how the life goes on.
          A                   E   F♯m7
Ob-la-di, ob-la-da, life goes on, bra,
A             E         A
La-la how the life goes on.
```

Verse 2
```
A                              E
Desmond takes a trolley to the jeweller's store,
E7                          A
Buys a twenty carat golden ring.
                                D
Takes it back to Molly waiting at the door,
          A                E             A
And as he gives it to her, she begins to sing:
```

Chorus 2 As Chorus 1

Middle 1

D
    In a couple of years,
                                                              A Asus2 A A7
They have built a home sweet home.
D
    With a couple of kids running in the yard
    A/E   E
Of Desmond and Molly Jones.

Verse 3

A   E
Happy ever after in the market place,
E7   A
Desmond lets the children lend a hand.
                                                        D
Molly stays at home and does her pretty face,
                  A   E   A
And in the evening she still sings it with the band:

Chorus 3

As Chorus 1

Middle 2

As Middle 1

Verse 4

A   E
Happy ever after in the market place,
E7   A
Molly lets the children lend a hand.
                                                              D
Desmond stays at home and does his pretty face,
                  A   E   A
And in the evening she's a singer with the band.

Chorus 4

              A   E   F♯m7
Ob-la-di, ob-la-da, life goes on, bra,
A   E   A
La-la how the life goes on.
              A   E   F♯m7
Ob-la-di, ob-la-da, life goes on, bra,
A   E   F♯m7
La-la how the life goes on,

And if you want some fun,
      E   A
Take Ob-la-di-bla-da.

Octopus's Garden

Words & Music by
Ringo Starr

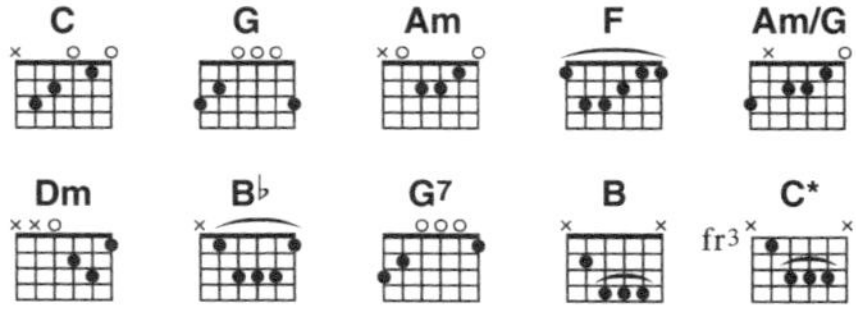

Capo fourth fret

Intro | (C) (G) | (C) || C | Am | F | G ||

Verse 1

```
C                   Am
  I'd like to be  under the sea,
      F                            G
In an octopus's garden in the shade.
C                  Am
  He'd let us in,  knows where we've been,
      F                            G
In his octopus's garden in the shade.
Am                                          Am/G
  I'd ask my friends to come and see
F                 G
  An octopus's garden with me.
```

Chorus 1

```
C                   Am
  I'd like to be  under the sea
      F          G                 C
In an octopus's garden in the shade.
```

Verse 2

```
C                          Am
  We would be warm  below the storm
       F                                 G
In our little hideaway beneath the waves.
C                        Am
  Resting our head  on the sea bed
      F                          G
In an octopus's garden near a cave.
```

```
        Am                                      Am/G
cont.      We would sing and dance around,
        F                         G
           Because we know we can't be found.

        C           Am
Chorus 2   I'd like to be   under the sea
           F          G              C
        In an octopus's garden in the shade.

Solo    | F          | Dm         | B♭         | C          |
          Ah,  ah,     ah.          Ah,  ah,     ah.

        | F          | Dm         | B♭   C     | F    G7    ||
          Ah,  ah,     ah.          Ah, ___      ah. ___

        C                 Am
Verse 3    We would shout   and swim about
          F                              G
        The coral that lies beneath the waves.
        C                 Am
           Oh, what joy for every girl and boy,
        F                                   G
        Knowing they're happy and they're safe.
        Am                                       Am/G
           We would be so happy, you and me,
        F                                 G
           No one there to tell us what to do.

        C           Am
Chorus 3   I'd like to be   under the sea
           F          G             Am   Am/G
        In an octopus's garden with you,
           F          G             Am   Am/G
        In an octopus's garden with you,
           F          G             C   B  C*
        In an octopus's garden with you.
```

Oh! Darling

Words & Music by
John Lennon & Paul McCartney

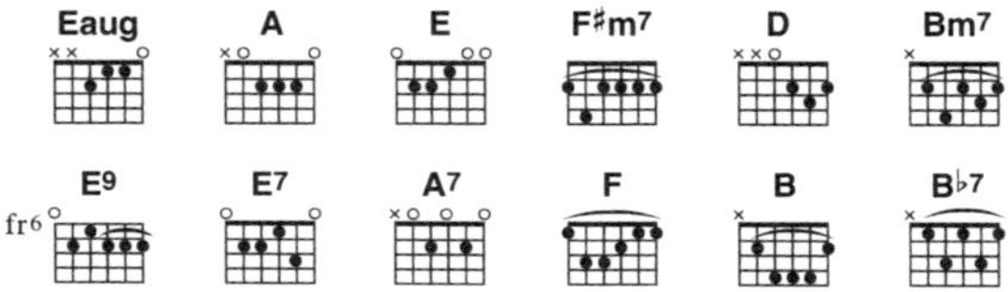

Intro | Eaug ||

Verse 1

```
    A                 E
Oh! darling, please believe me,
F♯m7              D
I'll never do you no harm.
   Bm7            E9
Believe me when I tell you,
Bm7       E9          A      D  A  E7
I'll never do you no harm.
```

Verse 2

```
     A           E
Oh!  darling, if you leave me,
F♯m7             D
I'll never make it alone.
   Bm7           E9
Believe me when I beg you,
Bm7        E9         A     D  A  A7
Don't ever leave me alone.
```

Bridge 1

```
             D                     F
When you told me you didn't need me anymore,
            A                              A7
Well, you know I nearly broke down and cried.
             B
When you told me you didn't need me anymore,
            E           F              E     Eaug
Well, you know I nearly broke down and died.
```

Verse 3

```
        A                E
Oh! darling, if you leave me,
F♯m7                   D
I'll never make it alone.
   Bm7                   E9
Believe me when I tell   you,
Bm7        E9          A       D
I'll never do you no harm.
A                        A7
(Believe me, darling.)
```

Bridge 2

```
            D                     F
When you told me you didn't need me anymore,
           A                                A7
Well, you know I nearly broke down and cried.
            B
When you told me you didn't need me anymore,
           E               F                E      Eaug
Well, you know I nearly broke down and died.
```

Verse 4

```
        A                 E
Oh! darling, please believe me,
F♯m7              D
I'll never let you down.

(Oh, believe me darling.)
   Bm7                E9
Believe me when I tell you,
Bm7          E9          A        D  A  B♭7  A7
  I'll never do you no harm.
```

One After 909

Words & Music by
John Lennon & Paul McCartney

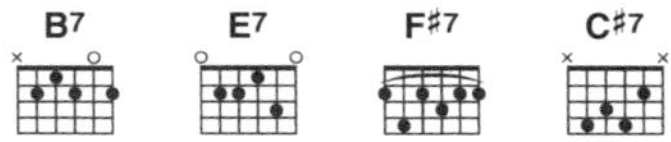

Intro | B7 | B7 | B7 | B7 | B7 | B7 ||

Verse 1
B7
My baby says she's travelling

On the one after 909.

I said, "Move over, honey,

I'm travelling on that line."

Chorus 1
B7 N.C.
I said, "Move over once,
B7 N.C.
Move over twice,
E7
Come on baby, don't be cold as ice."
B7
Said she's travelling
F♯7 B7
On the one after 909.

Verse 2
B7
I begged her not to go,

And I begged her on my bended knee.

You're only fooling around,

Only fooling around with me.

Chorus 2 As Chorus 1

Bridge 1

E7 B7
Pick up my bags, run to the station.
C♯7 F♯7
Railman says, “You’ve got the wrong location.”
E7 B7
Pick up my bags, run right home,
C♯7 F♯7
Then I find I’ve got the number wrong.

Verse 3

B7
Well, said she’s travelling
On the one after 909.
I said, “Move over, honey,
I’m travelling on that line.”

Chorus 3

As Chorus 1

Instrumental

𝄆 B7 | B7 | B7 | B7 𝄇 B7 | B7 |
| E7 | E7 | B7 | F♯7 | B7 | B7 ||

Bridge 2

As Bridge 1

Verse 4

B7
Well, she says she’s travelling
On the one after 909.
I said, “Move over, honey,
I’m travelling on that line.”

Chorus 4

As Chorus 1

Coda

(B7) F♯7
She said she’s travelling on the one after 90,
F♯7 B7
Said she’s travelling on the one after 909.

Only A Northern Song

Words & Music by
George Harrison

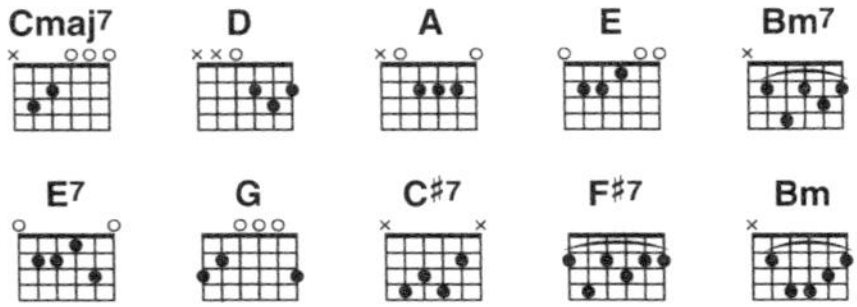

Intro | Cmaj7 | D A | E ||

Verse 1
A
If you're listening to this song,
Bm7
You may think the chords are going wrong.
E7
But they're not,
D
He just wrote it like that.

Verse 2
A
When you're listening late at night,
Bm7
You may think the band are not quite right.
E7
But they are,
D
They just play it like that.

Chorus 1
E Bm7 G C♯7
It doesn't really matter what chords I play,
F♯7
What words I say,
Bm F♯7
Or time of day it is,
D A E
'Cause it's only a northern song.

```
Link        | A   | A   | A   | A   | Bm7 |
            | Bm7 | E7  | E7  | D   | D   ||

               E               Bm7          G          C#7
Chorus 2    It doesn't really matter what clothes I wear,
              F#7
            Or how I fare,
              Bm           F#7
            Or if my hair is brown,
                        D     A        E
            When it's only a northern song.

            A
Verse 3        If you think the harmony
                                         Bm7
            Is a little dark and out of key.
                          E7
            You're correct,
                                  D
            There's nobody there.

            | E  Bm7 | G  C#7 | F#7 | Bm7 | F#7 |
                   D                     A       E
            And I told you there's no-one there.

Outro       | A   | A   | A   | A   | Bm7    | Bm7   |
            | E7  | E7  | D   | D   | E  Bm7 | G C#7 |
            | F#7 | Bm  | F#7 | D A | E      ||  Fade out
```

Old Brown Shoe

Words & Music by
George Harrison

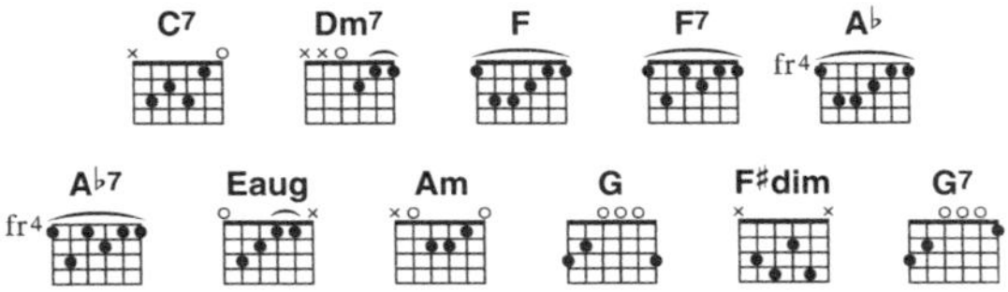

Intro | C7 | C7 | C7 | C7 ||

Verse 1
C7
I want a love that's right,

Right is only half of what's wrong.
Dm7
I want a short-haired girl

Who sometimes wears it twice as long.

Chorus 1
F F7
Now I'm stepping out this old brown shoe,
A♭ A♭7
Baby, I'm in love with you,
F
I'm so glad you came here,
Eaug Am
It won't be the same now, I'm telling you.

Link | C7 | C7 ||

Verse 2
C7
You know, you pick me up from where

Some try to drag me down.
Dm7
And when I see your smile

Replacing every thoughtless frown.

Chorus 2

F   F7
Got me escaping from this zoo,
A♭   A♭7
Baby, I'm in love with you,
F
I'm so glad you came here,
Eaug   Am
It won't be the same now, when I'm with you.

Bridge 1

G
If I grow up, I'll be a singer,
                        F
Wearing rings on every finger,
G
Not worrying what they or you say.
                          F
I'll live and love and maybe some day,
F♯dim   G   G7
Who knows, baby, you may comfort me. ____

Solo

C7	C7	C7	C7
Dm7	Dm7	Dm7	Dm7
F	F7	A♭	A♭7
F	Eaug	Am	Am

Bridge 2

G
I may appear to be imperfect,
                                   F
My love is something you can't reject,
G
I'm changing faster than the weather,
                              F
If you and me should get together,
F♯dim   G   G7
Who knows, baby, you may comfort me. ____

Verse 3

               C7
I want that love of yours,

To miss that love is something I'd hate.
                 Dm7
I'll make an early start,

I'm making sure that I'm not late.

Chorus 3

```
F                                      F7
   For your sweet top lip I'm in the queue,
Ab                      Ab7
   Baby, I'm in love with you,
F
I'm so glad you came here,
   Eaug                                 Am
It won't be the same now when I'm with you.
      F
I'm so glad you came here,
   Eaug                               Am
It won't be the same now that I'm with you.
```

Coda

```
||: C7        | C7        | C7        | C7        :||

||: C7        | C7        | C7        | C7        :||  Repeat to fade
    Do do,      do do do.   Do do,      do do do.
```

Polythene Pam

Words & Music by
John Lennon & Paul McCartney

D A E G B7 C C♯m E7/B

```
Intro     | D   A  | E      | D   A  | E      ||

                       D  A          E
Verse 1   Well, you should see Polythene Pam,
                    D              A        E
          She's so good-looking, but she looks like a man.
                       G                              B7
          Well, you should see her in drag, dressed in her polythene bag,
                     C  D         E
          Yes, you should see Polythene Pam,
          C    D     E
          Yeah, yeah, yeah.

Link      | D   A  | E      | D   A  | E      ||

               D               A          E
Verse 2   Get a dose of her in jackboots and kilt,
                     D                A          E
          She's killer-diller when she's dressed to the hilt.
                   G                         B7
          She's the kind of a girl that makes the News of the World,
                          C                D        E
          Yes, you could say she was attractively built.
          C    D     E
          Yeah, yeah, yeah.

Link      | D   A  | E      | D   A  | E      ||

Solo      |: D   A  | E      | D   A  | E      :|  Play 4 times

          | E   | E   | E   | D   | C♯m  | E7/B        ||
                                          Oh look out!
```

Paperback Writer

Words & Music by
John Lennon & Paul McCartney

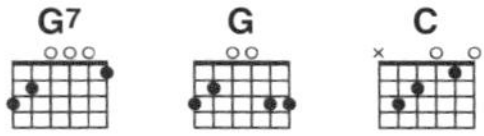

Intro
N.C.
Paperback writer, paperback writer.

Link
| G7 | G7 | G7 | G7 ||

Verse 1
G
Dear Sir or Madam, will you read my book,

It took me years to write, will you take a look?

It's based on a novel by a man named Lear,

And I need a job,

C
So I want to be a paperback writer,

G
Paperback writer.

Verse 2
G
It's a dirty story of a dirty man,

And his clinging wife doesn't understand.

His son is working for the Daily Mail,

It's a steady job,

C
But he wants to be a paperback writer,

G
Paperback writer.

N.C.
Paperback writer, paperback writer.

```
Link      | G7    | G7    | G7    | G7    ||

                 G
Verse 3   It's a thousand pages, give or take a few,

          I'll be writing more in a week or two.

          I can make it longer if you like the style,

          I can change it round,
                                      C
          And I want to be a paperback writer,
                     G      G7
          Paperback writer.

                  G
Verse 4   If you really like it, you can have the rights,

          It could make a million for you overnight,

          If you must return it, you can send it here,

          But I need a break,
                                      C
          And I want to be a paperback writer,
                     G
          Paperback writer.

          N.C.
          Paperback writer, paperback writer.

Link      | G7    | G7    | G7    | G7    ||

             G
Coda      |: Paperback writer, paperback writer. :|  Repeat to fade
```

Penny Lane

Words & Music by
John Lennon & Paul McCartney

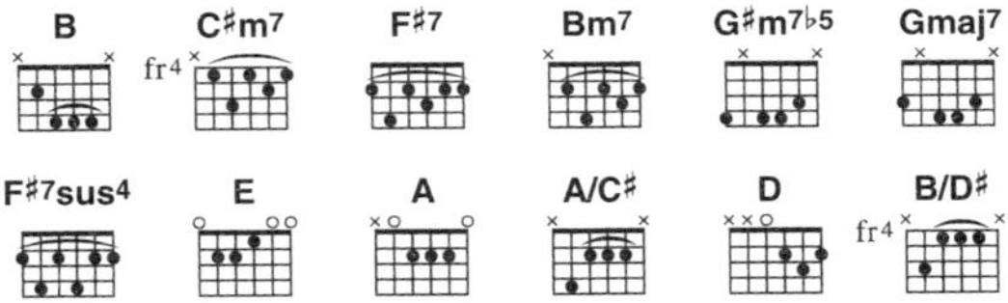

Verse 1

B C♯m7 F♯7
In Penny Lane there is a barber showing photographs
B Bm7
Of ev'ry head he's had the pleasure to know,
G♯m7♭5 Gmaj7
And all the people that come and go,
F♯7sus4 F♯7 F♯7sus4 F♯7
Stop and say hello.

Verse 2

B C♯m7 F♯7
On the corner is a banker with a motorcar,
B Bm7
The little children laugh at him behind his back,
G♯m7♭5 Gmaj7
And the banker never wears a mac
F♯7sus4 F♯7 E
In the pouring rain, – very strange.

Chorus 1

A A/C♯ D
Penny Lane is in my ears and in my eyes,
A A/C♯ D
There beneath the blue suburban skies
F♯7
I sit, and meanwhile back…

Verse 3

B C♯m7 F♯7
In Penny Lane there is a fireman with an hourglass,
B Bm7
And in his pocket is a portrait of the Queen.

cont.

G♯m7♭5 Gmaj7
He likes to keep his fire engine clean,

F♯7sus4 F♯7 F♯7sus4 F♯7
It's a clean machine.

Solo

| B | C♯m7 F♯7 | B | Bm7 |

| G♯m7♭5 | Gmaj7 | F♯7sus4 F♯7 | E ||

Chorus 2

A A/C♯ D
Penny Lane is in my ears and in my eyes,

A A/C♯ D
Full of fish and finger pies

F♯7
In summer, meanwhile back…

Verse 4

B C♯m7 F♯7
Behind the shelter in the middle of the roundabout

B Bm7
The pretty nurse is selling poppies from a tray,

G♯m7♭5 Gmaj7
And though she feels as if she's in a play,

F♯7sus4 F♯7 F♯7sus4 F♯7
She is anyway.

Verse 5

B C♯m7 F♯7
In Penny Lane the barber shaves another customer,

B Bm7
We see the banker sitting waiting for a trim,

G♯m7♭5 Gmaj7
And then the fireman rushes in

F♯7sus4 F♯7 E
From the pouring rain, – very strange.

Chorus 3

A A/C♯ D
Penny Lane is in my ears and in my eyes,

A A/C♯ D
There beneath the blue suburban skies

F♯7
I sit, and meanwhile back…

B B/D♯ E
Penny Lane is in my ears and in my eyes,

B B/D♯ E
There beneath the blue suburban skies…

B
Penny Lane.

Piggies

Words & Music by
George Harrison

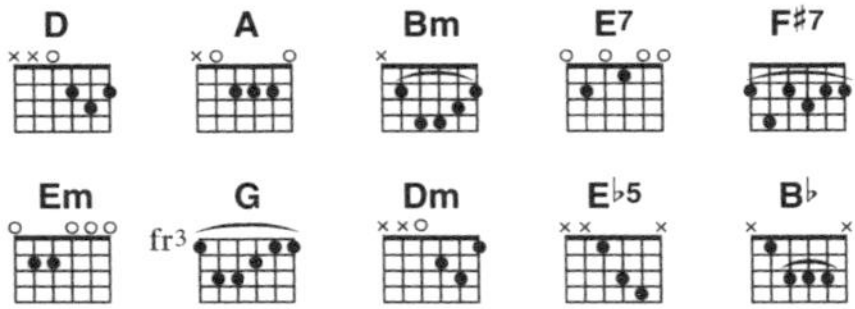

Capo sixth fret

Intro | D A | D A ||

Verse 1

D A D A
Have you seen the little piggies crawling in the dirt?
D A Bm E7
And for all the little piggies, life is getting worse,
Bm E7 A
Always having dirt to play around in.

Link 1 | D A | D A ||

Verse 2

D A D A
Have you seen the bigger piggies in their starched white shirts?
D A Bm E7
You will find the bigger piggies stirring up the dirt
Bm E7 A
Always have clean shirts to play around in.

Link 2 | D A | D F♯7 ||

```
            Em                  F♯7
*Bridge*    In their sties with all their backing,
            G          D          A
            They don't care what goes on around.
            Em                     F♯7
            In their eyes there's something lacking
            G                      A
            What they need's a damn good whacking!

*Solo*      | D   A   | D   A   | D   A   | Bm  E7  |
            | Bm  E7  | A       | D   A   | D   A   ||

            D                       A                D              A
*Verse 3*   Everywhere there's lots of piggies, living piggy lives,
            D                     A                  Bm                E7
            You can see them out for dinner with their piggy wives,
            Bm                      E7        A
            Clutching forks and knives to eat their bacon.

*Coda*      | D   A   | Dm   A  | Dm   A  | E7   A  |
            | N.C.            | E♭5      | B♭       ||
            (One more time.)
```

Please Please Me

Words & Music by
John Lennon & Paul McCartney

E A G B F♯m C♯m A* C

Intro | E | E | E | E ||

Verse 1

E   A   E   G A B
Last night I said these words to my girl,
E   A   E
I know you never even try, girl.

Chorus 1

A   F♯m
Come on, come on,
C♯m   A*
Come on, come on,
E   A
Please please me, woah yeah,
B   E   A   B
Like I please you.

Verse 2

E   A   E   G A B
You don't need me to show the way, love,
E   A   E
Why do I always have to say, love.

Chorus 2

A   F♯m
Come on, come on,
C♯m   A*
Come on, come on,
E   A
Please please me, woah yeah,
B   E
Like I please you.

Bridge

A
I don't want to sound complaining,
B   E
But you know there's always rain in my heart.
A
I do all the pleasing with you,
B   E
It's so hard to reason with you,
    A   B   E   A B
Oh yeah, why do you make me blue?

Verse 3

E   A E   G A B
  Last night I said these words to my girl,
E   A   E
  I know you never even try, girl.

Chorus 3

     A   F♯m
Come on, come on,
     C♯m   A*
Come on, come on,
       E   A
Please please me, woah yeah,
      B
Like I please you.
E   A
Please please me, woah yeah,
(you.)
      B
Like I please you,
E   A
Please please me, woah yeah,
(you.)
      B   E   G C B E
Like I please you. __________

P.S. I Love You

Words & Music by
John Lennon & Paul McCartney

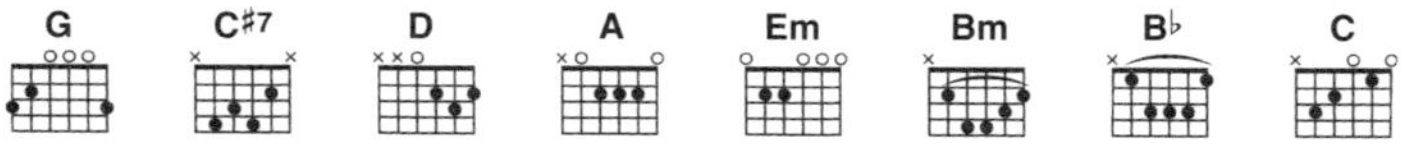

Intro

```
G     C♯7         D
As I write this letter,
G          C♯7    D
Send my love to you,
   G          C♯7    D
Remember that I'll always
      A         D
Be in love with you.
```

Verse 1

```
D                     Em                  D
Treasure these few words till we're together,
      A           Bm
Keep all my love forever,
A           B♭
P. S. I love you, ___
      C    D
You, you, you.
```

Verse 2

```
D                Em              D
I'll be coming home again to you love,
   A           Bm
Until the day I do love,
A           B♭
P. S. I love you, ___
      C    D
You, you, you.
```

Bridge 1

```
G                 D
As I write this letter,
G                 D
Send my love to you,
   G                 D
Remember that I'll always
      A         D
Be in love with you.
```

Verse 3

```
D                      Em                   D
Treasure these few words till we're together,
       A                 Bm
Keep all my love forever,
A            B♭
P. S. I love you, ___
      C    D
You, you, you.
```

Bridge 2

```
G                  D
As I write this letter, (oh,)
G                     D
Send my love to you, (you know I want you to)
   G                 D
Remember that I'll always, yeah,
       A         D
Be in love with you.
```

Verse 4

```
D                Em               D
I'll be coming home again to you love,
    A            Bm
Until the day I do love,
A            B♭
P. S. I love you, ___
      C    D
You, you, you,
B♭    C    D
You, you, you,
B♭ C   D
I  love you.
```

Rain

Words & Music by
John Lennon & Paul McCartney

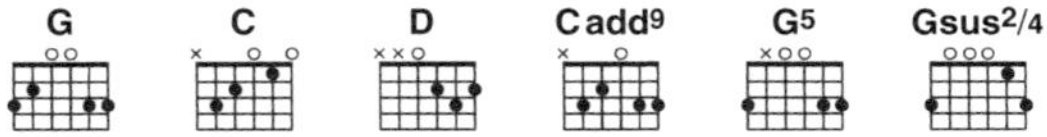

Intro | G | G | G | G ||

Verse 1

G
If the rain comes,
C D G
They run and hide their heads.
C D G
They might as well be dead,
Cadd9 G
If the rain comes, if the rain comes.

Verse 2

G
When the sun shines,
C D G
They slip into the shade,
C D G
And sip their lemonade,
Cadd9 G
When the sun shines, when the sun shines.

Chorus 1

G5 Gsus2/4 G5
Rain, ____ I don't mind.
G5 Gsus2/4 G5
Shine, ____ the weather's fine.

Verse 3

G
I can show you
C D G
That when it starts to rain,
C D G
Everything's the same,
Cadd9 G
I can show you, I can show you.

Chorus 2

```
G5      Gsus2/4   G5
Rain, ___ I don't mind.
G5      Gsus2/4          G5
Shine, ___ the weather's fine.
```

Verse 4

```
        G
Can you hear me
C             D       G
That when it rains and  shines,
    C    D      G
It's just a state of mind?
        Cadd9
Can you hear me?
        G
Can you hear me?
```

Coda

𝄆 G | G | G | G 𝄇 *Repeat ad lib. to fade*

Revolution 1

Words & Music by
John Lennon & Paul McCartney

```
Intro       | A   | A   | A   | A   | E7  ||

                 A                                  D
Verse 1     You say you want a revolution, well, you know,
                                        A
            We all want to change the world.
                                                   D
            You tell me that it's evolution, well, you know,
                                        E
            We all want to change the world.
            Bm                         E
              But when you talk about destruction,
            Bm                            G    A  F♯7   E
              Don't you know that you can count me out, in.

                                         A    D
Chorus 1    Don't you know it's gonna be all right,
                                         A    D
            Don't you know it's gonna be all right.
                                         A    D
            Don't you know it's gonna be all right.

            | E7  | E7  ||

                 A                                  D
Verse 2     You say you got a real solution, well, you know,
                                       A
            We'd all love to see the plan.

            (Ba-oh shoo-be-doo-wop, ba-oh shoo-be-doo-wop.)

            You ask me for a contribution, well, you know,
                                    E
            We all do it when we can.
            Bm                                    E
              But if you want money for people with minds that hate,
            Bm                                 G    A  F♯7  E
              All I can tell you is, brother, you have to  wait.
```

Chorus 2

```
                         A      D
Don't you know it's gonna be all right,
                         A      D
Don't you know it's gonna be all right.
                         A      D
Don't you know it's gonna be all right.

| E7    | E7    ||
```

Verse 3

```
    A                                              D
You say you'll change the constitution, well, you know,
                          A
We'd all love to change your head.

(Ba-oh shoo-be-doo-wop, ba-oh shoo-be-doo-wop)
                                        D
You tell me it's the institution, well, you know,
                               E
You'd better free your mind instead.

(Ba-oh shoo-be-doo-wop, ba-oh shoo-be-doo-wop)
Bm                                  E
   But if you go carrying pictures of Chairman Mao,
Bm                                      G   A  F#7  E
   You ain't gonna make it with anyone an - y - how.
```

Chorus 3

```
                         A      D
Don't you know it's gonna be all right,
                         A      D
Don't you know it's gonna be all right.
                         A      D
Don't you know it's gonna be all right.

| E7    | E7    ||
```

Coda

```
A
(Oh shoo-be-doo-wop.)
D
  Ah-ah-ah-ah,
A          D
  Ah-ah-ah-ah,
           A
Ah-ah all  right,
   D      A
All right, all right,
          D
All right, all right,
          A
All right, all right!
```

ad lib. to fade

Revolution (single version)

Words & Music by
John Lennon & Paul McCartney

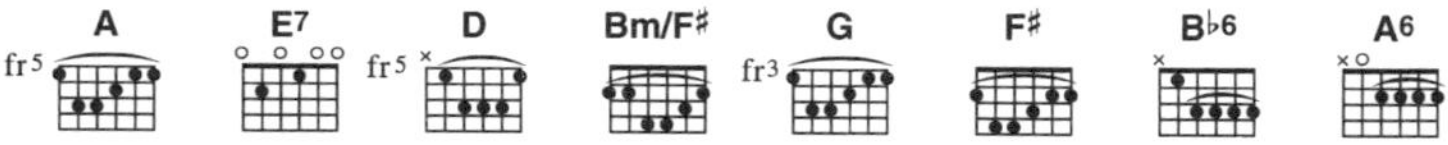

Capo first fret

Intro | A | A | A | E7 ||

Verse 1

A
You say you want a revolution,
D
Well, you know,
A
We all want to change the world.

You tell me that it's evolution,
D
Well, you know,
E7
We all want to change the world.
Bm/F♯ E7
But when you talk about destruction,
Bm/F♯ G A F♯
Don't you know that you can count me out.

Chorus 1

E7 A D
Don't you know it's going to be all right,
A D A D
All right, all right.

| E7 | E7 ||

Verse 2

A
You say you got a real solution,
D
Well, you know,
A
We'd all love to see the plan.

cont.

```
        (A)
You ask me for a contribution,
                 D
Well, you know,
                             E7
We're all doing what we can.
Bm/F#                                          E7
   But if you want money for people with minds that hate,
Bm/F#                                      G     A  F#
   All I can tell you is, brother, you'll have to   wait.
```

Chorus 2 As Chorus 1

Solo

| A | A | A | D | D |

| E7 | E7 | E7 | E7 ||

Verse 3

```
        A
You say you'll change the constitution,
                 D
Well, you know,
                              A
We all want to change your head.

You tell me it's the institution,
                 D
Well, you know,
                                E7
You'd better free your mind instead.
Bm/F#                                E7
   But if you go carrying pictures of Chairman Mao,
Bm/F#                                        G    A  F#
   You ain't gonna make it with anyone an - y - how.
```

Chorus 3 As Chorus 1

Coda

```
      A        D
All right, all right,
      A        D
All right, all right,
      A        D
All right, all right,
      E7               B♭6   A6
All right, all right!
```

Rocky Raccoon

Words & Music by
John Lennon & Paul McCartney

Am7 D7sus4 D7 G7 C C/B

Intro | Am7 | Am7 ||

Verse 1

```
           Am7
Now somewhere in the black mountain hills of Dakota
                 D7sus4                          D7
There lived a young boy named Rocky Racoon-na
G7                                      C
And one day his woman ran off with another guy,
C/B                        Am7
Hit young Rocky in the eye,

Rocky didn't like that,
                  D7sus4          D7
He said, "I'm gonna get that boy."
         G7
So one day he walked into town,
                                    C          C/B
Booked himself a room in the local saloon.
```

Verse 2

```
Am7                        D7sus4       D7
Rocky Racoon checked into his room,
G7                              C    C/B
Only to find Gideon's Bible.
Am7                   D7sus4            D7
Rocky had come, equipped with a gun,
   G7                              C      C/B
To shoot off the legs of his rival.
     Am7                     D7sus4         D7
His rival, it seems, had broken his dreams,
   G7                           C      C/B
By stealing the girl of his fancy.
     Am7                            D7sus4              D7
Her name was Magill, and she called herself Lil,
    G7                              C      C/B
But everyone knew her as Nancy.
```

Verse 3

        Am7   D7sus4   D7
Now she and her man, who called himself Dan,
       G7   C   C/B
Were in the next room at the hoedown.
Am7   D7sus4   D7
Rocky burst in, and grinning a grin,
            G7   C   C/B
He said, "Danny boy, this is a showdown."
     Am7   D7sus4   D7
But Daniel was hot, he drew first and shot,
     G7   C   C/B
And Rocky collapsed in the corner.

Piano break 𝄆 Am7 | D7sus4 D7 | G7 | C C/B 𝄇

Verse 4

            Am7   D7sus4   D7
Now, the doctor came in, stinking of gin,
            G7   C   C/B
And proceeded to lie on the table.
             Am7
He said, "Rocky, you met your match."
               D7sus4   D7
And Rocky said, "Doc, it's only a scratch,
               G7
And I'll be better, I'll be better, Doc,
                  C   C/B
As soon as I am   able."

Verse 5

        Am7   D7sus4   D7
Now Rocky Racoon he fell back in his room,
G7   C   C/B
Only to find Gideon's Bible.
Am7   D7sus4   D7
Gideon checked out and left in no doubt
    G7   C   C/B
To help with good Rocky's revival.

Piano break | Am7 | D7sus4 D7 | G7 | C C/B |
(Do do do do do do do do do) etc.

Coda | Am7 | D7sus4 D7 |
(Come on Rocky boy.) (Come on Rocky boy.)

| G7 | C G7 | C ||

Run For Your Life

Words & Music by
John Lennon & Paul McCartney

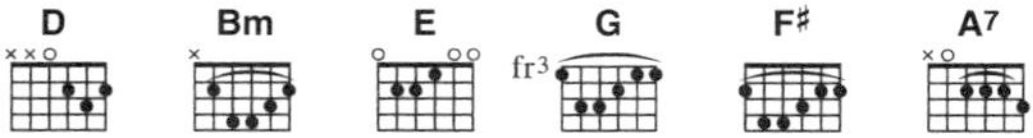

Intro | D | D | D ||

Verse 1

D
Well, I'd rather see you dead, little girl,
Bm
Than to be with another man.
D
You'd better keep your head, little girl,
Bm
Or I won't know where I am.

Chorus 1

Bm E
You'd better run for your life if you can, little girl,
Bm E
Hide your head in the sand, little girl,
Bm G
Catch you with another man,
F♯ Bm
That's the end, little girl.

Link | D | D ||

Verse 2

D
Well, you know that I'm a wicked guy
Bm
And I was born with a jealous mind.
D
And I can't spend my whole life trying
Bm
Just to make you tow the line.

Chorus 2 As Chorus 1

Solo | D | D | G | D | A7 | D ||

Verse 3

D
Let this be a sermon,
Bm
I mean everything I said,
D
Baby, I'm determined,
Bm
And I'd rather see you dead.

Chorus 3

Bm E
You'd better run for your life if you can, little girl,
Bm E
Hide your head in the sand, little girl,
Bm G
Catch you with another man,
F♯ Bm
That's the end, little girl.

Link | D | D ||

Verse 4

D
I'd rather see you dead, little girl,
Bm
Than to be with another man.
D
You'd better keep your head, little girl,
Bm
Or you won't know where I am.

Chorus 4

Bm E
You'd better run for your life if you can, little girl,
Bm E
Hide your head in the sand, little girl,
Bm G
Catch you with another man,
F♯ Bm
That's the end, little girl.

Coda | D | D |: D :| *Repeat to fade*
Na na na. Na na

Savoy Truffle

Words & Music by
George Harrison

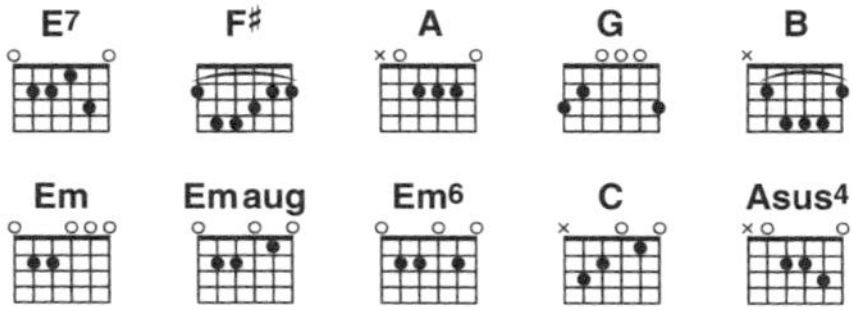

Intro | E7 | E7 ||

Verse 1
N.C. E7
Cream tangerine, a Montelimar,
F♯ A
A ginger sling with a pineapple heart,
G B
A coffee dessert, yes, you know it's good news:

Chorus 1
Em Emaug Em6
But you'll have to have them all pulled out
Emaug C G
After the Savoy truffle.

Link | E7 | E7 ||

Verse 2
N.C. E7
Cool cherry cream, nice apple tart.
F♯ A
I feel your taste all the time we're apart,
G B
Coconut fudge really blows down those blues:

Chorus 2
Em Emaug Em6
But you'll have to have them all pulled out
Emaug C G
After the Savoy truffle.

Bridge 1

```
Em                        A
   You might not feel it now,
                Asus4     A
But when the pain cuts through,
                  G         B
You're going to know, and how.
    Em                          A
The sweat is gonna fill your head,
          Asus4        A            G       B
When it becomes too much, you'll shout aloud…
```

Solo

```
| E7 | E7 | E7 | E7 | F♯ | F♯ |
| A  | A  | G  | G  | B  | B  ||
```

Chorus 3

```
             Em                  Emaug      Em6
But you'll have to have them all pulled out
            Emaug  C    G
After the Savoy truffle.
```

Bridge 2

```
    Em                       A
You know that what you eat you are,
              Asus4  A          G   B
But what is sweet   now, turns so  sour.
    Em                      A
We all know Ob-la-di-bla-da,
               Asus4 A          G    B
But can you show   me where you are?
```

Verse 3

```
E7
Cream tangerine and Montelimar,
F♯                                A
   A ginger sling with a pineapple heart,
G                                           B
   A coffee dessert, yes, you know it's good news:
```

Chorus 4

```
             Em                  Emaug      Em6
But you'll have to have them all pulled out
            Emaug  C    G
After the Savoy truffle.
             Em                  Emaug      Em6
Yes, you'll have to have them all pulled out
            Emaug  C    G
After the Savoy truffle.
```

Sexy Sadie

Words & Music by
John Lennon & Paul McCartney

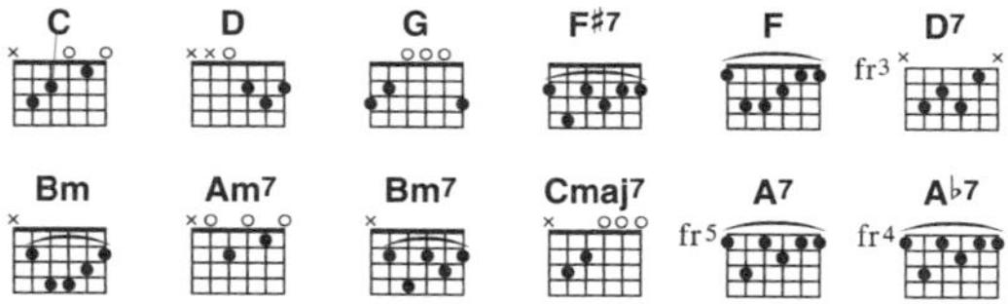

Intro | C D | G F♯7 | F D7 ||

Verse 1

G F♯7 Bm
Sexy Sadie, what have you done?
C D G F♯7
You made a fool of everyone, ____
C D G F♯7
You made a fool of everyone. ____
F D7 G
Sexy Sadie, oh, what have you done?

Verse 2

G F♯7 Bm
Sexy Sadie, you broke the rules
C D G F♯7
You laid it down for all to see,
C D G F♯7
You laid it down for all to see. ____
F D7 G
Sexy Sadie, oh, you broke the rules.

Bridge 1

G Am7 Bm7 Cmaj7
One sunny day the world was waiting for a lover,
G Am7 Bm7 C
She came along to turn on everyone. ______
A7 A♭7 G
Sexy Sadie, the greatest of them all.

Verse 3

G F#7 Bm
Sexy Sadie, how did you know?
C D G F#7
The world was waiting just for you, ___
C D G F#7
The world was waiting just for you, ___
F D7 G
Sexy Sadie, oh, how did you know?

Verse 4

G F#7 Bm
Sexy Sadie, you'll get yours yet,
C D G F#7
However big you think you are, ___
C D G F#7
However big you think you are. ___
F D7 G
Sexy Sadie, oh you'll get yours yet.

Bridge 2

G Am7 Bm7 Cmaj7
We gave her everything we owned just to sit at her table.
G Am7 Bm7 C
Just a smile would lighten everything. ___
A7 A♭7 G F#7
Sexy Sadie, she's the latest and the greatest of them all.

Coda

‖: Bm7 | C D | G F#7 |
Ooh, ___

| C D | G F#7 |
She made a fool of everyone, ___
How ever big you think you are, ___

| F D7 | G F#7 :‖ *Repeat to fade*
Sexy Sadie.
Sexy Sadie.

Sgt. Pepper's Lonely Hearts Club Band

Words & Music by
John Lennon & Paul McCartney

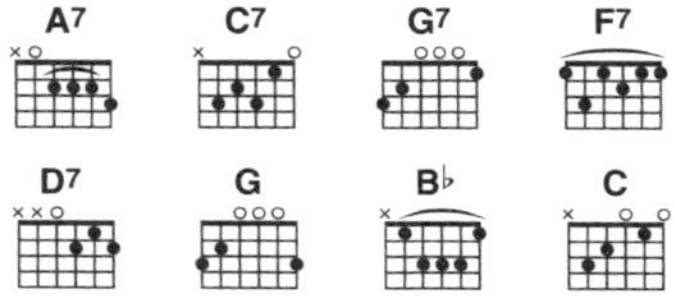

Intro | A7 | A7 | C7 | G7 ||

Verse 1

G7 A7
It was twenty years ago today,
C7 G7
Sergeant Pepper taught the band to play.
A7
They've been going in and out of style,
C7 G7
But they're guaranteed to raise a smile.
A7
So may I introduce to you
C7
The act you've known for all these years:
G7 C7 G7
Sergeant Pepper's Lonely Hearts Club Band.

Link | C7 | F7 | C7 | D7 | D7 ||

Chorus

G B♭ C7 G
We're Sergeant Pepper's Lonely Hearts Club Band,
C7 G7
We hope you will enjoy the show.
G B♭ C7 G
Sergeant Pepper's Lonely Hearts Club Band,
A7 D7
Sit back and let the evening go.
C7 G7
Sergeant Pepper's Lonely, Sergeant Pepper's Lonely,
A7 C7 G7
Sergeant Pepper's Lonely Hearts Club Band.

```
            C7
Bridge      It's wonderful to be here,
            F7
            It's certainly a thrill,
               C7
            You're such a lovely audience,
              D7
            We'd like to take you home with us,

            We'd love to take you home.

               G7                      A7
Verse 2     I don't really want to stop the show,
              C7                          G7
            But I thought you might like to know,
                                          A7
            That the singer's going to sing a song,
                C7                      G7
            And he wants you all to sing along.
             A7
            So let me introduce to you
             C7
            The one and only Billy Shears,
                G7                C7                 G7
            And Sergeant Pepper's Lonely Hearts Club Band, yeah!

Coda        | C     | C     ||
```

Sgt. Pepper's Lonely Hearts Club Band (Reprise)

Words & Music by
John Lennon & Paul McCartney

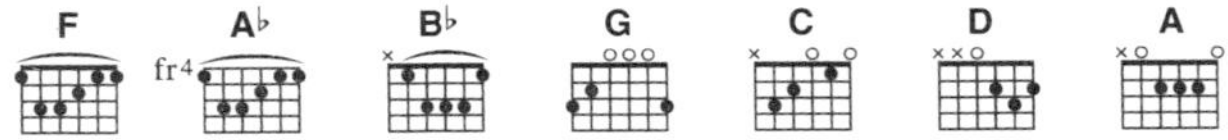

Intro | *Drums for 4 bars* || F | F | F | F ||

Verse 1

```
       F                     A♭         B♭          F
We're Sergeant Pepper's Lonely Hearts Club Band,
   B♭                             F
We hope you have enjoyed the show.
                        A♭         B♭          F
Sergeant Pepper's Lonely Hearts Club Band,
          G                    C
We're sorry, but it's time to go.
B♭                              F
Sergeant Pepper's Lonely, Sergeant Pepper's Lonely,
G                               D
Sergeant Pepper's Lonely, Sergeant Pepper's Lonely.
```

Verse 2

```
     G                  B♭          C           G
Sergeant Pepper's Lonely Hearts Club Band,
        C                         G
We'd like to thank you once again.
     G                  B♭               C                   G
Sergeant Pepper's one and only Lonely Hearts Club Band,
   A                         D
It's getting very near the end.
    C                             G
Sergeant Pepper's Lonely, Sergeant Pepper's Lonely,
    A                                C           G
Sergeant Pepper's Lonely Hearts Club Band.
```

Coda | B♭ | C | G ||

Sun King

Words & Music by
John Lennon & Paul McCartney

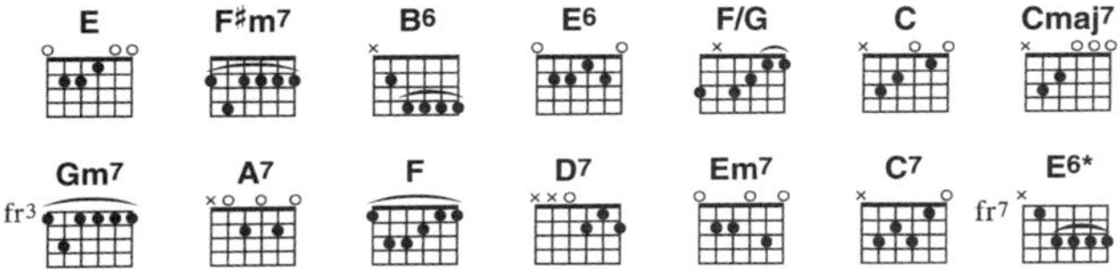

Intro

| E | E | E | E |

|: F♯m7 | F♯m7 B6 | E6 | E :| *Play 3 times*

F/G
Ah. ____

Chorus

C Cmaj7 Gm7 A7
Here come the Sun King,
C Cmaj7 Gm7 A7
Here come the Sun King,
F D7
Everybody's laughing,
F D7
Everybody's happy,
C Em7 C7 F
Here come the Sun King.

Verse 1

F♯m7 B6 E6 E
Quando paramucho mi amore de felice carafon,
F♯m7 B6 E6 E
Mundo paparazzi mi amore chicka ferdy parasol,
F♯m7 B6 E6 E6*
Cuesto obrigado tanta mucho que can eat it carousel.

She Came In Through The Bathroom Window

Words & Music by
John Lennon & Paul McCartney

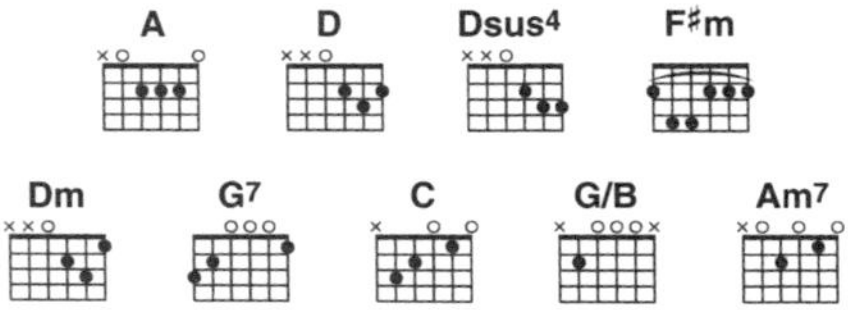

Verse 1

A D Dsus4 D
She came in through the bathroom window,
A F♯m D Dsus4 D
Protected by a silver spoon.
A F♯m D Dsus4
But now she sucks her thumb and wonders
D
By the banks of her own lagoon.

Bridge 1

A Dm
Didn't anybody tell her?
A Dm
Didn't anybody see? ___
G7 C G/B Am7
Sunday's on the phone to Monday,
G7 C A
Tuesday's on the phone to me.

Verse 2

(A) D Dsus4 D
She said she'd always been a dancer,
A F♯m D Dsus4 D
She worked at fifteen clubs a day,
A F♯m D Dsus4
And though she thought I knew the answer,
D
Well, I knew what I could not say.

Verse 3

```
A                                  D            Dsus4  D
   And so I quit the police department,
A                F#m               D      Dsus4  D
   And got myself a steady job.
A                     F#m                       D      Dsus4
   And though she tried her best to help me,
            D
She could steal, but she could not rob.
```

Bridge 2

```
A                         Dm
   Didn't anybody tell her?
A                            Dm
   Didn't anybody see? ___
G7                               C        G/B   Am7
Sunday's on the phone to Monday,
G7                               C
Tuesday's on the phone to me,
    A
Oh yeah.
```

She Loves You

Words & Music by
John Lennon & Paul McCartney

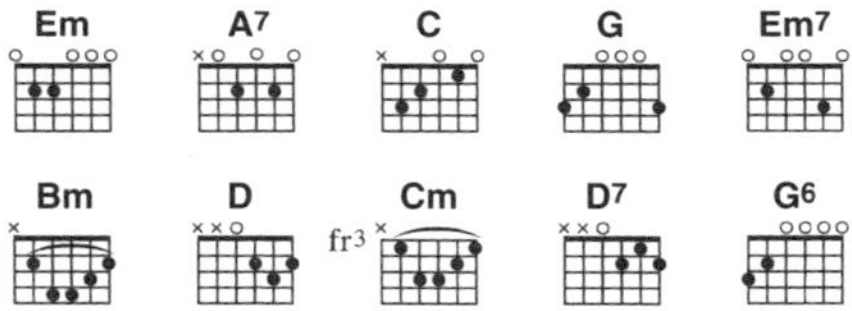


```
            Em
Intro       She loves you, yeah, yeah, yeah,
            A7
            She loves you, yeah, yeah, yeah,
            C                            G
            She loves you, yeah, yeah, yeah, yeah.


                (G)                  Em7
Verse 1     You think you lost your love,
                    Bm          D
            Well I saw her yesterday.
               G                 Em7
            It's you she's thinking of,
                      Bm          D
            And she told me what to say.
                           G                                   Em
            She says she loves you, and you know that can't be bad,
                      Cm                                  D
            Yes, she loves you, and you know you should be glad.


                G               Em7
Verse 2     She said you hurt her so,
                Bm             D
            She almost lost her mind.
                G              Em7
            But now she says she knows,
                        Bm          D
            You're not the hurting kind.
                           G                                   Em
            She says she loves you, and you know that can't be bad,
                      Cm                                  D
            Yes, she loves you, and you know you should be glad.   Ooh.
```

Chorus 1

```
    Em
She loves you, yeah, yeah, yeah,
    A7
She loves you, yeah, yeah, yeah.
         Cm
With a love like that,
    D7                       G
You know you should be glad.
```

Verse 3

```
    G                    Em7
You know it's up to you,
  Bm              D
I think it's only fair.
G                      Em7
Pride can hurt you too,
  Bm           D
Apologise to her.
                 G                                        Em
Because she loves you, and you know that can't be bad,
           Cm                                            D
Yes, she loves you, and you know you should be glad.   Ooh.
```

Chorus 2

```
    Em
She loves you, yeah, yeah, yeah,
    A7
She loves you, yeah, yeah, yeah.
         Cm
With a love like that,
    D7                        G     Em
You know you should be glad.
         Cm              N.C.
With a love like that,
    D                         G     Em
You know you should be glad.
         Cm              N.C.
With a love like that,
    D7                        G
You know you should be glad.
Em
   Yeah, yeah, yeah,
C                G6
Yeah, yeah, yeah, yeah.
```

She Said She Said

Words & Music by
John Lennon & Paul McCartney

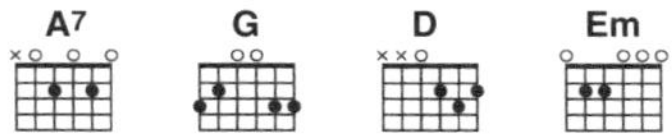

Capo first fret

Intro
```
| A7        | A7        ||
```

Verse 1
```
A7        G     D
She said,
                    A7        G      D
"I know what it's like to be dead.
                 A7       G       D
I know what it is to be sad."
            A7            G              D            A7
And she's making me feel like I've never been born.

| A7   G    | D    A7   ||
```

Verse 2
```
A7        G     D
I said,
                          A7             G        D
"Who put all those things in your head?
                            A7         G       D
Things that make me feel that I'm mad,
              A7            G              D            A7
And you're making me feel like I've never been born."

| A7   G    | D    A7   ||
```

Bridge 1
```
A7               G              A7
She said, "You don't understand what I said."
          G                     A7
I said, "No, no, no, you're wrong.
                Em         A7
When I was a boy
                 D      A7              D
Everything was right,   everything was right."
```

Verse 3

A7 G D
I said,

A7 G D
"Even though you know what you know,

A7 G D
I know that I'm ready to leave,

A7 G D A7
'Cause you're making me feel like I've never been born."

| A7 G | D A7 ||

Bridge 2

A7 G A7
She said, "You don't understand what I said."

G A7
I said, "No, no, no, you're wrong.

Em A7
When I was a boy

D A7 D
Everything was right, everything was right."

Verse 4

A7 G D
I said,

A7 G D
"Even though you know what you know,

A7 G D
I know that I'm ready to leave,

A7 G D A7
'Cause you're making me feel like I've never been born."

| A7 G | D A7 ||

Coda

A7
She said, (she said,)

"I know what it's like to be dead,"

(I know what it's like to be dead,)

"I know what it is to be sad,"

(I know what it is to be sad,)

"I know what it's like to be dead." *Fade out*

She's A Woman

Words & Music by
John Lennon & Paul McCartney

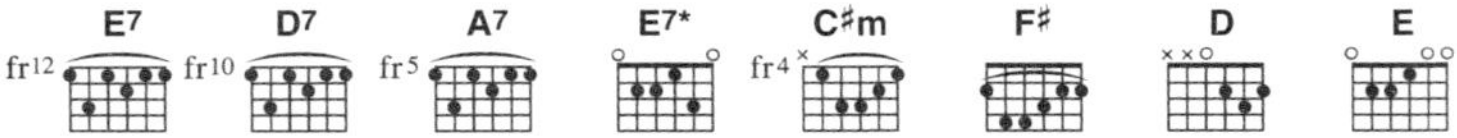

Intro | E7 | E7 | D7 | D7 | A7 | A7 | A7 | A7 ||

Verse 1
A7 D7 A7
My love don't give me presents,
D7 A7
I know that she's no peasant,
D7
Only ever has to give me love forever and forever.
A7 D7 A7
My love don't give me presents,
E7
Turn me on when I get lonely,
D7 A7
People tell me that she's only foolin',
D7 A7 E7*
I know she isn't.

Verse 2
A7 D7 A7
She don't give boys the eye,
D7 A7
She hate to see me cry,
D7
She is happy just to hear me say that I will never leave her.
A7 D7 A7
She don't give boys the eye,
E7
She will never make me jealous,
D7 A7
Give me all her time as well as lovin',
D7 A7
Don't ask me why.

Bridge 1

C♯m F♯
She's a woman who understands,
C♯m D E
She's a woman who loves her man.

Verse 3

As Verse 1

Intro

| A7 | A7 | A7 | A7 | D7 | D7 |

| A7 | A7 | E7 | D7 | A7 | E7* ||

Bridge 2

C♯m F♯
She's a woman who understands,
C♯m D E
She's a woman who loves her man.

Verse 4

A7 D7 A7
My love don't give me presents,
D7 A7
I know that she's no peasant,
D7
Only ever has to give me love forever and forever.
A7 D7 A7
My love don't give me presents,
E7
Turn me on when I get lonely,
D7 A7
People tell me that she's only foolin',
D7 A7
I know she isn't.

Coda

A7
She's a woman, she's a woman,
D7 A7
She's a woman, she's a woman… *Fade out*

She's Leaving Home

Words & Music by
John Lennon & Paul McCartney

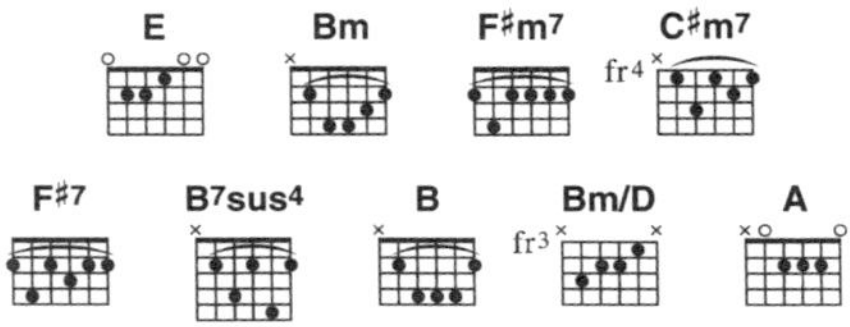

Intro | E | E | E | E ||

Verse 1
E Bm F♯m7 C♯m7 F♯7
Wednesday morning at five o'clock, as the day begins.
B7sus4 B
Silently closing her bedroom door,
B7sus4 B
Leaving the note that she hoped would say more.

Verse 2
E Bm F♯m7 C♯m7 F♯7
She goes downstairs to the kitchen clutching her handkerchief.
B7sus4 B
Quietly turning the back door key,
B7sus4 B
Stepping outside she is free.

Chorus 1
E
She (We gave her most of our lives)

Is leaving (Sacrificed most of our lives)
Bm/D (C♯m7)
Home. (We gave her everything money could buy.)
C♯m7 F♯7
She's leaving home after living alone (Bye, bye)
C♯m7 F♯7
For so many years.

Verse 3

E   Bm   F♯m7   C♯m7   F♯7
Father snores as his wife gets into her dressing gown.
B7sus4   B
Picks up the letter that's lying there.
B7sus4   B
Standing alone at the top of the stairs.

Verse 4

              E   Bm   F♯m7
She breaks down and cries to her husband,
              C♯m7   F♯7
"Daddy, our baby's gone!"
B7sus4   B
"Why would she treat us so thoughtlessly?
B7sus4   B
How could she do this to me?"

Chorus 2

E
She (We never thought of ourselves)

Is leaving (Never a thought for ourselves)
                              Bm/D   (C♯m7)
Home. (We've struggled hard all our lives to get by.)
C♯m7   F♯7
She's leaving home after living alone (Bye, bye)
        C♯m7   F♯7
For so many years.

Verse 5

E   Bm   F♯m7   C♯m7   F♯7
Friday morning at nine o'clock, she is far away.
B7sus4   B
Waiting to keep the appointment she made,
B7sus4   B
Meeting a man from the motor trade.

Chorus 3

E
She (What did we do that was wrong?)

Is having (We didn't know it was wrong)
                     Bm/D   (C♯m7)
Fun. (Fun is the one thing that money can't buy)
C♯m7   F♯7
Something inside that was always denied (Bye, bye)
        C♯m7   F♯7
For so many years.
C♯m7   F♯7
She's leaving home.
        A   E
(Bye, bye.)

Something

Words & Music by
George Harrison

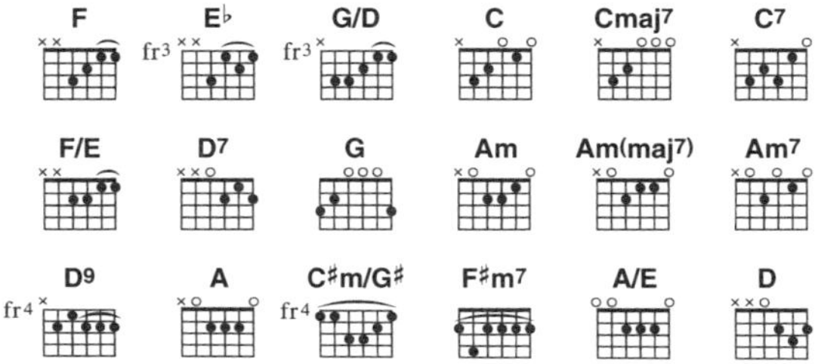

Intro | F E♭ G/D ||

Verse 1

```
C                                   Cmaj7
Something in the way she moves
C7                                F              F/E
  Attracts me like no other lover.
D7                                 G
Something in the way she woos me.
 Am                                 Am(maj7)
I don't want to leave her now,
    Am7                        D9
You know I believe, and how.
```

| F E♭ G/D ||

Verse 2

```
C                                     Cmaj7
Somewhere in her smile she knows
C7                                  F            F/E
  That I don't need no other lover.
D7                                   G
Something in her style that shows me.
 Am                                 Am(maj7)
I don't want to leave her now,
    Am7                        D9
You know I believe, and how.
```

| F E♭ G/D | A ||

Bridge

```
A                 C♯m/G♯            F♯m7  A/E
   You're asking me will my love grow,
        D      G        A
I don't know, I don't know.
A              C♯m/G♯              F♯m7  A/E
   You stick around now, it may show,
        D      G        C
I don't know, I don't know.
```

Solo

```
| C        | Cmaj7 | C7       | F  F/E | D7       | G        |
| Am  Am(maj7)     | Am7  D9  | F    E♭  G/D ||
```

Verse 3

```
C                                 Cmaj7
Something in the way she knows,
C7                         F              F/E
   And all I have to do is think of her.
D7                                 G
Something in the things she shows me.
  Am                                Am(maj7)
I don't want to leave her now,
    Am7                       D9
You know I believe, and how.
```

Coda

```
| F   E♭  G/D | A          | F   E♭  G/D | C          ||
```

Strawberry Fields Forever

Words & Music by
John Lennon & Paul McCartney

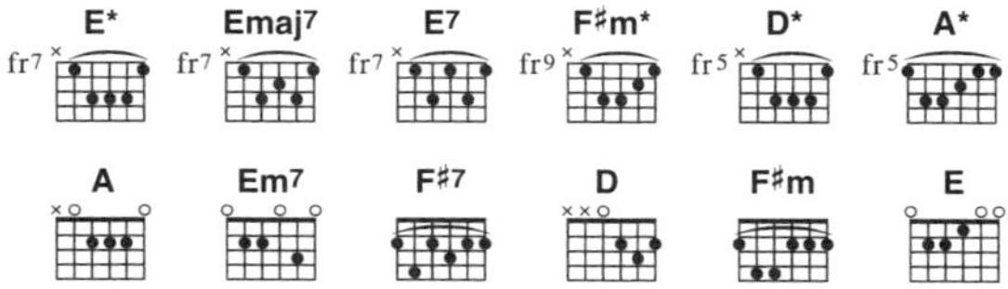

Capo first fret

Intro | E* Emaj7 | E7 | F♯m* E* | D* A* ||

Chorus 1

(A)
Let me take you down,
Em7
'Cause I'm going to

Strawberry Fields.
F♯7
Nothing is real,
D F♯7
And nothing to get hung about.
D A
Strawberry Fields forever.

Verse 1

E* Emaj7 E7
Living is easy with eyes closed,
F♯m E D
Misunderstanding all you see.
E A
It's getting hard to be someone,
F♯m
But it all works out;
D E D A
It doesn't matter much to me.

Chorus 2 As Chorus 1

Verse 2

```
E*          Emaj7      E7
No-one I think is in my tree,
F#m            E                D
   I mean, it must be high or low.
               E                    A
That is, you can't, you know, tune in,
             F#m
But it's all right.
D              E                D      A
   That is, I think it's not too bad.
```

Chorus 3 As Chorus 1

Verse 3

```
E*        Emaj7       E7
Always know, sometimes think it's me,
F#m                     E                  D
   But you know, I know when it's a dream.
             E             A
I think a 'No', I mean a'Yes',
             F#m
But it's all wrong.
D              E          D     A
   That is, I think I disagree.
```

Chorus 4

```
(A)
   Let me take you down,
                        Em7
'Cause I'm going to

Strawberry Fields.
F#7
   Nothing is real,
      D                F#7
And nothing to get hung about.
D                       A       F#m
Strawberry Fields forever,
D                       A
Strawberry Fields forever,
D              E        D
Strawberry Fields forever.
```

Coda |: A | A | A | A :| *Repeat to fade*

Taxman

Words & Music by
George Harrison

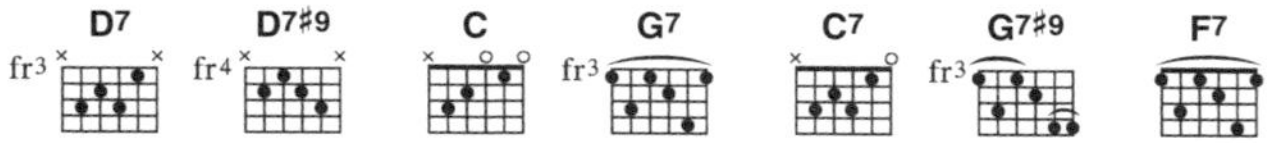

Intro | D7 | D7 ||

Verse 1

```
          D7                           D7♯9
Let me tell you how it will be:
D7                                        D7♯9
   There's one for you, nineteen for me,
D7              C
   'Cause I'm the Taxman,
                G7        D7
Yeah, I'm the   Taxman. ___
```

Verse 2

```
          D7                              D7♯9
Should five percent appear too small,
D7                                D7♯9
   Be thankful I don't take it all.
D7              C
   'Cause I'm the Taxman,
                G7        D7
Yeah, I'm the   Taxman. ___
```

Bridge

```
          D7
(If you drive a car, car,)  I'll tax the street,
                              C7
(If you try to sit, sit,) I'll tax your seat,
          D7
(If you get too cold, cold,) I'll tax the heat,
                                   C7
(If you take a walk, walk,) I'll tax your feet…
D7
Taxman!
```

```
Solo      | D7     | D7♯9  D7 | D7     | D7     | D7     | D7♯9  D7 ||
                          C
          'Cause I'm the Taxman,
                        G7♯9       D7
          Yeah, I'm the   Taxman.

                D7
Verse 3   Don't ask me what I want it for.
          D7♯9      D7
          (A-ah Mister Wilson!)

          If you don't want to pay some more.
          D7♯9      D7
          (A-ah Mister Heath!)
                          C
          'Cause I'm the Taxman,
                        G7♯9       D7
          Yeah, I'm the   Taxman.

              D7
Verse 4   Now my advice for those who die,
          D7♯9        D7
          (Taxman!)

          Declare the pennies on your eyes.
          D7♯9        D7
          (Taxman!)
                          C
          'Cause I'm the Taxman,
                        G7♯9       D7
          Yeah, I'm the   Taxman,
                         F7
          And you're working for no-one but me.

Solo      | D7     | D7     | D7♯9  D7 |
           (me.)
           (Taxman!)
          | D7     | D7     | D7     | D7♯9   || Fade out
```

Tell Me What You See

Words & Music by
John Lennon & Paul McCartney

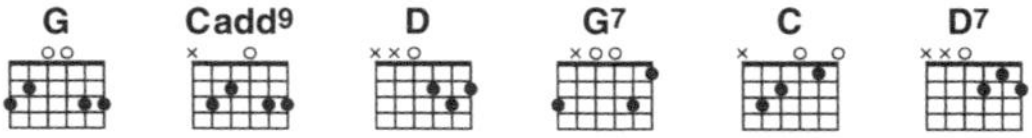

Intro | G | G ||

Verse 1

G Cadd9 D G
If you let me take your heart,
Cadd9 G
I will prove to you,
Cadd9 D G
We will never be apart
Cadd9 D G
If I'm part of you.

Chorus 1

Cadd9 G Cadd9 G
Open up your eyes now, tell me what you see,
Cadd9 G Cadd9 D G
It is no surprise now, what you see is me.

Verse 2

G Cadd9 D G
Big and black the clouds may be,
G Cadd9 G
Time will pass away,
Cadd9 D G
If you put your trust in me,
Cadd9 D G
I'll make bright your day,

Chorus 2

Cadd9 G Cadd9 G
Look into these eyes now, tell me what you see,
Cadd9 G Cadd9 D G
Don't you realise now, what you see is me?

Bridge 1

G7 C
Tell me what you see.

| G | D7 | G | G ||

Verse 3

```
G       Cadd9 D          G
Listen to  me  one more time,
           Cadd9 G
How can I   get   through?
            Cadd9 D       G
Can't you try  to   see that I'm
Cadd9     D     G
Trying to get to you?
```

Chorus 3

```
Cadd9        G             Cadd9            G
Open up your eyes now, tell me what you see,
Cadd9      G          Cadd9    D     G
It is no surprise now, what you see is me.
```

Bridge 2

```
G7                  C
Tell me what you see.

| G      | D7     | G      | G      ||
```

Verse 4

```
G       Cadd9 D          G
Listen to me one more time,
           Cadd9 G
How can I get through?
            Cadd9 D       G
Can't you try  to   see that I'm
C          D     G
Trying to get to you?
```

Chorus 4

```
Cadd9        G             Cadd9            G
Open up your eyes now, tell me what you see,
Cadd9      G          Cadd9    D     G
It is no surprise now, what you see is me.
G7                          C       G
Mmm-mmm-mmm-mmm-mmm.
```

Tell Me Why

Words & Music by
John Lennon & Paul McCartney

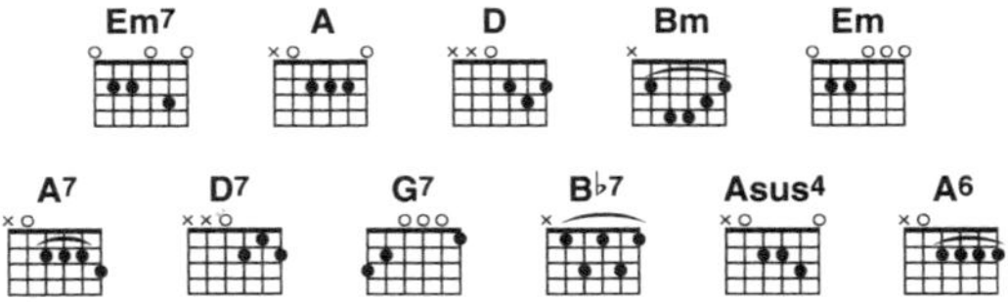

Intro | Em7 A | Em7 A | Em7 A ||

Chorus 1

Em7 A D
Tell me why you cried,
Em7 A D Em7
And why you lied to me.
A D
Tell me why you cried,
Em7 A D Em7 A
And why you lied to me.

Verse 1

D Bm
Well I gave you everything I had,
Em A7
But you left me sitting on my own,
D Bm
Did you have to treat me oh so bad?
Em A7
All I do is hang my head and moan.

Chorus 2

A D
Tell me why you cried,
Em7 A D Em7
And why you lied to me.
A D
Tell me why you cried,
Em7 A D Em7 A
And why you lied to me.

Verse 2

D Bm
If it's something that I've said or done,
Em A7
Tell me what and I'll apologise.
D Bm
If you don't, I really can't go on,
Em A7
Holding back these tears in my eyes.

Chorus 3

D
Tell me why you cried,
Em7 A D Em7
And why you lied to me.
A D
Tell me why you cried,
Em7 A D D7
And why you lied to me.

Bridge

G7
Well I beg you on my bended knees,
A7
If you'll only listen to my pleas,
Bm
Is there anything I can do?
Em7
'Cause I really can't stand it,
A7 D
I'm so in love with you.

Chorus 4

N.C. D
Tell me why you cried,
Em7 A D Em7
And why you lied to me.
A D
Tell me why you cried,
Em7 A Bm B♭7 Asus4 A6 D
And why you lied to me.

Thank You Girl

Words & Music by
John Lennon & Paul McCartney

A7 G D Bm Em

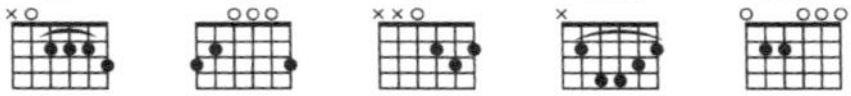

Intro | A7 | G ||

Verse 1

A7 G
Oh, oh,
D G D G
You've ___ been good to me,
D A7 D G
You made me glad ___ when I was blue.
D G D G
And ___ eternally,
D A7 D
I'll always be ___ in love with you,

Chorus 1

G A7 G
And all I gotta do is thank you girl,
A7
Thank you girl.

Verse 2

D G D G
I ___ could tell the world
D A7 D G
A thing or two ___ about our love.
D G D G
I ___ know little girl,
D A7 D
Only a fool ___ would doubt our love,

Chorus 2

G A7 G
And all I gotta do is thank you girl,
A7
Thank you girl.

Bridge

Bm   D   A7
Thank you girl for loving me the way that you do,

(Way that you do,)

Em   A7   D
That's the kind of love that is too good to be true,

Chorus 3

     G   A7   G
And all I gotta do is thank you girl,

A7
Thank you girl.

Link

| A7 | G ||

Verse 3

A7   G
Oh,   oh,

D   G   D   G
You've ___ been good to me,

                D   A7   D   G
You made me glad ___ when I was blue.

D   G   D   G
And ___ eternally, ___

              D   A7   D
I'll always be ___ in love with you,

Chorus 4

     G   A7   G
And all I gotta do is thank you girl,

A7
Thank you girl.

Link

| A7 | G ||

Coda

A7 G D G D G
Oh, oh, oh!

A7 G D G D G
Oh, oh, oh!

A7 G D
Oh, oh!

That Means A Lot

Words & Music by
John Lennon & Paul McCartney

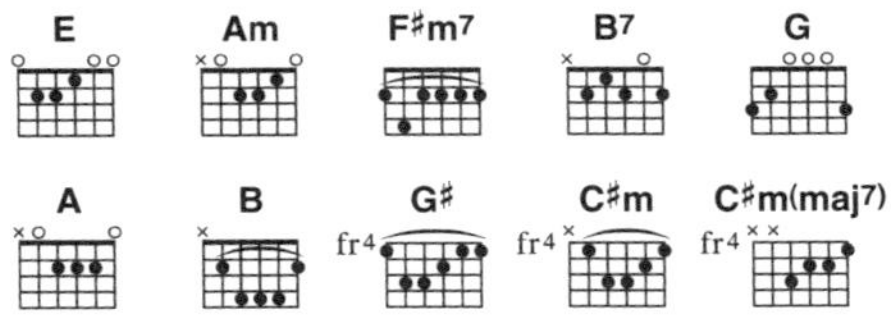

Intro | E | E ||

Verse 1

E   Am   E
A friend says that your love won't mean a lot,
                                        Am   F♯m7   B7
But you know that your love is all you've got.
  G   Am   G   F♯m7   B7
At times, things are so fine, and at times they're not,
     E   A
But when she says she loves you,
B
That means a lot.

| E | E ||
(lot.)

Verse 2

E   Am   E
A friend says that a love is never true,
                                        Am   F♯m7   B7
But you know that does not apply to you. ___
  G   Am   G   F♯m7   B7
A touch can mean so much when it's all you've got
      E   A
And when she says she loves you,
B
That means a lot.

| E | E ||
(lot.)   (Love can.)

```
           E      G♯   C♯m
Bridge     Love can be,    deep inside,
           E      G♯   C♯m
           Love can be,    suicide,
                C♯m(maj7)  E              B7
           Can't you       see you can't  hide
                    C♯m          G♯
           What you feel when it's real?

             E                        Am              E
Verse 3    A friend says that your love won't mean a lot,
                                       Am              F♯m7  B7
           But you know that your love is all you've got. ___
             G                  Am              G  F♯m7  B7
           A touch can mean so much when it's all you've got
              E                            A
           But when she says she loves you,
           B              E
           That means a lot.

           C♯m    C♯m(maj7)   E     C♯m
Coda          Can't you       see, yeah.
                  C♯m(maj7)   E     C♯m
           ||: Can't you      see, yeah.   :||  Repeat to fade
```

There's A Place

Words & Music by
John Lennon & Paul McCartney

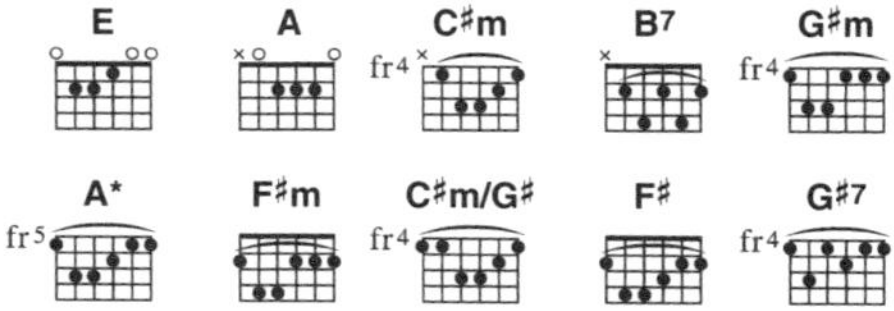

Intro | E | A | E | A ||

Verse 1

N.C.
There

    E   A   E
Is a place   where I can go,

A   E
   When I feel low,

C♯m   B7
   When I feel blue,

               G♯m   A*
And it's my mind,

                 E   A
And there's no time

        F♯m C♯m/G♯
When I'm alone.

Verse 2

N.C.
I

          E
Think of you

A   E
   And things you do

A   E
   Go round my head,

C♯m   B7
   The things you've said,

        A   B7
Like, I love only you.

Bridge

C♯m F♯
In my mind there's no sorrow,
E G♯7
Don't you know that it's so?
C♯m F♯
There'll be no sad tomorrow,
E G♯7 C♯m
Don't you know that it's so?

Verse 3

N.C.
There
E A E
Is a place where I can go,
A E
When I feel low,
C♯m B7
When I feel blue,
G♯m A*
And it's my mind,
E A
And there's no time
F♯m C♯m/G♯
When I'm alone.

Coda

N.C. E A
There's a place,
E A
There's a place,
E A
There's a place,
E A
𝄆 There's a place. 𝄇 *Repeat to fade*

Things We Said Today

Words & Music by
John Lennon & Paul McCartney

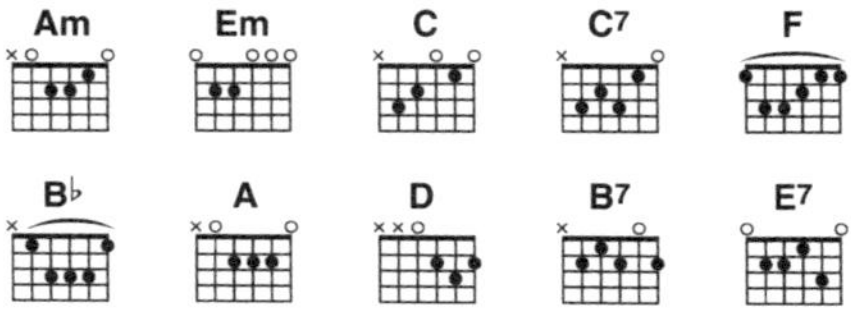

Intro | Am | Am ||

Verse 1

Am   Em   Am   Em   Am
You say you will love me if I have to go,
              Em   Am   Em   Am
You'll be thinking of me, somehow I will know.
C   C7
Someday when I'm lonely,
F   B♭
Wishing you weren't so far away,
Am   Em   Am   Em   Am
Then I will remember things we said today.

Verse 2

Am   Em   Am   Em   Am
You say you'll be mine, girl, till the end of time,
               Em   Am   Em   Am
These days, such a kind girl seems so hard to find.
C   C7
Someday when we're dreaming
F   B♭
Deep in love, not a lot to say,
Am   Em   Am   Em   A
Then we will remember things we said today.

Bridge 1

```
A                D
Me, I'm just the lucky kind,
B7                E7                A
Love to hear you say that love is love,
              D
And though we may be blind,
B7              B♭
Love is here to stay, and that's
```

Verse 3

```
  Am      Em        Am                 Em   Am
Enough to make you mine, girl, be the only one.
        Em      Am                   Em  Am
Love me all the time, girl, we'll go on and on.
C                  C7
Someday when we're dreaming,
F                   B♭
Deep in love, not a lot to say,
Am      Em   Am                 Em   A
Then we will remember things we said today.
```

Bridge 2 As Bridge 1

Verse 4

```
  Am      Em        Am                 Em   Am
Enough to make you mine, girl, be the only one.
        Em      Am                   Em  Am
Love me all the time, girl, we'll go on and on.
C                  C7
Someday when we're dreaming,
F                   B♭
Deep in love, not a lot to say,
Am      Em   Am                 Em
Then we will remember things we said to-day.
```

Coda

```
|: Am     | Am     | Am     | Am     :|
(-day.)
```
Repeat to fade

Think For Yourself

Words & Music by
George Harrison

G7 Am Dm B♭ C C7 E♭/B♭ D7

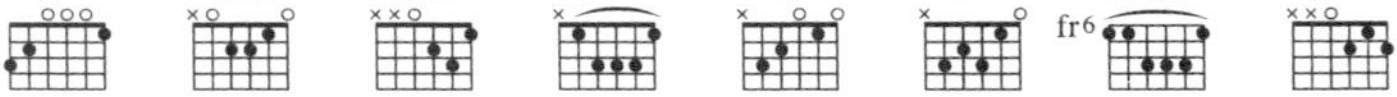

Intro | G7 | G7 ||

Verse 1

Am Dm
I've got a word or two
B♭ C G7
To say about the things that you do.
Am Dm
You're telling all those lies
B♭ C G7
About the good things that we can have
Am
If we close our eyes.

Chorus 1

C7
Do what you want to do,
G7
And go where you're going to,
E♭/B♭
Think for yourself,
D7 G7
'Cause I won't be there with you.

Verse 2

Am Dm
I left you far behind
B♭ C G7
The ruins of the life that you have in mind.
Am Dm
And though you still can't see,
B♭ C
I know your mind's made up,
G7 Am
You're gonna cause more misery.

Chorus 2

C7
Do what you want to do,
    G7
And go where you're going to,
E♭/B♭
Think for yourself,
           D7   G7
'Cause I won't be there with you.

Verse 3

Am   Dm
   Although your mind's opaque,
B♭   C
   Try thinking more,
                  G7
   If just for your own sake.
Am   Dm
   The future still looks good,
B♭   C   G7
   And you've got time to rectify
                    Am
All the things that you should.

Chorus 3

C7
Do what you want to do,
    G7
And go where you're going to,
E♭/B♭
Think for yourself,
           D7   G7
'Cause I won't be there with you.

Chorus 4

C7
Do what you want to do,
    G7
And go where you're going to,
E♭/B♭
Think for yourself,
           D7   C7   G7
'Cause I won't be there with you.
E♭/B♭
Think for yourself,
            D7   C7   G7
'Cause I won't be there with you.

This Boy

Words & Music by
John Lennon & Paul McCartney

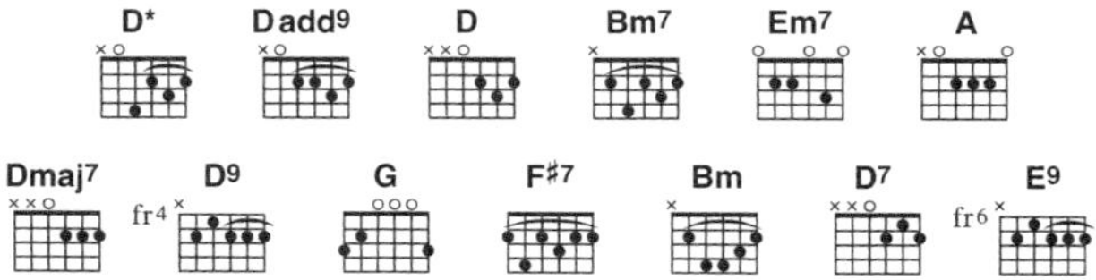

Intro | D* Dadd9 D* || D Bm7 | Em7 A ||

Verse 1

Dmaj7 Bm7 Em7
That boy ____
A Dmaj7 Bm7
Took my love away, ___
Em7 A Dmaj7 Bm7
Though he'll regret it someday, ___
Em7 N.C.
But this boy
A N.C D Bm7 Em7 A
Wants you back again. _____

Verse 2

Dmaj7 Bm7 Em7
That boy ____
A Dmaj7 Bm7
Isn't good for you, ___
Em7 A Dmaj7 Bm7
Though he may want you too, ___
Em7 N.C.
This boy
A N.C D D9
Wants you back again.

```
                G                   F#7
Bridge      Oh, and this boy would be happy,
                Bm                 D      D7
            Just to love you, but oh my-hi-hi-hi-a,
            G                E9
            That boy won't be happy
            A                  N.C.
            Till he's seen you cry. ___

            Dmaj7   Bm7   Em7
Verse 3     This boy ___
                    A       Dmaj7  Bm7
            Wouldn't mind the pain, ___
            Em7             A      Dmaj7  Bm7
              Would always feel the same, ___
              Em7 N.C.
            If this boy
            A   N.C.       D     Bm7  Em7  A
            Gets you back again.

            Dmaj7 Bm7    Em7  A
Coda        This boy, ___
              Dmaj7 Bm7    Em7  A
            |: This boy, ___          :|  Repeat to fade
```

Tomorrow Never Knows

Words & Music by
John Lennon & Paul McCartney

C
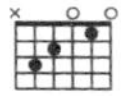
C11
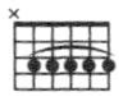

Intro | (C) | (C) | (C) | (C) ||

Verse 1

```
C
Turn off your mind,

Relax and float downstream,
          C11              C
It is not dying, it is not dying.
```

Verse 2

```
C
Lay down all thought,

Surrender to the void,
      C11           C
It is shining, it is shining.
```

Verse 3

```
C
That you may see

The meaning of within,
      C11         C
It is being, it is being.
```

Solo ||: C | C | C | C :|| *Play 4 times*

Verse 4

```
C
That love is all

And love is everyone,
      C11             C
It is knowing, it is knowing.
```

Verse 5

```
C
That ignorance and hate

May mourn the dead,
         C11            C
It is believing, it is believing.
```

Verse 6

```
C
But listen to the

Colour of your dreams,
         C11              C
It is not living, it is not living.
```

Verse 7

```
   C
Or play the game existence to the end
           C11                C
Of the beginning, of the beginning,
           C11                C
Of the beginning, of the beginning,
           C11                C
Of the beginning, of the beginning,
           C11       C
Of the beginning.          Fade out
```

Twist And Shout

Words & Music by
Bert Russell & Phil Medley

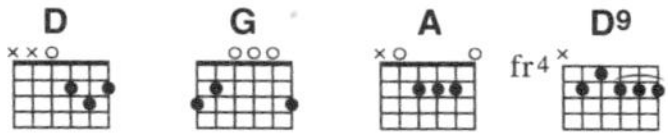

Intro

```
| D    G   | A         | D    G   | A         ||
```

Chorus 1

```
                   D          G          A
Well, shake it up, baby now, (shake it up, baby,)
            D      G       A
Twist and shout, (twist and shout.)
                                 D          G         A
C'mon, c'mon, c'mon, c'mon baby now, (come on baby,)
                            D  G           A
Come on and work it on out, (work it on out.)
```

Verse 1

```
                  D  G         A
Well, work it on out, (work it on out,)
                         D       G       A
You know you look so good, (look so good.)
                          D          G       A
You know you got me goin' now, (got me goin',)
                          D              G           A
Just like I knew you would, (like I knew you would.)
```

Chorus 2

As Chorus 1

Verse 2

```
                                D    G            A
You know you twist it, little girl, (twist little girl,)
                          D    G        A
You know you twist so fine, (twist so fine.)
                                D                G            A
Come on and twist a little closer now, (twist a little closer,)
                                D                G               A
And let me know that you're mine, (let me know you're mine, ooh.)
```

```
Middle       | D   G   | A   G   | D   G   | A   G   |

             | D   G   | A   G   | D   G   | A       |
             (A)
             Ah, ah, ah, ah.

                                 D           G             A
Chorus 3     Well, shake it up, baby now, (shake it up, baby,)
                       D        G          A
             Twist and shout, (twist and shout.)
                                             D            G          A
             C'mon, c'mon, c'mon, c'mon baby now, (come on baby,)
                                         D  G          A
             Come on and work it on out, (work it on out.)

                                             D   G          A
Verse 3      You know you twist it, little girl, (twist little girl,)
                                        D     G        A
             You know you twist so fine, (twist so fine.)
                                          D             G              A
             Come on and twist a little closer now, (twist a little closer,)
                                              D              G                  A
             And let me know that you're mine, (let me know you're mine, ooh.)

                                                D            G             A
Outro        Well, shake it, shake it, shake it baby now, (shake it up baby,)
                                                D            G             A
             Well, shake it, shake it, shake it baby now, (shake it up baby,)
                                                D            G             A
             Well, shake it, shake it, shake it baby now, (shake it up baby,)
             A               D D9
             Ah, ah, ah, ah.
```

Two Of Us

Words & Music by
John Lennon & Paul McCartney

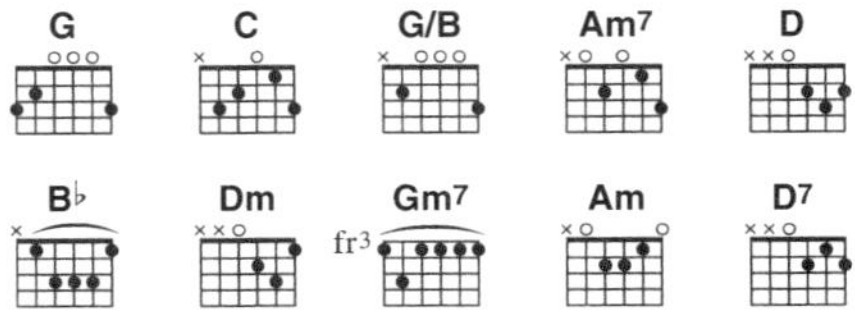

Intro | (G) | (G) | G | G ||

Verse 1

G
Two of us riding nowhere,
                              C   G/B   Am7
Spending someone's hard-earned pay.
G
You and me Sunday driving,
                        C   G/B   Am7   G
Not arriving on our   way back home.

Chorus 1

D   C   G
   We're on our way home,
D   C   G
   We're on our way home,
C   G
   We're going home.

Link | (G) | (G) | G | G ||

Verse 2

G
Two of us sending postcards,
                         C G/B Am7
Writing letters on my   wall.
G
You and me burning matches,
                          C   G/B   Am7   G
Lifting latches, on our   way back home.

```
Chorus 2     D                C    G
               We're on our way home,
             D                C    G
               We're on our way home,
             C                G
               We're going home.

Bridge 1     B♭               Dm
             You and I have memories,
             Gm7                Am                          D7
             Longer than the road that stretches out ahead.

Verse 3      G
             Two of us wearing raincoats,
                              C  G/B  Am7
             Standing solo in  the    sun.
             G
             You and me chasing paper,
                                 C   G/B  Am7      G
             Getting nowhere on  our   way back home.

Chorus 3     D                C    G
               We're on our way home,
             D                C    G
               We're on our way home,
             C                G
               We're going home.

Bridge 2     B♭               Dm
             You and I have memories,
             Gm7                Am                          D7
             Longer than the road that stretches out ahead.

Verse 4      G
             Two of us wearing raincoats,
                              C  G/B  Am7
             Standing solo in  the    sun.
             G
             You and me chasing paper,
                                 C   G/B  Am7      G
             Getting nowhere on  our   way back home.

Chorus 4     As Chorus 3

Coda         | (G)  | (G)  |: G  | G  | G  | G  :|  Repeat to fade
```

Ticket To Ride

Words & Music by
John Lennon & Paul McCartney

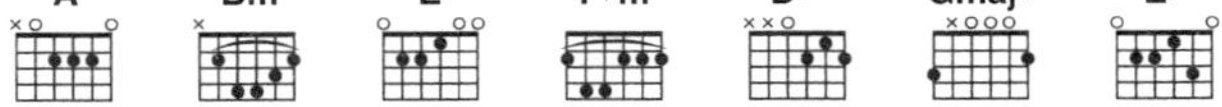

Intro | A | A | A | A ||

Verse 1

A
I think I'm gonna be sad, I think it's today, yeah!
Bm E
The girl that's driving me mad is going away.

Chorus 1

F♯m D7 F♯m Gmaj7
She's got a ticket to ride, she's got a ticket to ride.
F♯m E A
She's got a ticket to ride, and she don't care.

Verse 2

She said that living with me was bringing her down, yeah!
A Bm E
She would never be free when I was around.

Chorus 2 As Chorus 1

Bridge 1

D7
I don't know why she's riding so high.
E E7
She ought to think twice, she ought to do right by me.

Before she gets to saying goodbye,
D7 E
She ought to think twice, she ought to do right by me.

Verse 3 As Verse 1

Chorus 3 As Chorus 1

Bridge 2 As Bridge 1

Verse 4 As Verse 2

Chorus 4 As Chorus 1

Outro

‖: A
My baby don't care. :‖ *Repeat to fade*

Why Don't We Do It In The Road

Words & Music by
John Lennon & Paul McCartney

D7 G7 A7

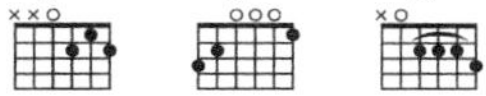

Intro *Drums for 3 bars*

Verse 1

```
N.C.                            D7
Why don't we do it in the road?

Why don't we do it in the road?
                                G7
Why don't we do it in the road?
                                D7
Why don't we do it in the road?
A7
No-one will be watching us,
G7                                 D7
Why don't we do it in the road?
```

Verse 2 As Verse 1

Verse 3

```
N.C.                            D7
Why don't we do it in the road?

Why don't we do it in the road?
                                G7
Why don't we do it in the road?
                                D7
Why don't we do it in the road?
A7                              G7
No-one will be watching us,
N.C.                               D7
Why don't we do it in the road?
```

Wait

Words & Music by
John Lennon & Paul McCartney

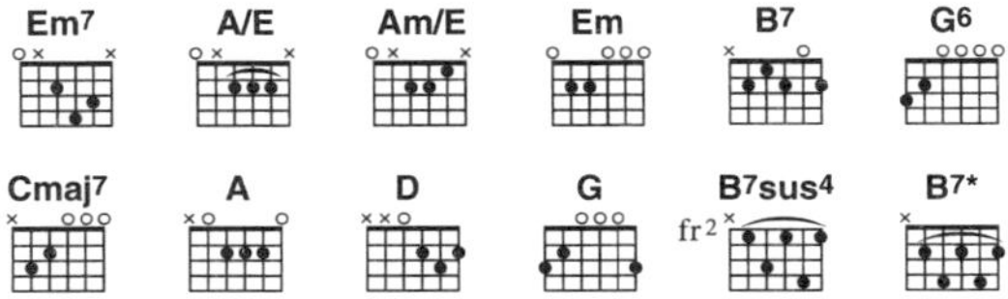

Capo second fret

Verse 1

Em7 A/E
It's been a long time,
Am/E Em B7 Em
Now I'm coming back home,
Em7 A/E
I've been away now,
Am/E Em B7 Em
Oh, how I've been alone.

Chorus 1

G6 Cmaj7 G6 Cmaj7 G6 Cmaj7
Wait till I come back to your side,
G6 B7 Em
We'll forget the tears we cried.

Verse 2

Em7 A/E
But if your heart breaks,
Am/E Em B7 Em
Don't wait, turn me away,
Em7 A/E
And if your heart's strong,
Am/E Em B7 Em
Hold on, I won't delay.

Chorus 2

G6 Cmaj7 G6 Cmaj7 G6 Cmaj7
Wait till I come back to your side,
G6 B7 Em
We'll forget the tears we cried.

Bridge 1

```
               A                        D
I feel as though you ought to know
                  G                              Em
That I've been good, as good as I can be.
                A                 D
And if you do, I'll trust in you,
                  G                        B7sus4   B7*
And know that you will wait for me.
```

Verse 3

```
                Em7  A/E
It's been a long time,
Am/E  Em   B7            Em
Now   I'm  coming back home,
                Em7   A/E
I've been away   now,
Am/E  Em   B7         Em
Oh,    how I've been alone.
```

Chorus 3

```
G6    Cmaj7  G6          Cmaj7   G6   Cmaj7
Wait  till I  come back to your side,
            G6     B7          Em
We'll forget the tears we cried.
```

Bridge 2

As Bridge 1

Verse 4

```
                  Em7  A/E
But if your heart breaks,
Am/E  Em   B7        Em
Don't wait, turn me away,
                 Em7    A/E
And if your heart's strong,
Am/E  Em   B7        Em
Hold  on,  I won't delay.
```

Chorus 4

As Chorus 3

Verse 5

```
                Em7  A/E
It's been a long time,
Am/E  Em   B7            Em
Now   I'm  coming back home,
                Em7   A/E
I've been away   now,
Am/E  Em   B7              Em
Oh,    how I've been alone.
```

We Can Work It Out

Words & Music by
John Lennon & Paul McCartney

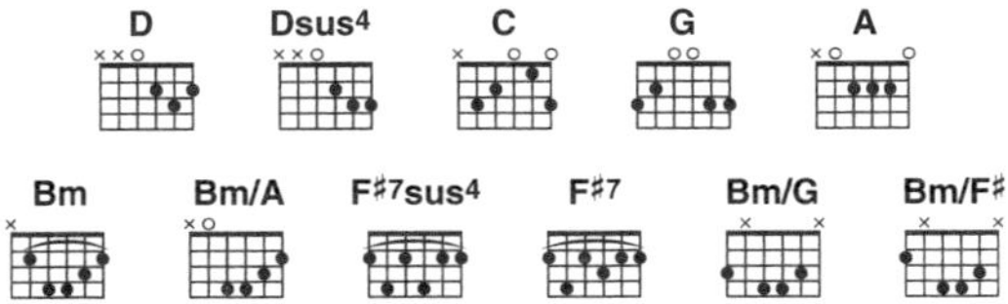

Verse 1

D   Dsus4 D
  Try to see it my   way,
                 Dsus4   C   D
Do I have to keep on talking till I can't go on?
                      Dsus4 D
While you see it your   way,
                     Dsus4   C   D
Run the risk of knowing that our love may soon be gone.

Chorus 1

G   D
We can work it out,
G   A
We can work it out.

Verse 2

D   Dsus4 D
  Think of what you're say   -   ing,
                    Dsus4   C   D
You can get it wrong and still you think that it's alright.
                        Dsus4 D
Think of what I'm say   -   ing,
                      Dsus4   C   D
We can work it out and get it straight, or say goodnight.

Chorus 2

G   D
We can work it out,
G   A
We can work it out.

```
            Bm                         Bm/A      G      F#7sus4
Bridge 1    Life is very short, and there's no time
                F#7         Bm              Bm/A  Bm/G  Bm/F#
            For fussing and fighting, my friend.
            Bm                            Bm/A  G        F#7sus4
            I have always thought that it's a   crime,
               F#7   Bm      Bm/A    Bm/G  Bm/F#
            So I will ask you once a - gain.

            D               Dsus4  D
Verse 3       Try to see it my      way,
                              Dsus4      C              D
            Only time will tell if I am right or I am wrong.
                               Dsus4  D
            While you see it your     way,
                                    Dsus4          C                D
            There's a chance that we might fall apart before too long.

            G               D
Chorus 3    We can work it out,
            G               A
            We can work it out.

Bridge 2    As Bridge 1

            D               Dsus4  D
Verse 4       Try to see it my      way,
                              Dsus4      C              D
            Only time will tell if I am right or I am wrong.
                               Dsus4  D
            While you see it your     way,
                                    Dsus4          C                D
            There's a chance that we might fall apart before too long.

            G               D
Chorus 4    We can work it out,
            G               A
            We can work it out.

            | D        | D        ||
```

What Goes On

Words & Music by
John Lennon, Paul McCartney & Ringo Starr

Intro | E7 B7 | E7 ||

Chorus 1
```
                E7
What goes on in your heart?
                         A7
What goes on in your mind?
            E7
You are tearing me apart,
                              A7
When you treat  me so unkind.
              B7sus4   B7*           E
What goes on           in your mind?
```

Verse 1
```
     E7
The other day I saw you
      Am
As I walked along the road.
     E7
But when I saw him with you
          Am
I could feel my future fold.
                    B7                E7
It's so easy for a girl like you to lie
          B7
Tell me why.
```

Chorus 2 As Chorus 1

Verse 2

E7
I met you in the morning,
Am
Waiting for the tides of time.
E7
But now the tide is turning,
Am
I can see that I was blind.
B7 E7
It's so easy for a girl like you to lie
B7
Tell me why.
E7
What goes on in your heart?

Solo

| E7 | A7 | E7 | E7 |

| E7 | A7 | B7 | E7 ||

Verse 3

E7
I used to think of no one else,
Am
But you were just the same,
E7
You didn't even think of me
Am
As someone with a name.
B7 E7
Did you mean to break my heart and watch me die?
B7
Tell me why.

Chorus 3

As Chorus 1

Coda

| E7 | E7 | E ||

What You're Doing

Words & Music by
John Lennon & Paul McCartney

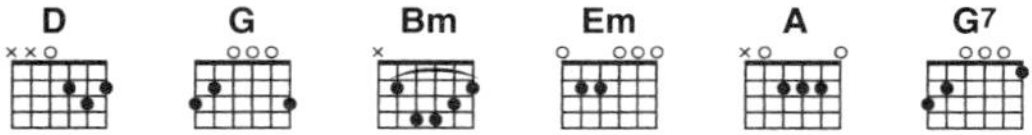


```
Intro      | Drums for 4 bars || D      | G      | D      | G      ||

           D                  G
Verse 1    Look what you're doing,
           D           G
           I'm feeling blue and lonely,
                   Bm              G
           Would it be too much to ask of you,
                                D      G
           What you're doing to me?

           D          G
Verse 2    You got me running
           D              G
           And there's no fun in it,
                            Bm             G
           Why should it be so much to ask of you,
                                D
           What you're doing to me?

           G                     Bm
Bridge 1     I've been waiting here for you,
           G                            Bm
             Wondering what you're gonna do,
           Em
             And should you need a love that's true,
              A
           It's me. _____
```

Verse 3

D   G
Please stop your lying,
D   G
You've got me crying, girl,
                            Bm   G
Why should it be so much to ask of you,
                                        D   G
What you're doing to me?

Solo

| D | G7 | D | G7 |
| Bm | G7 | G7 | D ||

Bridge 2

G   Bm
I've been waiting here for you,
G   Bm
Wondering what you're gonna do,
Em
And should you need a love that's true,
  A
It's me. _____

Verse 4

D   G
Please stop your lying,
D   G
You've got me crying, girl,
                            Bm   G
Why should it be so much to ask of you,
                                        D
What you're doing to me?
                          G   D
What you're doing to me?
                          G   D   G
What you're doing to me?

| D | *(Drums)* | (A) | (A) ||

Coda

|: D | G7 | D | G7 :| *Repeat to fade*

What's The New Mary Jane?

Words & Music by
John Lennon & Paul McCartney

D G/B Gm/B♭ A7 G7/A A Asus2 A add9

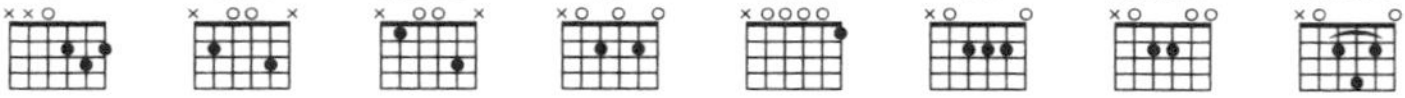

Intro | D G/B Gm/B♭ | A7 | D G/B Gm/B♭ | A7 ||

Verse 1

```
    D               G/B    Gm/B♭ A7
She looks as an Afri - can      queen.
    D                   G/B    Gm/B♭ A7
She eating twelve chapattis and      cream.
    D                G/B   Gm/B♭ A7
She taste as Mon - go  -  lian    lamb.
    D                G/B   Gm/B♭ A7
She coming from Alde - be   -   ran.
```

Chorus 1

```
G7/A                                                  A    Asus2  A
   What a shame Mary Jane had a pain at the party.
G7/A
   What a shame Mary Jane,
                                                    A    Asus2  A
What a shame Mary Jane had a pain at the party.
```

Verse 2

```
    D              G/B       Gm/B♭  A7
She like to be married with      Yeti.
   D                    G/B      Gm/B♭   A7
He grooving such cookie spagh  -  etti.
    D              G/B       Gm/B♭  A7
She jumping as Mexi - can       bean,
   D                     G/B  Gm/B♭ A7
To make that her body more    thin.
```

Chorus 2 As Chorus 1

Verse 3

```
    D              G/B     Gm/B♭  A7
She catch Patagonian pan   -   cakes,
     D              G/B      Gm/B♭   A7
With that one and gin party          makes.
```

cont.

D G/B Gm/B♭ A7
She having always good contacts,
D G/B Gm/B♭ A7
She making with apple and contract.

Chorus 3

G7/A A Asus2 A
What a shame Mary Jane had a pain at the party.
G7/A
What a shame Mary Jane,
A Asus2 A
What a shame Mary Jane had a pain at the party.

(All together now!)

Chorus 4

G7/A A Asus2 A
What a shame Mary Jane had a pain at the party.
G7/A
What a shame,
A Asus2 A
What, what a shame Mary Jane had a pain at the party.
G7/A
What a shame, what a shame,
A
What a shame Mary Jane had a pain at the party.
G7/A
What a shame, what a shame, what a shame,
A
What a shame Mary Jane had a pain at the party…

Ad lib. with sound effects.

Instrumental |: A Aadd9 A Aadd9 | A Aadd9 A Aadd9 :| *Repeat ad lib.*

Coda

D G/B Gm/B♭ A7
She looks as an Afri - can queen.
D G/B Gm/B♭ A7
She taste as Mon - go - lian lamb. *Sound effects*
G7/A
What a shame Mary Jane,
A Asus2 A
What a shame Mary Jane had a pain at the party.

(All together now!)

Continue as Chorus 3 and fade out to sound effects.

When I Get Home

Words & Music by
John Lennon & Paul McCartney

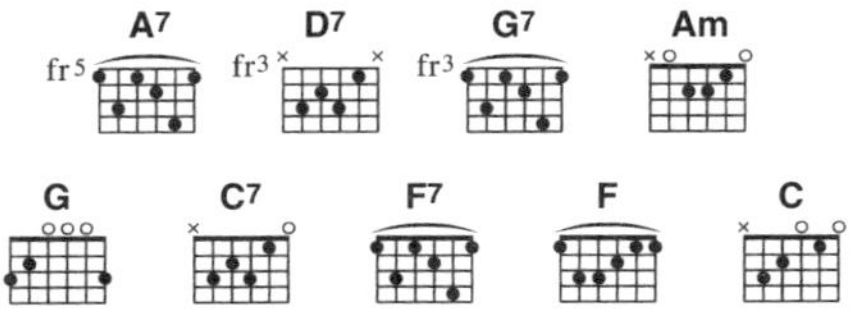

Chorus 1

N.C. A7
Woh-ah, woh-ah,
D7 G7
I got a whole lot of things to tell her
Am G
When I get home.

Verse 1

C7 F7
Come on, out my way,
C7 F7
'Cause I'm a-gonna see my baby today,
C7 F7 G7
I've got a whole lot of things I've gotta say to her.

Chorus 2

As Chorus 1

Verse 2

C7 F7
Come on if you please,
C7 F7
I've got no time for triviality,
C7 F7 G7
I've got a girl who's waiting home for me tonight.

Chorus 3

N.C. A7
Woh-ah, woh-ah,
D7 G7
I got a whole lot of things to tell her
Am
When I get home.

Bridge

```
                 C7
When I'm getting home tonight,
          Am
I'm gonna hold her tight,
          C7                           Am
I'm gonna love her till the cows come home.
      F             G
I bet I'll love her more
       F             G      Am    G
Till I walk out that door, again.
```

Verse 3

```
     C7         F7
Come on, let me through,
         C7                          F7
I've got so many things I've got to do,
         C7                           F7       G7
I've got no business being here with you this way.
```

Chorus 4

```
      A7
Woh-ah, woh-ah,
        D7                          G7
I got a whole lot of things to tell her
           A7
When I get home, yeah.
        D7                          G7
I got a whole lot of things to tell her
           C
When I get home.
```

When I'm Sixty Four

Words & Music by
John Lennon & Paul McCartney

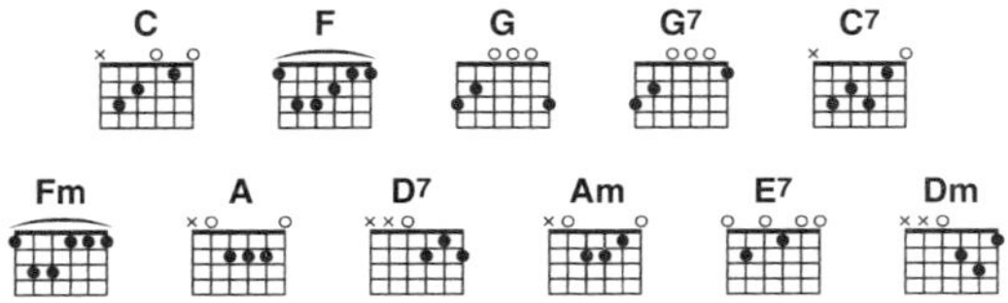

Capo first fret

Intro | C | C | F G | C | C | C ||

Verse 1

C
When I get older, losing my hair,
G
Many years from now,
G7
Will you still be sending me a valentine,
N.C. (C)
Birthday greetings, bottle of wine?
C
If I'd been out till quarter to three,
C7 F
Would you lock the door?
Fm C A
Will you still need me, will you still feed me,
D7 G7 C G C
When I'm sixty-four?

Link | Am | Am | G | Am ||

Bridge 1

Am E7
You'll be older too.
Am Dm
And if you say the word
F G C G
I could stay with you.

```
             C
Verse 2      I could be handy, mending a fuse
                                   G
             When your lights have gone.
             G7
             You can knit a sweater by the fireside,
             N.C.             (C)
             Sunday mornings, go for a ride.
             C
             Doing the garden, digging the weeds,
             C7                F
             Who could ask for more?
                           Fm       C              A
             Will you still need me, will you still feed me
             D7       G7       C G C
             When I'm sixty-four?

             Am
Bridge 2     Every summer we can rent a cottage
                           G                     Am
             In the Isle of Wight, if it's not too dear.
                                    E7
             We shall scrimp and save.
             Am              Dm
               Grandchildren on your knee,
             F    G          C       G
             Vera, Chuck and Dave.

             C
Verse 3      Send me a postcard, drop me a line,
                                G
             Stating point of view.
             G7
             Indicate precisely what you mean to say,
             N.C.            (C)
             Yours sincerely, wasting away.
             C
             Give me your answer, fill in a form,
             C7          F
             Mine for evermore.
                           Fm       C              A
             Will you still need me, will you still feed me
             D7       G7       C G C
             When I'm sixty-four?

Coda         | C    | C    | F  G | C G C  ||
```

While My Guitar Gently Weeps

Words & Music by
George Harrison

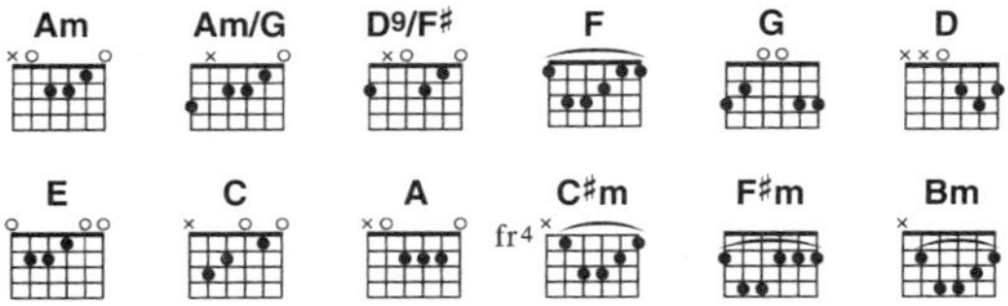

Intro

| Am | Am/G | D9/F♯ | F |

| Am | G | D | E ||

Verse 1

   Am   Am/G   D9/F♯   F
I look at you all, see the love there that's sleeping,
Am   G   D   E
   While my guitar gently weeps.
   Am   Am/G   D9/F♯   F
I look at the floor, and I see it needs sweeping,
Am   G   C   E
   Still my guitar gently weeps.

Bridge 1

A   C♯m   F♯m   C♯m
   I don't know why   nobody told you
Bm   E
   How to unfold your love.
A   C♯m   F♯m   C♯m
   I don't know how   someone controlled you,
Bm   E
   They bought and sold you.

Verse 2

   Am   Am/G   D9/F♯   F
I look at the world and I notice it's turning,
Am   G   D   E
   While my guitar gently weeps.
         Am   Am/G   D9/F♯   F
With every mistake, we must surely be learning,
Am   G   C   E
   Still my guitar gently weeps.

Solo

Am	Am/G	D9/F♯	F
Am	G	D	E
Am	Am/G	D9/F♯	F
Am	G	C	E	

Bridge 2

A C♯m F♯m C♯m
I don't know how you were diverted,
Bm E
You were perverted too.
A C♯m F♯m C♯m
I don't know how you were inverted,
Bm E
No-one alerted you.

Verse 3

Am Am/G D9/F♯ F
I look at you all, see the love there that's sleeping,
Am G D E
While my guitar gently weeps.
Am Am/G D9/F♯ F
I look at you all.
Am G C E
Still my guitar gently weeps. ____

Outro

Am	Am/G	D9/F♯	F
Am	G	D	E
Am	Am/G	D9/F♯	F
Am	G	C	E
|: Am	Am/G	D9/F♯	F
Am	G	C	E :|| *Repeat to fade*

With A Little Help From My Friends

Words & Music by
John Lennon & Paul McCartney

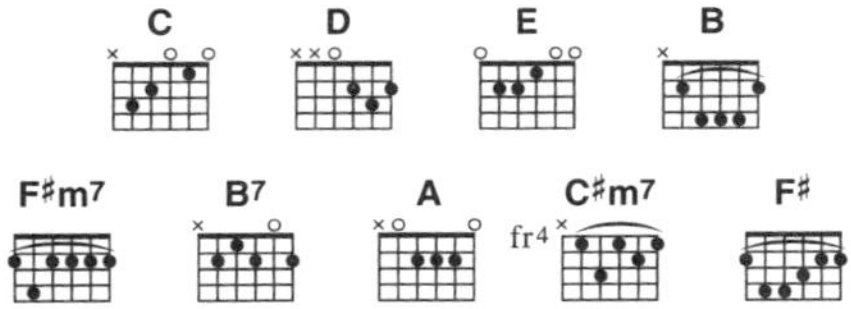

Intro

C D E
Bil - ly Shears.

Verse 1

E B F♯m7
What would you think if I sang out of tune,
B7 E
Would you stand up and walk out on me?
B F♯m7
Lend me your ears and I'll sing you a song,
B7 E
And I'll try not to sing out of key.

Chorus 1

D A E
Oh, I get by with a little help from my friends,
D A E
Mm, I get high with a little help from my friends,
A E B
Mm, I'm gonna try with a little help from my friends.

Verse 2

E B F♯m7
What do I do when my love is away?
B7 E
(Does it worry you to be alone?)
B F♯m7
How do I feel by the end of the day?
B7 E
(Are you sad because you're on your own?)

```
                    D                   A               E
Chorus 2   No, I get by with a little help from my friends,
                       D                   A               E
           Mm, I get high with a little help from my friends,
                        A                                  E
           Mm, gonna try with a little help from my friends.

                    C#m7    F#
Bridge 1   Do you need anybody?
            E          D       A
           I need somebody to love.
                     C#m7  F#
           Could it be anybody?
            E          D       A
           I want somebody to love.

           E               B              F#m7
Verse 3    Would you believe in a love at first sight?
                                     B7            E
           Yes I'm certain that it happens all the time.
                           B               F#m7
           What do you see when you turn out the light?
                                 B7        E
           I can't tell you, but I know it's mine.

                    D                   A               E
Chorus 3   Oh, I get by with a little help from my friends,
                   D                   A               E
           Mm, get high with a little help from my friends,
                             A                                  E
           Oh, I'm gonna try with a little help from my friends.

Bridge 2   As Bridge 1

                    D                   A               E
Chorus 4   Oh, I get by with a little help from my friends,
                         D                   A               E
           Mm, gonna try with a little help from my friends,
                    A                                     E
           Oh, I get high with a little help from my friends.
                     D                                     A
           Yes I get by with a little help from my friends,
                                          C    D  E
           With a little help from my friends. ___
```

The Word

Words & Music by
John Lennon & Paul McCartney

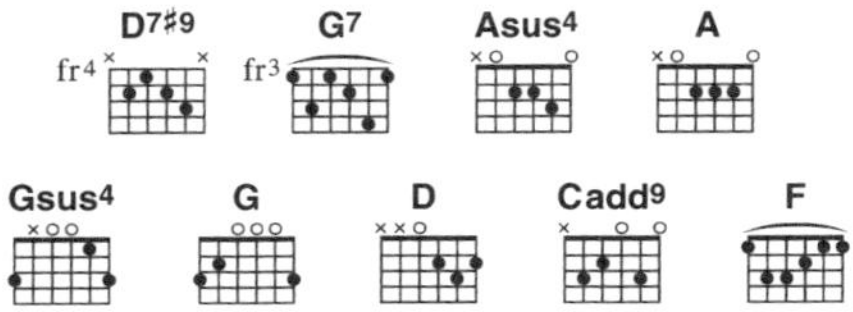

Intro | D7♯9 | D7♯9 ||

Chorus 1

            D7♯9
Say the word and you'll be free,

Say the word and be like me.
            G7
Say the word I'm thinking of,
                 D7♯9
Have you heard? The word is love.
      Asus4 A   Gsus4   G
It's so   fine, it's sun - shine,
            D7♯9
It's the word love.

Verse 1

D   Cadd9
    In the beginning, I misunderstood,
F   G
    But now I've got it, the word is good.

Chorus 2

                 D7♯9
Spread the word and you'll be free,

Spread the word and be like me.
                 G7
Spread the word I'm thinking of,
                 D7♯9
Have you heard? The word is love.
      Asus4 A   Gsus4   G
It's so   fine, it's sun - shine,
            D7♯9
It's the word love.

Verse 2

D Cadd9
Everywhere I go I hear it said,
F G
In the good and the bad books that I have read.

Chorus 3

As Chorus 1

Verse 3

D Cadd9
Now that I know what I feel must be right,
F G
I'm here to show everybody the light.

Chorus 4

D7♯9
Give the word a chance to say,

That the word is just the way.
G7
It's the word I'm thinking of,
D7♯9
And the only word is love.
Asus4 A Gsus4 G
It's so fine, it's sun - shine,
D7♯9
It's the word love.

Solo

| D | Cadd9 | F | G | D7♯9 | D7♯9 ||

Coda

D7♯9
Say the word love,
G7
Say the word love,
D7♯9
Say the word love,
Asus4 A Gsus4 G D7♯9
Say the word ______________ love.

| D | Cadd9 | F | *Fade out*

Within You Without You

Words & Music by
George Harrison

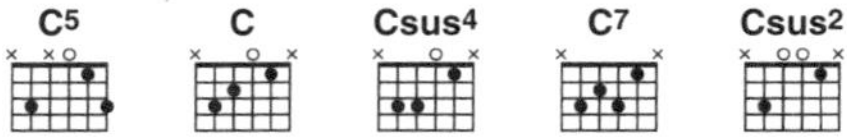

Capo first fret

Intro ‖: (C5) | (C5) | (C5) | (C5) | (C5) :‖ (C) ‖

Verse 1
```
C   Csus4 C5  C7
We were   talk-ing
 C                Csus2 C     Csus4 C
About the space be  -   tween us      all,
      Csus4  C5  C7
And the      peo-ple
      C                     Csus2  C    Csus4  C        Csus4  C
Who hide themselves be  -   hind a       wall of illu  -  sion,
   Csus4 C
Never    glimpse the truth,
      Csus4  C7  C                        Csus4   C
Then it's far  too  late, when they pass away. ___
```

Verse 2
```
C   Csus4 C5  C7
We were   talk-ing
 C              Csus2  C Csus4  C
About the love we      all would  share
       Csus4   C5  C7
When we        find it,
   C           Csus2  C     Csus4  C
To try our best to      hold it      there.
      Csus4   C       Csus4     C7
With our      love, with our    love ___
C   Csus4  C    C7 C
We could   save the world, if they only knew.
```

Bridge 1

C5
Try to realise it's all within yourself,
C Csus4 C
No-one else can make you change.
C5
And to see you're really only very small,
C Csus4 C Csus2
And life flows on within you and with - out you.

Solo

|: (C5) | (C5) | (C5) | (C5) :| *Play 8 times*

| (C5) | (C5) | (C5) ||

Verse 3

C Csus4 C C7
We were talk-ing
C Csus2 C Csus4 C
About the love that's gone so cold
Csus4 C C7
And the peo - ple
C Csus2 C Csus4 C
Who gain the world and lose their soul.
Csus4 C
They don't know,
Csus4 C
They can't see,
Csus4 C C7 C
Are you one of them?

Link

| C5 | C5 | C5 | C5 | C5 | C5 | C5 ||

Bridge 2

C5
When you've seen beyond yourself,
C Csus4 C
Then you may find peace of mind is wait - ing there.
C5
And the time will come when you see we're all one,
C Csus4 C Csus2
And life flows on within you and with - out you.

Wild Honey Pie

Words & Music by
John Lennon & Paul McCartney

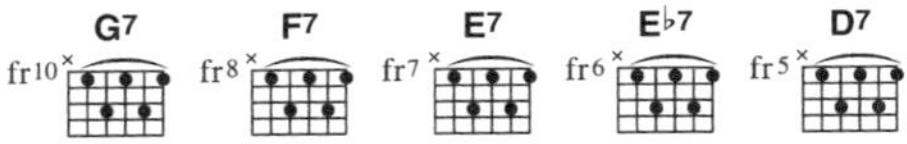

Intro | G7 | F7 | E7 E♭7 | D7 ||

Verse 1
G7
Honey Pie,

Honey Pie.

Link | G7 | F7 | E7 E♭7 | D7 ||

Verse 2
G7
Honey Pie,

Honey Pie.

Link | G7 | F7 | E7 E♭7 | D7 ||

Verse 3
G7
Honey Pie,
F7
Honey Pie,
G7
Honey Pie,
F7
Honey Pie,
G7
I love you, Honey Pie.

You Know My Name (Look Up The Number)

Words & Music by
John Lennon & Paul McCartney

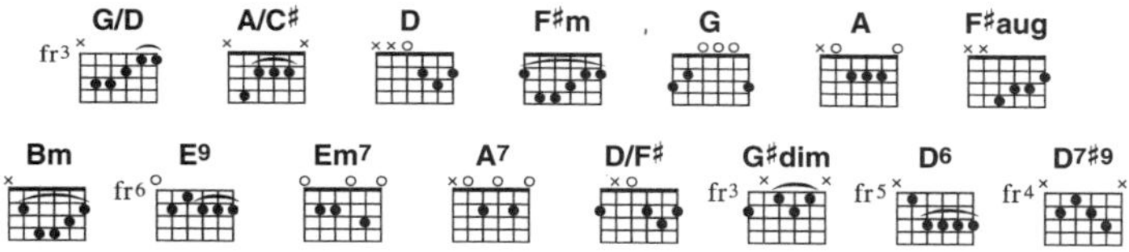

Intro | G/D | A/C♯ || D F♯m | G A | D F♯m | G A ||

Verse 1

G F♯aug Bm E9
You know my name, look up the number.
G D Em7 A
You know my name, look up the number.
D F♯m G A
You, you know, you know my name,
D F♯m G A D
You, you know, you know my name.

(spoken)

N.C
Good evening and welcome to Slaggers,
D
Featuring Denis O'Bell
Em7
And Ringo, Hey, Ringo!
D
Let's hear it for Denis! Ha-hay!
Em7
(Good evening.)

Verse 2

G F♯aug Bm E9
You know my name, better look up my number.
G D Em7 A
You know my name, that's right, look up my number.

Verse 3

```
D     D/F♯        G                A
You, you know, you know my name,
D     D/F♯        G                A
You, you know, you know my name,
G                  F♯aug                          Bm
   You know my name, ba-ba-ba-ba-ba-ba-ba-ba-pum,
             E9
Look up my number.
G              D
You know my name… hah!
Em7                          A
   That's right, look up my number.
```

Verse 4

```
     D                        Em7
Oh, you know, you know,   you know my name,
D                 Em7
   You know, you know, you know my name,
               G
Huh huh huh huh,
               F♯aug           Bm
You know my name, ba-ba-ba-pum,
             E9
Look up the number.
G              D        Em7          A
You know my   name,   look up the number.
D               Em7          A
You, you know, you know my name, baby,
D               Em7          A
You, you know, you know my name,
D             A7
   You know, you know my name,
D                            A7
   You know, you know my name.
```

(spoken)

```
Oh let's hear it!
          (D) N.C.
Go on, Denis, let's hear it for Denis O'Bell.
```

Verse 5

```
D              D/F♯          G                  A
   You know,   you know,   you know my name,
D              D/F♯          G                  A
   You know,   you know,   you know my name,
G  N.C.                   F♯aug  N.C.
   You know my name,             look up the number,
Bm  N.C.                    E9  N.C.               G
      You know my name,       look up the number,
D              Em7                     A
   You know,   you know my name,   look up the number.
```

Verse 6

```
D                 D/F♯
   You know my name,
     G               A
You know my number too,
     D                  D/F♯
You know my number three,
          G                  A
And you know my number four,
D                 D/F♯
   You know my name,
     G                G♯dim
You know my number too,
     A
You know my name,

You know my number,
                          D6
What's up with you? Ha!
N.C.
You know my name,

That's right.

Yeah…
```

Outro

```
| D   D/F♯ | G   A | D   D/F♯ | G   A |
 Vocal ad lib.
| G   | F♯aug | Bm   | E9   | G  D | Em7 | A   ||

| D   F♯m | G   A | D   F♯m | G   A |

| G   | F♯aug | Bm   | E9   | G  D | Em7 | A   ||
```

Sax solo

```
| D   F♯m | G   A | D   F♯m | G   A |

| D   F♯m | G  G♯dim | A7   | D7♯9   ||
```

Yellow Submarine

Words & Music by
John Lennon & Paul McCartney

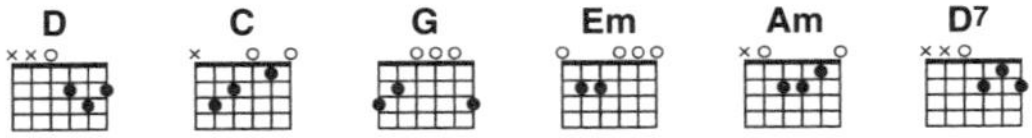

Tune guitar down one semitone

Verse 1

D C G
In the town where I was born,
Em Am C D7
Lived a man who sailed to sea,
G D C G
And he told us of his life,
Em Am C D7
In the land of submarines.

Verse 2

G D C G
So we sailed on to the sun,
Em Am C D7
Till we found the sea of green,
G D C G
And we lived beneath the waves,
Em Am C D7
In our yellow submarine.

Chorus 1

G D
We all live in a yellow submarine,
G
Yellow submarine, yellow submarine.
D
We all live in a yellow submarine,
G
Yellow submarine, yellow submarine.

Verse 3

(G) D C G
And our friends are all aboard,
Em Am C D7
Many more of them live next door,
G D C G D
And the band begins to play.

Link | G G | D7 G ||

Chorus 2
```
G                   D
We all live in a yellow submarine,
                        G
Yellow submarine, yellow submarine.
                    D
We all live in a yellow submarine,
                        G
Yellow submarine, yellow submarine.
```

Instrumental | D7 C | G Em | Am C | D7 G |
| D C | G Em | Am C | D7 G ||

Verse 4
```
(G)   D7   C    G
As we live a life of ease,
Em    Am          C      D7
Every one of us has all we need,
G     D      C    G
Sky of blue and sea of green,
Em    Am    C      D7
In our yellow submarine.
```

Chorus 3
```
G                   D
We all live in a yellow submarine,
                        G
Yellow submarine, yellow submarine.
                      D
||: We all live in a yellow submarine,
                        G
Yellow submarine, yellow submarine. :||   Repeat to fade
```

Yer Blues

Words & Music by
John Lennon & Paul McCartney

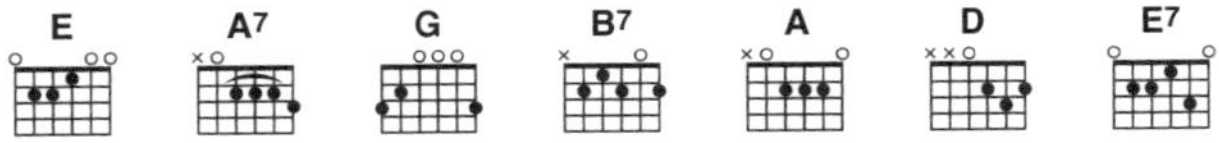

Verse 1

```
        E
Yes, I'm lonely, wanna die,
        A7               E
Yes, I'm lonely, wanna die,
          G
If I ain't   dead already,
B7                               E    A  E  B7
Whoo, girl, you know the reason why.
```

Verse 2

```
       E
In the morning, wanna die,
       A7               E
In the evening, wanna die,
          G
If I ain't   dead already,
B7                               E    A  E  B7
Whoo, girl, you know the reason why.
```

Bridge 1

```
     E   N.C.
My mother was of the sky,
D     E  N.C.
   My father was of the earth,
D     E N.C.
   But I  am of the universe,
       E7
And you know what it's worth.
```

Verse 3

```
     A7             E
I'm lonely, wanna die,
          G
If I ain't   dead already,
B7                               E    A  E  B7
Whoo, girl, you know the reason why.
```

```
Bridge 2         E  N.C.
            The eagle picks my eyes,
            D       E  N.C.
               The worm, he licks my bones,
            D E    N.C.
               Feel so suicidal,
                       E7
            Just like Dylan's Mr. Jones.

            A7                 E
Verse 4        Lonely, wanna die,
                       G
            If I ain't   dead already,
            B7                                E     A  E  B7
            Whoo, girl, you know the reason why.

            E      N.C.
Verse 5     Black cloud crossed my mind,
            D E    N.C.
               Blue mist from my soul,
            D E    N.C.
               Feel so suicidal,
                  E7
            Even hate my rock and roll.
                     A7               E
            Wanna die, yeah, wanna die,
                        G
            If I ain't   dead already,
            B7                                E     A  E  B7
            Whoo, girl, you know the reason why.

Solo        | E    | E    | E    | E    | A7   | A7   |
            | E    | E    | G    | B7   | E  A | E  B7 ||
            | E    | E    | E    | E    | A7   | A7   |
            | E    | E    | G    | B7   | E    ||

                          E
Verse 6     (Yes, I'm lonely, wanna die,
                       A7            E
            Yes, I'm lonely, wanna die,
                        G
            If I ain't   dead already,
            B7                             E  A  E  B7
            Girl, you know the reason why.)              Fade out
```

Yes It Is

Words & Music by
John Lennon & Paul McCartney

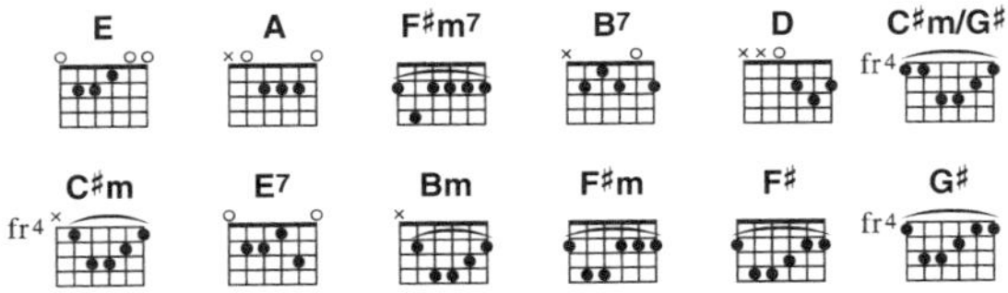

Intro | E ||

Verse 1

E A F♯m7 B7
If you wear red tonight,
E A D B7
Remember what I said tonight,
C♯m/G♯ A
For red is the colour that my baby wore,
D C♯m
And what's more, it's true,
E
Yes it is.

Verse 2

E A F♯m7 B7
Scarlet were the clothes she wore,
E A D B7
Everybody knows I'm sure,
C♯m/G♯ A
I would remember all the things we planned,
D C♯m
Understand, it's true,
E E7
Yes it is, it's true,
(E7)
Yes it is.

```
             Bm         E            A             F#m
Bridge 1     I could be happy with you by my side,
             Bm          E
             If I could forget her,
                C#m
             But it's my pride,
                     E
             Yes it is, yes it is,
                      F#   B7
             Oh yes it is,   yeah.

             E                       A       F#m7  B7
Verse 3      Please don't wear red tonight,
             E                  A      D        B7
             This is what I said tonight,
                C#m/G#                          A
             For red is the colour that will make me blue,
                D                    C#m
             In spite of you, it's true,
             E
             Yes it is, it's true,
             E7
             Yes it is.

Bridge 2     As Bridge 1

             E                       A       F#m7  B7
Verse 4      Please don't wear red tonight,
             E                  A      D        B7
             This is what I said tonight,
                C#m/G#                          A
             For red is the colour that will make me blue,
                D                    C#m
             In spite of you, it's true,
             E               G#
             Yes it is, it's true,
             A               E
             Yes it is, it's true.
```

Yesterday

Words & Music by
John Lennon & Paul McCartney

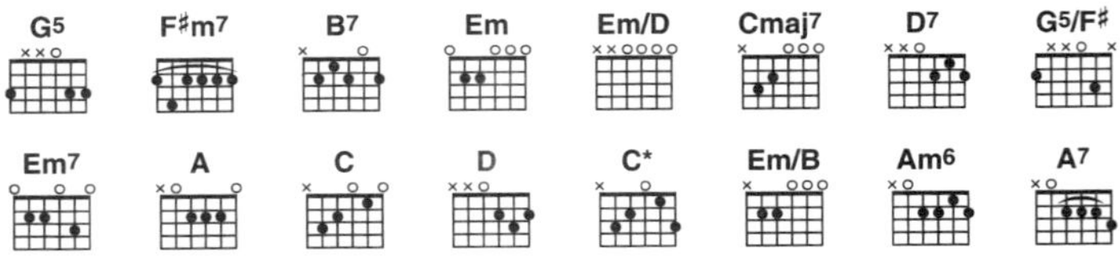

Tune guitar down one whole tone

Intro | G5 | G5 ||

Verse 1

G5 F♯m7
Yesterday,
B7 Em Em/D
All my troubles seemed so far away,
Cmaj7 D7 G5 G5/F♯
Now it looks as though they're here to stay,
Em7 A C G5
Oh, I be - lieve in yesterday.

Verse 2

G5 F♯m7
Suddenly,
B7 Em Em/D
I'm not half the man I used to be,
Cmaj7 D7 G5 G5/F♯
There's a shadow hanging over me,
Em7 A C G5
Oh, yesterday came suddenly.

Bridge 1

F♯m7 B7 Em D C*
Why she had to go
Em/B Am6 D7 G5
I don't know, she wouldn't say.
F♯m7 B7 Em D C*
I said some-thing wrong
Em/B Am6 D7 G5
Now I long for yesterday.

Verse 3

G5 F#m7
Yesterday,
B7 Em Em/D
Love was such an easy game to play,
Cmaj7 D7 G5 G5/F#
Now I need a place to hide away
Em7 A C G5
Oh, I be - lieve in yesterday.

Bridge 2

F#m7 B7 Em D C*
Why she had to go
Em/B Am6 D7 G5
I don't know, she wouldn't say.
F#m7 B7 Em D C*
I said some-thing wrong
Em/B Am6 D7 G5
Now I long for yesterday.

Verse 4

G5 F#m7
Yesterday,
B7 Em Em/D
Love was such an easy game to play,
Cmaj7 D7 G5 G5/F#
Now I need a place to hide away,
Em7 A C G5
Oh, I be - lieve in yesterday,
G A7 C* G5
Mmm. ______

You Can't Do That

Words & Music by
John Lennon & Paul McCartney

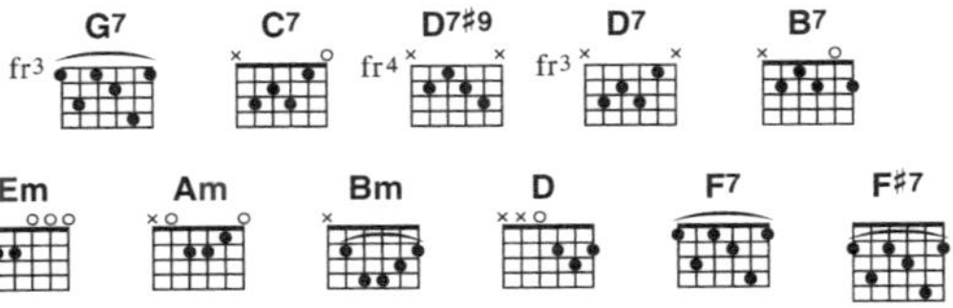

Intro | (G7) | (G7) | G7 | G7 ||

```
            G7
Verse 1     I got something to say that might cause you pain,

            If I catch you talking to that boy again,
                     C7
            I'm gonna let you down
                         G7
            And leave you flat.
                     D7#9
            Because I told you before,
            C7                G7   D7
            Oh, you can't do that.

                       G7
Verse 2     Well, it's the second time I've caught you talking to him,

            Do I have to tell you one more time, I think it's a sin.
                     C7
            I think I'll let you down, (let you down,)
                         G7
            And leave you flat.

            (Gonna let you down and leave you flat.)
                       D7#9
            Because I've told you before,
            C7                G7
            Oh, you can't do that.
```

Bridge 1

B7 Em
Everybody's green ______
Am Bm G7
'Cause I'm the one who won your love.
B7 Em
But if they'd seen ______
Am
You talking that way,
Bm D
They'd laugh in my face.

Verse 3

G7
So please listen to me if you wanna stay mine,

I can't help my feelings, I'll go out of my mind,
C7
I'm gonna let you down, (let you down,)
G7
And leave you flat.

(Gonna let you down and leave you flat.)
D7♯9
Because I've told you before,
C7 G7 D7
Oh, you can't do that.

Solo

G7	G7	G7	G7	C7	C7
G7	G7	D7	C7	G7	G7

Bridge 2

As Bridge 1

Verse 4

G7
So please listen to me if you wanna stay mine,

I can't help my feelings, I'll go out of my mind,
C7
I'm gonna let you down, (let you down,)
G7
And leave you flat.

(Gonna let you down and leave you flat.)
D7♯9
Because I've told you before,
C7 G7 F7 F♯7 G7
Oh, you can't do that.

You Know What To Do

Words & Music by
George Harrison

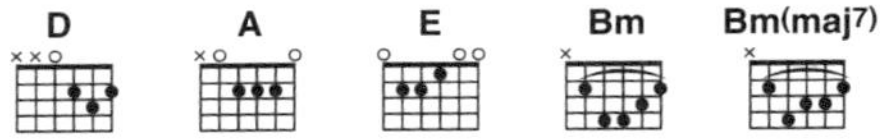

Intro | D | D ||

Verse 1

A E
When I see you, I just don't know what to say,
A E
I like to be with you every hour of the day.

Chorus 1

A E
So if you want me,
A E
Just like I need you,
A D
You know what to do.

Verse 2

A E
I watched you walking by, and you looked all alone,
A E
I hope that you won't mind if I walk you back home.

Chorus 2

A E
And if you want me,
A E
Just like I need you,
A D
You know what to do.

Bridge 1

Bm
Just call on me when you are lonely,
Bm(maj7)
I'll keep my love for you only.
A D
I'll call on you if I'm lonely too.

```
            A                                  E
Verse 3     Understand, I'll stay with you every day,
            A                                E
            Make you love me more in every way.

                              A    E
Chorus 3    So if you want me,
                              A    E
            Just like I want you,
                     A          D
            You know what to do.

            Bm
Bridge 2      Just call on me when you are lonely,
            Bm(maj7)
              I'll keep my love for you only.
            A                               D
              I'll call on you if I'm lonely too.

            A                                  E
Verse 4     Understand, I'll stay with you every day,
            A                                E
            Make you love me more in every way.

                              A    E
Chorus 4    So if you want me,
                              A    E
            Just like I need you,
                     A          D
            You know what to do.

Coda        | D    | D    | D    | D        ||
```

You Like Me Too Much

Words & Music by
George Harrison

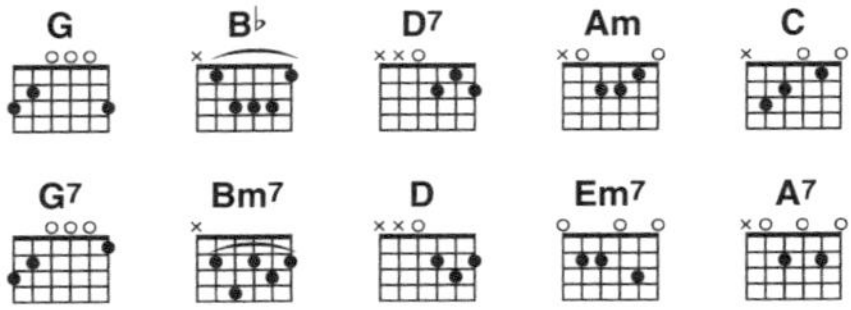

Intro | G | B♭ D7 | G ||

Verse 1

(G) Am
Though you've gone away this morning,
C G7
You'll be back again tonight,
Am
Telling me there'll be no next time
C G7
If I just don't treat you right.

Chorus 1

Bm7 D7
You'll never leave me and you know it's true,
G C D
'Cause you like me too much and I like you.

Verse 2

Am
You've tried before to leave me,
C G7
But you haven't got the nerve,
Am
To walk out and make me lonely,
C G7
Which is all that I deserve.

Chorus 2

Bm7 D7
You'll never leave me and you know it's true,
G C D
'Cause you like me too much and I like you.

Bridge 1

Em7 A7
I really do,
Bm7 A7
And it's nice when you believe me.
Em7 A7 D7
If you leave me:

Verse 3

Am
I will follow you and bring you
C G7
Back where you belong,
Am
'Cause I couldn't really stand it,
C G7
I'd admit that I was wrong.

Chorus 3

Bm7 D7
I wouldn't let you leave me, 'cause it's true,
G C D7
'Cause you like me too much and I like you.

Solo

| G | G | G | G | C | C |
| G | G | D7 | D7 | D7 | D7 ||
(D7) G C D
'Cause you like me too much and I like you.

Bridge 2

As Bridge 1

Verse 4

Am
I will follow you
C G7
And bring you back where you belong,
Am
'Cause I couldn't really stand it,
C G7
I'd admit that I was wrong.

Chorus 4

Bm7 D7
I wouldn't let you leave me, 'cause it's true,
G C D
'Cause you like me too much and I like you,
G C D
'Cause you like me too much and I like you.

Coda

| G | G | B♭ D7 | G ||

You Never Give Me Your Money

Words & Music by
John Lennon & Paul McCartney

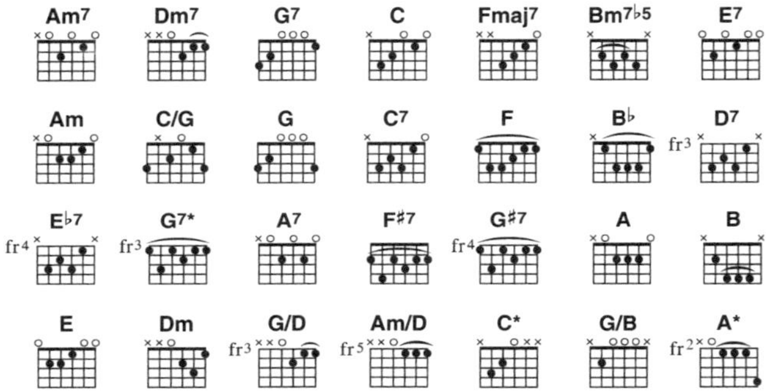

Intro

| Am7 | Dm7 | G7 | C |
| Fmaj7 | Bm7♭5 E7 | Am | Am ||

Verse 1

```
Am7                          Dm7
   You never give me your money,
G7                           C
   You only give me your funny paper,
Fmaj7                        Bm7♭5  E7
   And in the middle of negot - i - ations
     Am
You break down.
```

Verse 2

```
Am7                      Dm7
   I never give you my number,
G7                       C
   I only give you my situation,
Fmaj7                        Bm7♭5   E7
   And in the middle of invest - i - gation
   Am         C/G  G
I break down.
```

Bridge

C E7
Out of college, money spent,
Am C7
See no future, pay no rent,
F G C
All the money's gone, nowhere to go.

C E7
Any jobber got the sack,
Am C7
Monday morning turning back,
F G C
Yellow lorry slow, nowhere to go.

B♭ F C
But oh, that magic feeling, nowhere to go!
B♭ F C
Oh, that magic feeling, nowhere to go!

Nowhere to go!

Link

𝄆 B♭ | F | C 𝄇 *Play 3 times*
Ah, ____________ ooh. _____

| D7 | E♭7 G7* | C7 A7 | E♭7 C7 | F♯7 E♭7 | A7 F♯7 G7* G♯7 ‖

Verse 3

A B
One sweet dream,
C E A
Pick up the bags and get in the limousine.
Dm G/D
Soon we'll be away from here,
Am/D G/D A
Step on the gas and wipe away that tear away,
B C* G/B A*
One sweet dream came true today,
C* G/B A*
Came true today,
C* G/B A*
Came true today,
C* G/B A*
Yes it did…

Coda

C* G/B
𝄆 One two three four, five, six, seven,
A*
All good children go to heaven. 𝄇 *Repeat to fade*

You Won't See Me

Words & Music by
John Lennon & Paul McCartney

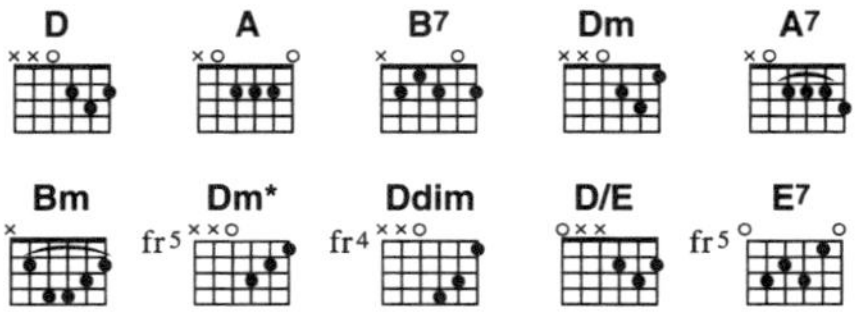

Intro | D A | A ||

Verse 1
A B7 D A
When I call you up, your line's engaged,
B7 D A
I have had enough, so act your age.
A7 D Dm A
We have lost the time that was hard to find,
B7
And I will lose my mind
D A
If you won't see me,

(You won't see me,)
D A
You won't see me.

Verse 2
A B7 D A
I don't know why you should want to hide,
B7 D A
But I can't get through, my hands are tied.
A7 D Dm A
I won't want to stay, I don't have much to say,
B7
But I can turn away,
D A
And you won't see me,

(You won't see me,)
D A
You won't see me.

Bridge 1

```
Bm              Dm*            Ddim          A
Time after time, you refuse to even listen,
B7                          D/E                  E7
I wouldn't mind if I knew what I was missing.
```

Verse 3

```
              A                B7           D          A
Though the days are few, they're filled with tears,
                       B7       D        A
And since I lost you, it feels like years,
           A7          D      Dm                         A
Yes, it seems so long, girl, since you've been gone,
                           B7
And I just can't go on,
     D    A
If you won't see me,

(You won't see me,)
D    A
You won't see me.
```

Bridge 2 As Bridge 1

Verse 4

```
              A                B7           D          A
Though the days are few, they're filled with tears,
                       B7       D        A
And since I lost you, it feels like years,
           A7          D      Dm                         A
Yes, it seems so long, girl, since you've been gone,
                           B7
And I just can't go on,
     D    A
If you won't see me,

(You won't see me,)
D    A
You won't see me,

(You won't see me.)
```

Coda

```
𝄆 A        | B7       | D        | A        𝄇   Repeat to fade
```

Your Mother Should Know

Words & Music by
John Lennon & Paul McCartney

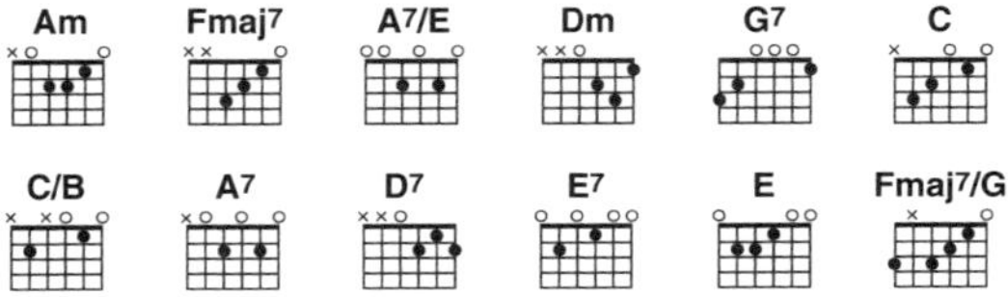


```
Intro      | Am        | Am        ||

           Am                    Fmaj7
Verse 1    Let's all get up and dance to a song
                       A7/E             Dm
           That was a hit before your mother was born.
           G7                        C        C/B    A7
           Though she was born a long, long time ago,
                                  D7
           Your mother should know,
           G7                        C
             Your mother should know.
           E7
           Sing it again.

           Am                    Fmaj7
Verse 2    Let's all get up and dance to a song
                       A7/E             Dm
           That was a hit before your mother was born.
           G7                        C        C/B    A7
           Though she was born a long, long time ago,
                                  D7
           Your mother should know,
           G7                        C
             Your mother should know.

Link 1     | E   | Am   | Fmaj7 | Fmaj7 | Fmaj7/G | C   | E7   ||
```

Verse 3

Am   Fmaj7
Lift up your hearts and sing me a song
                     A7/E   Dm
That was a hit before your mother was born.
G7   C   C/B   A7
Though she was born a long, long time ago,
                                     D7
Your mother should know,
G7   C
    Your mother should know.
A7   D7
    Your mother should know,
G7   C
    Your mother should know.

Link 2 | E | Am | Fmaj7 | Fmaj7 | Fmaj7/G | C |

E7
Sing it again…

Verse 4

Am   Fmaj7
Da da da da da, da da da da
                 A7/E   Dm
Da da da, da da da da, da da da da.
G7   C   C/B   A7
Though she was born a long, long time ago,
                                     D7   G7
Your mother should know, (your mother should,)
                                 C   A7
Your mother should know, ye - eah.
                                     D7   G7
Your mother should know, (your mother should,)
                                 C   A7
Your mother should know, ye - eah.
                                     D7   G7
Your mother should know, (your mother should,)
                                 C
Your mother should know, ye - eah.

You're Going To Lose That Girl

Words & Music by
John Lennon & Paul McCartney

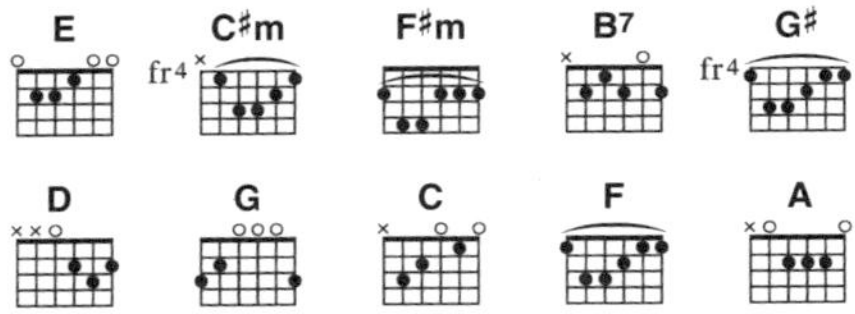

Chorus 1

(E)
You're gonna lose that girl, (C♯m)
(Yes, yes, you're gonna lose that girl.)

(F♯m) (B7)
You're gonna lose ________ that girl,
(Yes, yes, you're gonna lose that girl.)

Verse 1

E G♯
If you don't take her out tonight,

F♯m
She's gonna change her mind, B7
(She's gonna change her mind.)

E G♯
And I will take her out tonight,

F♯m
And I will treat her kind. B7
(I'm gonna treat her kind.)

Chorus 2

As Chorus 1

Verse 2

E G♯
If you don't treat her right, my friend,

F♯m
You're gonna find her gone, B7
(You're gonna find her gone,)

E G♯
'Cause I will treat her right and then

F♯m
You'll be the lonely one. B7
(You're not the only one.)

```
                             E
Chorus 3     { You're gonna lose that girl,                    C#m
             {                  (Yes, yes, you're gonna lose that girl.)
                             F#m                  B7
             { You're gonna lose __________ that  girl,
             {               (Yes, yes, you're gonna lose that girl.)
                             F#m                                  D
               You're gonna lose _______ (yes, yes, you're gonna lose that girl.)

               G                   C                    G
Bridge 1         I'll make a point of taking her away from you,

               (Watch what you do,) yeah.
                                   C            F
               The way you treat her, what else can I do?

Solo           |: E       | G#       | F#m       | B7        :|

Chorus 4       As Chorus 3

Bridge 2       As Bridge 1

Verse 3        As Verse 1

                             E
Chorus 5     { You're gonna lose that girl,                    C#m
             {                  (Yes, yes, you're gonna lose that girl.)
                             F#m                  B7
             { You're gonna lose __________ that  girl,
             {               (Yes, yes, you're gonna lose that girl.)
                             F#m       D     A  E
               You're gonna lose ___________ that girl.
```

You've Got To Hide Your Love Away

Words & Music by
John Lennon & Paul McCartney

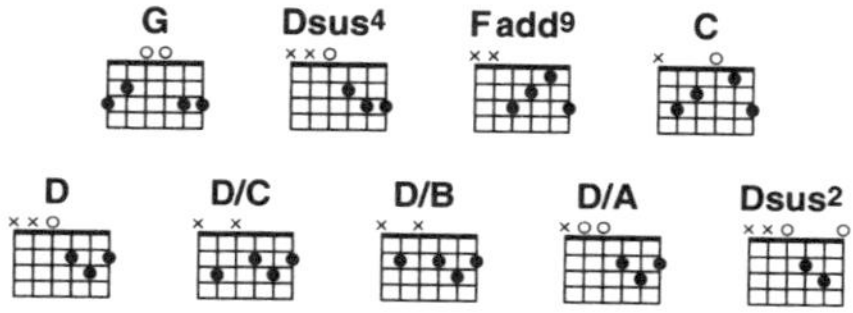

Verse 1

G Dsus4 Fadd9 C G
Here I stand, head in hand,
C Fadd9 C
Turn my face to the wall.
G Dsus4 Fadd9 C G
If she's gone I can't go on
C Fadd9 C D
Feeling two foot small.

Verse 2

G Dsus4 Fadd9 C G
Ev'rywhere peo - ple stare,
C Fadd9 C
Each and ev'ry day.
G Dsus4 Fadd9 C G
I can see them laugh at me,
C Fadd9 C D D/C D/B D/A
And I hear them say:

Chorus 1

G C Dsus4 D Dsus2 D
Hey, you've got to hide your love away.
G C Dsus4 D Dsus2 D
Hey, you've got to hide your love away.

```
              G           Dsus4 Fadd9 C   G
Verse 3       How can I          ev  -  en  try?
              C              Fadd9   C
              I can never win.
              G          Dsus4  Fadd9 C   G
              Hearing them,  see  -  ing them
              C                  Fadd9   C   D
              In the state I'm in.

              G              Dsus4  Fadd9 C  G
Verse 4       How could she       say      to  me
              C                   Fadd9  C
              Love will find a way?
              G        Dsus4  Fadd9  C G
              Gather round,  all    you clowns,
              C                   Fadd9  C  D  D/C  D/B  D/A
              Let me hear you say:

              G                    C                   Dsus4  D  Dsus2  D
Chorus 2      Hey, you've got to hide your love away.
              G                    C                   Dsus4  D  Dsus2  D
              Hey, you've got to hide your love away.

Flute solo    | G Dsus4 Fadd9   C   G | C      Fadd9 C |

              | G Dsus4 Fadd9   C   G | C      Fadd9 C | G        ||
```

You'll Be Mine

Words & Music by
John Lennon & Paul McCartney

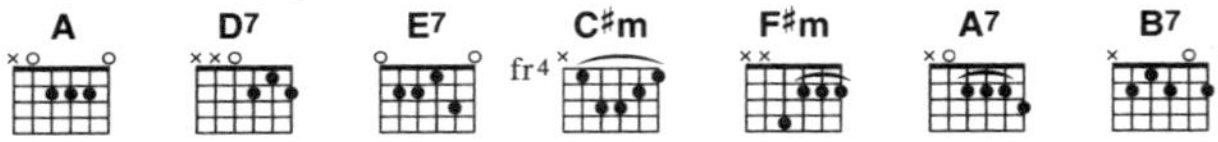

Capo first fret

Intro | A D7 | A E7 ||

```
                        A           C♯m           F♯m          A
Verse 1    When the stars fall at night, you'll be mine, yes I know
                     E7        D7
           You'll be mine, until you die,
                     A      E7
           You'll be mine.

                   A        C♯m       F♯m            A
Verse 2    And so all the night, you'll be mine,   you'll be mine.
                      E7              D7              A
           And the stars gonna shine, you'll be mine,
           A7
           Now. _____

              D7
Spoken     My darling, when you brought me that toast the other morning,
           A                          A7
           I, I looked into your eyes   and I could see
                        D7
           A National Health eyeball.
                                             B7
           And I loved you like I have never done,
                                     E7
           I have never done before.

                   A             C♯m
Verse 3    Yes, the stars gonna shine
                           F♯m             A
           And you'll be mine, and you'll be mine.
                     E7          D7            A
           You'll be mine, and the stars gonna shine.
```


7 8 9 10 11 12 13 14 15 16 17 18 19